THE POLITICAL ECONOMY OF PONDOLAND 1860–1930

To Jenny and Katie

THE POLITICAL ECONOMY OF PONDOLAND 1860–1930

WILLIAM BEINART

Queen Elizabeth House, Oxford

CAMBRIDGE UNIVERSITY PRESS

CAMBRIDGE
LONDON NEW YORK NEW ROCHELLE
MELBOURNE SYDNEY

Published by the Press Syndicate of the University of Cambridge
The Pitt Building, Trumpington Street, Cambridge CB2 1RP
32 East 57th Street, New York, NY 10022, USA
296 Beaconsfield Parade, Middle Park, Melbourne 3206, Australia

© Cambridge University Press 1982

First published 1982

Printed in Malta by Interprint Limited

Library of Congress catalogue card number: 81–21619

British Library cataloguing in publication data

Beinart, William
The political economy of Pondoland 1860–1930. –
(African studies series; 33)
1. Pondoland (South Africa) – Economic conditions
2. Pondoland (South Africa) – Politics and government
I. Title II. Series
330.9687 HC517.57

ISBN 0 521 24393 9

Contents

Contents

Maps

vi

Preface

My interest in Pondoland was initially stimulated by an event which is not addressed at all in this book: the revolt of 1960.[1] None of the studies dealing with the emergence of mass nationalist movements in South Africa after the Second World War seemed to have come to terms with the links between urban-based action and the series of rural rebellions which spread through the countryside, and particularly the African 'reserves', in the 1950s. Pondoland, the scene of one of the most significant and sustained popular movements, was clearly an important vantage point from which to analyse such issues. I soon became convinced, however, that the revolts could not be explained merely by reference to the broader nationalist movements nor by the specific state policies, land rehabilitation and the 'Bantu Authorities' which triggered them off. Ultimately, an understanding of the position in the African reserves had to be located in an analysis of the way in which formerly independent African chiefdoms had been transformed by the development of industrial capitalism in South Africa.

The problems raised in this exercise soon became central to the project, and the focus for research moved to the early colonial and even pre-colonial periods. Discussion of the process of colonisation in Pondoland seemed particularly important, for its people had what may be considered an atypical experience: it was one of the last annexed areas of South Africa, it was not conquered by force of arms, and little land was taken for white settlement. Studies of African societies in the region taken over by the Cape Colony have tended to concentrate on the Xhosa and Mfengu peoples. Some of the former fought a long series of wars against colonial encroachment and found themselves progressively pushed out of their lands by settlers. Some of the latter became allies of the Colony and were beneficiaries of the frontier wars. The Mpondo experience differed markedly from that of both Xhosa and Mfengu, yet arguably it was as significant in shaping

vii

the relationships between colonisers and colonised, between capital and labour in the region.

The central focus of the book is on Eastern Pondoland, seat of the senior branch of Mpondo paramountcy, although comparative information from Western Pondoland has been introduced in various sections. Analysis of the Mpondo chiefdom prior to annexation (1894) is based on a wide variety of sources: the papers of the colonial governments, Methodist missionaries, traders and travellers, and oral traditions.[2] As the treatment of the nineteenth century is restricted to one initial chapter, the result is schematic. The pre-colonial Mpondo chiefdom is not as well documented as the Zulu, Xhosa or Sotho polities. But there is certainly sufficient material for a revision of the only detailed study of Pondoland at this time – a diplomatic history which gives little attention to social relationships within the area.[3] The thrust of the book deals with the process of colonisation. It draws extensively on the voluminous papers of the officials who administered the Transkeian Territories, valuable collections which had been little used at the time when research was done. As a corrective to a view of the society diffused through official eyes, oral material collected in a spell of interviewing in Pondoland in 1976 and 1977 has been incorporated. Monica Hunter's classic ethnography of the Mpondo, for which the fieldwork was done in the early 1930s, has provided invaluable background material.[4] Though her approach, in common with that of other anthropologists of the period, makes it difficult to use all her evidence in historical analysis, her eye for detail illuminates areas of life which are often not recorded elsewhere.

The bulk of the research for this study was done in 1976 and 1977 during my tenure of the Argus Research Fellowship at the Institute of Social and Economic Research, Rhodes University; I would like to thank the Directors for giving me the freedom to pursue the questions which seemed most important to me. The Human Sciences Research Council, Pretoria, provided some funds for fieldwork, and the School of Oriental and African Studies, London University, awarded a post-graduate scholarship for the writing up of material. My present employers, Queen Elizabeth House, Oxford, allowed me to spend some months completing the study. Without the resources provided by these institutions, the work could not have been done; none, of course, are responsible for the product. My major intellectual debt is to Shula Marks, who stimulated my interest in African history, shaped my thinking about the research and supervised the thesis on which this book is based. The approach has been worked out with Peter Delius over the last few years; his own research has constantly illuminated issues which I have had to confront. Jeff Peires, Colin Bundy, Monica Wilson and Terence Ranger have commented on various sections of the draft and contributed much to my understanding of the problems involved. The seminars at the Institute of Commonwealth Studies, London, and Queen Elizabeth House, Oxford, and a period of work with Stan Trapido and others on the Southern African rural history project have provided a constant source of inspiration when my mental horizon could stretch only with difficulty beyond the Mtamvuna river. Interviewing in Pondoland not only gave me an immediate sense of the area, but influenced my approach to the documents. It would have been infinitely more difficult without the help of Frank Deyi; Jameson Mgoduka, who translated Victor Poto's book; Mr and Mrs S. Ntloko; Mr and Mrs N. Webb; and most of all those who talked about their experiences to a relative stranger. Considerably more time was spent in the more impersonal environment of archives and libraries: the staffs at all the centres visited, particularly those at the Cape Archives, contributed much in the search for material. Diane Steer-Jones ably typed the various drafts.

Abbreviations

APS	British and Foreign Anti-Slavery and Aborigines Protection Society papers, Rhodes House, Oxford
Asst	Assistant
BBNA	Cape of Good Hope, *Blue Book on Native Affairs*
BPP	British Parliamentary Papers
CA 1/LBE	Cape Archives, papers of the Resident Magistrate, Libode
CA 1/LSK	Cape Archives, papers of the Resident Magistrate, Lusikisiki
CA 1/QBU	Cape Archives, papers of the Resident Magistrate, Qumbu
CA CMK	Cape Archives, papers of the Chief Magistrate of East Griqualand
CA CMT	Cape Archives, papers of the Chief Magistrate of the Transkeian Territories
CA NA	Cape Archives, Native Affairs papers
CA O'D	Cape Archives, papers of the M. H. O'Donnell trading firm
CA PMO	Cape Archives, Prime Minister's Office
CMK	Chief Magistrate of East Griqualand
CMT	Chief Magistrate of the Transkeian Territories
C of M	Chamber of Mines Archive, Johannesburg
DNL	Director of Native Labour
GNLB	Government Native Labour Bureau
ICS, SA Seminar	Institute of Commonwealth Studies, University of London, Collected Seminar Papers on the Societies of Southern Africa in the 19th and 20th Centuries
MLO	Mine Labour Organisation (formerly Native Recruiting Corporation)
NRC	Native Recruiting Corporation

PGC	*Pondoland General Council, Proceedings and Reports*
PRO CO	Public Records Office, London, Colonial Office
PTA SA NA	Union Archives, Pretoria, Secretary of Native Affairs
PTA TAB SNA	Transvaal Archives Depot, Pretoria, Secretary of Native Affairs
RM	Resident Magistrate
SANNC	South African Native National Congress
SNA	Superintendent *or* Secretary of Native Affairs
TTGC	Transkeian Territories General Council
TTGC	*Transkeian Territories General Council, Debates and Proceedings*
WMMS	Wesleyan Methodist Missionary Society Archives
WNLA	Witwatersrand Native Labour Association

Introduction

In the 1860s, the point at which this analysis begins, the region that was to become South Africa had already been deeply affected by successive waves of European expansion over two centuries.[1] Each of the four settler states, the Cape, Natal and the Boer Republics, had conquered, displaced or incorporated some African societies and, except in the case of the Transvaal, had established a reasonably secure hegemony within its effective boundary. Yet the impact of colonisation was uneven. Between the settler states and to their north, a number of African polities remained, by reason of their power and size or by reason of their geographic position in relation to the thrust of settler expansion, relatively free from colonial control. The Zulu, Swazi, Sotho, Tswana and Pedi chiefdoms, as well as some of those which lay along the coast between the Cape and Natal, all forged to a greater or lesser degree in the indigenous revolution precipitated by the Mfecane, were by no means immune from penetration by the agents of metropolitan and colonial merchant and religious enterprise. Yet despite the gradual consolidation of imperial and settler power in the region, they were able to defend their political and economic independence with some success.

In the next seventy years, however, the period covered by this book, the region as a whole was deeply transformed by a rapid and far-reaching industrial revolution based initially on the mining of diamonds and gold. The exploitation of minerals heralded a new phase of metropolitan investment and intervention; the pace of accumulation within the colonies quickened. It was these basic changes in the nature of production that lay behind the increasing integration of the separate colonial economies, the eventual conquest of the Boer Republics (1902) and the establishment of a unified South African state (1910). It was such changes, also, which hastened the incorporation of the remaining independent African polities during the last few decades of the nineteenth century. Industrialisation and the accompanying development of transport, urban communities and large-scale agriculture set the terms on which the people of these chiefdoms were absorbed. During the first few decades of the twentieth century, the areas they inhabited were reduced by uneven but increasingly uniform processes of change to reservoirs of labour for capitalist enterprises in the region. This book discusses the effects of and response to merchant penetration and South Africa's industrial revolution in the last-annexed, and perhaps largest, of the African polities between the Cape and Natal, the Mpondo chiefdom.

The approach adopted is geared to an exploration of change in the political economy of Pondoland itself during the years 1860–1930. Broader developments are dealt with only in passing, and only insofar as they made an important impact within the area. It is thus a limited set of questions which are addressed: How was Pondoland penetrated by merchant capital and how did it become a supplier of migrant labour? What were the implications of both these phases of incorporation for the nature of production in the area? What effect did these processes have on the form of political authority, the chieftaincy, which previously dominated Pondoland, what new patterns of rural differentiation emerged, and how did the people and the chiefs respond to and shape the forces of change? As these questions have been asked of the historical material relating to but one former chiefdom, the result can be no more than a case study. For while the overarching changes in southern Africa left none untouched, the diversity of experience in each African community is becoming increasingly apparent. At best this study can argue that the existing analyses of incorporation are inadequate when applied to the case of Pondoland. However, the approach adopted may serve to raise questions which are applicable throughout the region.

Rural ideology is not a central concern in this analysis, but one remarkably persistent theme in popular consciousness in Pondoland serves to illustrate the thrust of the argument.[2] When Mhlangaso, chief councillor to the paramount of Eastern Pondoland, pursued a policy of encouraging the activities of traders and concessionaires in the 1880s, rumours spread among the people that he was 'selling' them and the land for his own benefit. When, twenty years later, Sigcau, the paramount chief, promised to help mobilise migrants and was thought to have taken gifts from labour recruiters, he heard that certain headmen had brought the same charge against him. Over half a century on, in 1960, popular opposition to rehabilitation schemes and Bantu Authorities coalesced around the belief 'that chief Botha [Sigcau's grandson] sold the Pondos and the country for his own ends'. At one level this recurrent concern indicated suspicion about any unilateral initiative on the part of chiefs, the intermediaries in colonial society, which implied collaboration with external agents to the detriment of their people. The people did not want to be 'sold out' in the political sense. But the stress on the notion of selling also reflected a deeper concern about the threat posed to the independence of the homesteads by commoditisation through trade, by entry on unfavourable terms into the labour market and by state intervention to change the patterns of land occupation. It should not be taken to suggest complete opposition to the process of absorption into the capitalist world; as will be illustrated, the people of Pondoland were by no means unresponsive to the opportunities and pressures which accompanied colonisation. At issue were the terms on which they were incorporated, the degree of control which they could exercise within their own community in the face of larger social forces which they could hardly influence. Protection of communal access to resources provided one of the best means of defence. This element in popular ideology highlights important issues which have been neglected in the literature on the peasantry in southern Africa: the ambiguity of the response to colonial markets; the continuing importance of relationships between chiefs and people in 'reserve' areas such as Pondoland; and the trajectory of popular rural struggle.

The infusion of comparative literature on peasantries and theories of underdevelopment into the Africanist debate helped to liberate scholars of southern Africa from the intellectual bonds which inhibited a dynamic view of African society set in the context of the changing regional political economy.[3] While approaches rooted in this literature have opened new terrains for research, and indeed provided a major stimulus to this study, they have produced a set of propositions in which the capitalist market is moved to the centre of the stage. In breaking down the view of African agriculture and rural society as tradition-bound and unresponsive, studies have stressed the destruction of the old chiefdoms and the vitality of early responses to colonial markets. Not only were African peasants innovative, a point stressed by literature in a more neo-classical mould on the history of cash cropping in West and East Africa,[4] but at certain times and places they outproduced settler farmers. The penetration of merchant capital, however, implied new patterns of class differentiation linked to productive and marketing capacity. While a small group of wealthier peasants were able to accumulate resources and survive on the land, the majority became more marginalised. It was the very dependence on the wider colonial economies in which the terms of trade turned against the peasant, rather than the absence of involvement in markets, which first constrained the development of peasant agriculture. And the operation of capitalist markets, coupled with the action of colonial states favouring capitalist and settler interests, ultimately crushed the peasantry on a wider scale. Underdevelopment, in the context of southern Africa, meant not a

3

skewing of production in the rural economy through the necessity to produce cash crops, but mass dependence on wage labour.

It is not suggested that these propositions, even in so oversimplified a form, are without a good deal of foundation as a schematic view of the experience of many rural African communities. But they did not seem adequate to capture the particularities of change in Pondoland; the first clues to a critique of more formalist approaches to the process of incorporation are contained in the popular response to successive phases of penetration outlined above. An analysis of Pondoland indicated that the people of the area certainly engaged with colonial markets from the mid-nineteenth century onwards, adopted new technology and changed their methods of production. But they were highly selective about the commodities they imported; the rhythms and relationships of pre-colonial society, as much as the momentum of penetration, shaped their response. Because the chiefdom was able to escape the direct effect of settler expansion for much of the nineteenth century, these changes took place under the political authority of the chiefs. While the arrival of traders modified the social organisation of production and the relationships between chiefs and people, it by no means dissolved central institutions in the society. And capitalist penetration was met with resistance when it began to threaten communal access to land and resources; constraints on accumulation arose partly from internal forces. It was indeed the continued availability of such resources which limited differentiation in the area. No simple division between rich and poor peasant households, nor between peasants and proletarians, emerged as the process of incorporation became more advanced in the early decades of the twentieth century. The majority of homesteads both maintained production and sent certain of their members out to work as wage labourers. Any understanding of the effects of incorporation on rural society demanded an analysis of relationships within the homesteads, and of the domestic cycle, as much as of differentiation between them.[5] Proletarianisation appeared to be a more complex process than suggested in analyses which stress the collapse of peasant production; homestead heads attempted to control the wages of those who went to work, and the origins of mass migrancy coincided with a major phase of expanded crop production.

These features of the response to colonisation in Pondoland suggest that the experience of the people in the area differed considerably from that of the Mfengu, who have provided the model for the analysis of peasants in the region.[6] Some of the latter, having fled in diverse groups from Natal and Zululand in the 1820s, became wards of the missionaries and allies of the Colony in its frontier wars. Their chiefdoms destroyed, they were more highly receptive to elements of colonial culture, and it was

4

essentially from their number that the progressive peasantry of the Cape Province, the producers of wool and crops on a large scale, were drawn. Further, their position grew out of the specific political conjuncture in the Eastern Cape during the second half of the nineteenth century where the relationship between merchants, missionaries, officials and peasants provided the social basis for a significant 'liberal' and assimilationist thrust in Colonial policy. The experience of those in areas such as Pondoland also differed from the many communities which became absorbed as tenants on land owned by settlers.[7] In part, such variations grew out of differential access to colonial markets. But they call for an explanatory underpinning which is not provided by bodies of literature which stress the centrality of the market. Specific processes of change must be rooted in an understanding of the social forms and productive relationships which characterised pre-colonial societies and the earlier phases of colonisation.[8] The penetration of merchant capital did not necessarily dissolve these relationships, and the trajectory of class formation and change in each rural community in twentieth-century South Africa was moulded out of these relationships. An analysis of capitalist markets can contextualise the processes of change but not explain the shape of rural communities, the political conflicts within them and their response to absorption into a capitalist world. It is because the term 'peasant' has been generalised to cover all African communities on the land, and because it is so blunt an instrument in identifying specific processes of change, that it has been dropped for the purpose of this analysis.[9]

If the character of rural society requires more rigorous analysis, so too the particular pattern of capitalist growth, industrialisation and state policy in the region.[10] Indeed, out of the debate on the state and capital in South Africa a more differentiated and ambiguous policy towards the African areas has emerged. Certainly those tenants on land owned by settler farmers were increasingly squeezed for labour and restricted in their access to independent productive resources during the early decades of this century, but these pressures had more limited effects on the reserve areas. The mining industry, it has been argued, demanded a large but cheap and unskilled labour force; a system of migrant labour, in which the wages paid did not have to cover the costs of maintaining the workers' families, was a means to that end. It was not therefore in the interests of the dominant classes in South Africa to further undermine reserve society once the flow of labour had been stimulated. Hence the elaboration of policies which entrenched the African reserves, a cornerstone of segregation, and communal tenure. Segregationist policy also provided for the bolstering of certain political features of pre-capitalist society, in particular the chieftaincy. Partially destroyed in earlier phases of colonisation, chieftaincy in a modified form came to be seen by segregationist ideologues as a means to defuse agrarian and industrial class conflict in the 1920s.[11] These two strands in the pattern of dominance, partly shaped by sectoral competition for labour in the economy, were closely linked.

Such analyses, influenced by the theoretical literature dealing with the 'articulation of modes of production', provide a more convincing context against which to set the continuities and changes in patterns of production and social relationships in Pondoland in the early twentieth century.[12] By submitting peacefully to colonial rule, the Mpondo initially saved themselves from conquest and more destructive state intervention. When colonial rule was imposed, industrialisation was under way and the state was reluctant to restructure radically at least certain forms of pre-capitalist society. By allowing communal tenure to remain entrenched, the state guaranteed access to at least some productive resources for the vast majority of homesteads in the area; at the same time, the possibility of accumulation by a minority, which threatened the underpinning of the migrant labour system, was constrained. Yet, these analyses, while providing a better means of explaining the form taken by different rural communities during the process of industrialisation, have as yet concentrated on establishing the general structures of South African society, rather than the specific local processes out of which it was born, and have tended to assign too determinant a role to capital and the state. As has been mentioned, evidence from Pondoland suggests that the people and chiefs maintained considerable pressure on the state to entrench reserve status and protect communal tenure. The homesteads fought to retain access to land and control over cattle. The system of early migrancy, in which labour was paid for by an advance to homestead heads, ensured that men returned to their rural homes. Migrancy, as a specific form of proletarianisation, arose initially out of the dynamic relationships of power and authority within rural society as much as from the specific demands of capital.[13] Similarly, the ability of chiefs to maintain their authority, although in a modified form, was not merely the result of state attempts to use them in controlling semi-proletarianised communities. They themselves waged a determined battle to secure their place within the colonial hierarchy. Moreover, in an area where pre-capitalist society was only partially transformed, where communal tenure remained intact, there was a significant degree of coincidence between chiefly interests and popular demands to protect rural resources. The chiefs could, on some issues, serve as a spearhead of popular opinion. It was partly for this very reason that the state found it necessary to incorporate them into the administrative hierarchy. The political forms that emerged in the reserves had further implications for patterns of production.

6

The changing nature of rural society in Pondoland in the early decades of the century arose from the way in which its people had been absorbed into the larger capitalist economy and also, critically, from the way in which they struggled to defend their resources. It is these points which have been central to the analysis of the complex historical processes under discussion. The book traces the history of the people of Pondoland from their first regular contacts with colonial traders to the period in which labour migrancy had become entrenched. It describes their experience of new technology, of devastating natural disasters, of successive phases of state intervention and of the necessity to work for wages outside Pondoland. In so doing it attempts to establish a framework to analyse the dynamic relationships that arose in the colonisation of South Africa and to understand how dominated groups contributed to shaping not only their own local world but also the wider society of which they were becoming part.

1

The political economy of Pondoland in the nineteenth century

1 The material basis of the Mpondo chiefdom, c. 1820–60

Although it is clear that the Mpondo chiefdom had been located as a recognisable entity on the eastern side of the Mzimvubu river for at least a couple of centuries, and probably longer, before the Mfecane, sources on the area are too sparse to provide a picture of the society in this period.[1] The few reports and traditions that have survived affirm that the Mpondo resembled other 'Nguni' peoples who inhabited the whole of the east coast of South Africa. Each Nguni polity had its own distinctive character: linguistically and culturally, the Mpondo fell somewhere between the Xhosa, Thembu, Bomvana and Mpondomise to the south-west, later dubbed the 'Cape Nguni', and the many small units in pre-Mfecane Natal, whose way of life has been reconstructed by Bryant from traditions. Yet all shared basic features of social organisation and material culture which distinguished them from other African societies in southern Africa. They had been forged in a relatively similar environment – the undulating coastal strip, with a high rainfall and broken by many rivers and streams, between the Drakensberg and the sea. Settlement was usually in dispersed homesteads, rather than the concentrated villages of the Sotho and Tswana; cattle played a central role in subsistence and social relationships; land was cultivated by means of wooden digging sticks or, more rarely, metal hoes. A similar pattern of kinship, lineage and clan organisation, patrilineal succession and exogamous marriage, in which cattle were used as bridewealth, recurred throughout. And all, at least in the early nineteenth century, had a similar political structure; they consisted of a number of subchiefdoms, each under their own hereditary leaders, subordinated in varying degrees to a royal lineage with which most claimed a direct genealogical link.

By the early nineteenth century, the Mpondo had probably achieved some position of dominance in the region of the Mzimvubu river. But it was essentially during the reign of Faku (c. 1820–67) that the chiefdom

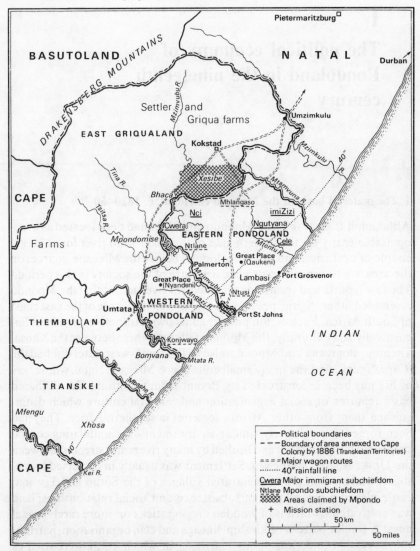

1 Sketch map of Pondoland and the Transkeian Territories in the 1880s.

emerged as the largest and most powerful south of the Zulu themselves.[2] Faku's paramountcy can be divided clearly into two phases. Up to the early 1840s, he led the Mpondo through a period of intense conflict initiated by the wave of invaders fleeing south from Shaka's Zulu kingdom. Their settlements to the east of the Mzimvubu destroyed by Zulu impis in 1828, their cattle lost, the Mpondo retreated to the forests and valleys

10

on the western side of the river. Perhaps 10,000 people, half the chiefdom, huddled in dense settlements around Faku's new homestead. Yet Faku was soon able to reconstitute his followers into a formidable military force. Although there is no record of age regiments, male circumcision was abolished, an innovation which suggests some of the changes in military organisation that took place in Zululand. Responding to the loss of their cattle, the Mpondo intensified raiding, hunting and agricultural activities. They traded both products of the hunt and surplus grain – Faku's country was described as 'the granary of the eastern parts of Caffreland' – to recoup their losses.[3] Within about fifteen years, they had reaccumulated a significant number of cattle. Close settlement and the importance of communally organised labour for hunting and raiding controlled by the paramount gave Faku considerable new powers. Refugees and immigrants moved in under his authority as he established his pre-eminence on the southern periphery of the Zulu kingdom, thus providing both more cattle, in the shape of tribute, and followers. Through control of military and hunting activities, trade and tribute, the paramount was able to secure access to many of the cattle which came into the chiefdom. Faku's polity was constituted in a similar way to those of the other large centralised chiefdoms, such as the Swazi, Sotho and Ndebele, that emerged in the wake of the Mfecane.[4] His personal power was greater than that of the chiefs to the south-west, and by the 1840s he 'governed a people composed of fragments of many different tribes . . . held together and harmonised in a surprising manner by his influence'.[5] The population under his authority was variously estimated at between 35,000 and 50,000 people.

In the second phase of Faku's reign, from the mid-1840s, many of the Mpondo people returned to the eastern side of the river and re-established their old scattered settlements. Faku was anxious to stake his claim to the land which was now threatened not by Zulu regiments but by the trekker state recently established in Natal. His authority over the area recognised and protected by a treaty with the Cape Colonial government in 1844, a period of expansion ensued as the subchiefdoms moved in search of grazing land for their newly restored herds. Further groups were incorporated, and by the 1860s estimates of population, perhaps reflecting the greater visibility of settlement, were around 100,000. With the reincorporation of cattle, pastoralism again became central to the society. Communal activities controlled by the paramount receded in importance and production became increasingly atomised to the level of the homesteads. Though Faku was able to exert some control over cattle and labour in the pastoral economy, partial reversion to older forms of subsistence and productive organisation was accompanied by a decline in the immediate authority of the paramountcy. The period of close settlement left its imprint on the

11

society, but, especially after Faku's death, the relative importance of various subchiefs increased. These two phases of Faku's reign, then, saw remarkable changes in the nature and organisation of productive activities and in the relationship between paramount, chiefs and people. An appreciation of this flexibility is essential if later responses are to be understood. What follows is a short description of some of the major features of Mpondo society before extensive penetration by colonial traders (from *c.* 1860). Relationships and points of conflict which became central in colonial Pondoland are pinpointed, and, in moving from the apex of the paramountcy to the base of the homesteads, an attempt is made to recognise the dynamic forces which shaped the society.[6]

In the 1840s, most of the Mpondo subchiefdoms moved back to the areas they had occupied before the Mfecane, while some remained where they were west of the Mzimvubu.[7] Yet Faku played an important role in controlling expansion and siting new centres of settlement. Major Mpondo groups were settled in an inner ring around his Great Place at Qaukeni, about twenty miles from the sea. Large immigrant groups, such as the Nci, Cwera, imiZizi and Cele, under their own chiefs, formed an outer ring on the periphery of the chiefdom. The intention was that the Great Place should be well protected. Further, Faku was able to extend his authority by placing members of the royal family in key locations well away from Qaukeni. The process of placing was physically manifested in the act of establishing a royal homestead housing a brother or son of the paramount and his mother. Followers would be attached to this 'house', but the influence of such newly established royal chiefs would usually extend beyond those people specifically allocated to them. Especially in areas where there was no powerful local subchief, the royal house would assume chiefly functions over already established settlements. After the return east of the Mzimvubu, for example, Faku placed Cingo, a younger son of his mother, about fifteen miles north of Qaukeni on the edges of some of the most numerous Mpondo subchieftaincies. Sitata, son of another of his father's wives, was established about forty miles north-west of the Great Place. It was an important location between two large immigrant chiefdoms and near the point at which a wagon route, already being broken by traffic passing between the Cape and Natal, entered Pondoland from the north-east. While all royal brothers and sons could become significant chiefs, not all of them did. This would depend on the complex interplay of rank and power in competition for followers, cattle and military leadership.

While the placing of brothers and sons served to extend the influence of the paramount, it was at the same time necessitated by the conflicts which arose between royal sons competing for power in anticipation of

12

succession.[8] There were, according to tradition, clear rules governing succession. Nyawuza, paramount two generations before Faku, is credited with instituting a great house, already a feature of some Nguni chiefdoms. The paramount would, when well established, marry a wife whose bride-wealth was paid by the people as a whole rather than from the royal herds. The eldest son of this publicly designated great wife would be the presumed heir; other wives were ranked in relation to the great wife and the first wife married and would later be placed in new royal subchieftaincies. While such rules provided the language of legitimacy, they did not determine the political process. Faku himself was apparently not of the great house, and though his successor, Mqikela (1867–87), was, Sigcau, the next paramount, was not. (Both Faku and Sigcau were adopted into the great house to legitimise their position.) Even during Faku's rule the chiefdom faced civil conflict between two of his sons. Ndamase, eldest son of his first wife and commander of Mpondo armies in the 1820s and 1830s, achieved a powerful position by the time of dispersion. In the mid-1840s, he was challenged by Mqikela, eldest son in the great house, who was probably born only in the late 1820s. In order to avert serious conflict, Faku sent Ndamase and his followers back to the western side of the Mzimvubu and established him as chief over all the Mpondo and immigrant subchiefdoms there. Ndamase was given great independence, a recognition of his power. But this case of virtual fission of the polity was exceptional; royal conflict was generally subsumed in the process of placing out.

After the subchiefdoms had become re-established, Faku's power to intervene in the relations between the more powerful chiefs and their people was limited. This was particularly so in the case of large immigrant groups: the chiefs acknowledged his paramountcy, attended his councils, exchanged wives with him and mobilised men for his campaigns but were by and large left to regulate their own internal affairs.[9] They too attempted to expand their authority and followings in the manner of the paramount. Disputed claims, particularly over groups peripheral to the major centres of power in the chiefdom, were a constant trigger for conflict between paramount and other chiefs and between the lesser chiefs. It was the paramount's task to regulate such internal conflict by imposing peace, and fines, on conflicting parties; his authority rested on his ability to threaten intervention with forces mobilised from his own followers and those of his chiefs. Each new paramount attempted to extend his authority through placing royal brothers and sons and controlling the alliances formed between other subchiefdoms. Such attempts could create conflict between the new paramount's nominees and those royal chiefs established by the previous paramount. Faku's successor, Mqikela, was not able to expand his immediate authority in the manner of his father. The degree of control

13

from the centre was uneven, but, as the nineteenth century progressed, centrifugal forces became more dominant within the chiefdom. The successors of Faku's own brothers, and allied groups of Mpondo and immigrant subchiefs, not only limited Mqikela's authority but gradually established a hold over the paramount's councils.[10]

The points of tension in the polity will become clearer if chiefly conflict is situated in the context of the material relations between chiefs and people. By the 1860s, the paramount's ability to exact either male or female labour directly from the homesteads had declined. Men could be mobilised for military purposes, and groups marshalled to work the chief's fields and herd his cattle, but only for short periods. Though specific clans did have certain responsibilities at the Great Place, there is no evidence of a group of 'serfs', such as in the Tswana chiefdoms, on whom the chiefs could call regularly for services.[11] Far more important than direct exactions of labour were the social relationships surrounding the circulation of cattle in the society. In a pastoral economy where the only fodder available was the stubble left in fields after harvest, herds had to be widely distributed in order to safeguard against overgrazing in any one spot. Faku and other leading chiefs had been able to secure control over many of the cattle coming into Pondoland from the 1830s, but they could not keep the animals in large herds around their homesteads. To some extent, the chiefs could meet the necessity for dispersion without losing direct control over their cattle. Herds were divided amongst the various royal homesteads, and some were put at cattle posts – the coastal plain of Lambasi was used for winter grazing by the paramount – with men who managed the animals in fulfilment of services owed to the chief.[12] But the pattern of distribution was not determined by ecological considerations alone; there is nothing to suggest that chiefs were able to command male labour on a scale sufficient to keep a large number of animals at their own posts. It was essential for them to distribute cattle to the homesteads if they were to maintain their followings and secure access to services. It was necessary for them to part with cattle if they were to secure wives to expand their homesteads. While the relationships surrounding the circulation of cattle gave the chiefs differential access to both male and female labour, they also contributed to a gradual decentralisation of stockholding and political authority in the chiefdom in the particular circumstances faced by the Mpondo after the Mfecane.

Although cattle were sometimes given outright to lesser chiefs and commoners, after military campaigns for example, the most common form of distribution was through loans.[13] Men would come to the chiefs to request animals, take them home, supervise their grazing and have full rights to use them, but ownership would not pass. After a period, the

14

cattle would be repossessed by the owner; in the ceremony which marked reclamation, at least some of the increase would be given to the borrower outright. The frequency and terms of loans no doubt varied through time, and type of transaction depended on the parties involved; sources are not sufficiently informative for such variations to be specified and periodised. The traditions of the Mpondo paramountcy in the early twentieth century claim that in earlier times every man, both chief and commoner, could have cattle on loan from the paramount. While such a tradition may have been constructed in order to stress the centrality of the chieftaincy in pre-colonial society, it probably did reflect the position in Pondoland in the second phase of Faku's reign with some accuracy. The control of the leading chiefs over communal labour in the period of close settlement was translated into control over stock and thus over labour in pastoral production. For they were able to use commoner homesteads to herd animals which they could reclaim with interest materialised in the portion of the increase they retained. Loans also usually entailed services to the chief. These were often expressed as aid in the construction of the chief's cattle kraal but could take a wide variety of forms. The borrower could, for a time, become an *induna* at the Great Place, a term that could mean anything from a close advisor to a messenger or herd. Conversely, men of status who attended regularly at the Great Place to officiate in cases or participate in councils' might cement their position by taking cattle. Immigrants would often enter into such relationships while establishing their own homesteads. It was not, at least in later years, chiefs alone who could loan cattle. Such transactions were replicated through all levels of the society, and thus most homesteads were able to acquire animals for use and build up the nucleus of a herd. From the 1860s, evidence suggests that cattle ownership, while still far from equal, had become more decentralised.[14]

Loaning relationships involved the passage of stock in return for services and support by men; in marriage, it was women that passed against cattle. Traditions claim that grain was used for bridewealth at the time of close settlement – they may merely symbolise the deprivation experienced – but it seems that cattle, and perhaps small stock for poorer homesteads, were the usual means of bridewealth payment in Pondoland.[15] In a society where the bulk of cultivation, at least after the period of close settlement, was the task of women, and where agricultural technology was limited to the wooden digging stick and iron hoe, the productive capacity of the homestead was critically dependent on access to women through marriage. At the same time, it was through women's reproductive powers that the future of the homestead and lineage was assured, and it was through female children that future bridewealth payments could be

15

expected. The productive and reproductive capacity of each homestead was thus directly linked to access to cattle.

There is little doubt that the centralised nature of control over cattle after the period of close settlement gave the leading chiefs differential access to wives. This was particularly so in the case of the paramount, who, it appears, received wives from the immigrant chiefs as an acknowledgement of his political hegemony. When asked whether a certain group were in his country, Mqikela replied: 'yes I have a daughter of [the Cele chief] here'.[16] Not only did the chiefs have greater access to wives, but they could in turn command larger payments for their daughters; bridewealth was linked to rank, and whereas commoners could expect something under ten head, twenty to thirty head was expected for a royal bride. (Bridewealth payment was usually a process spread over a long period of time so that it created a long-term relationship between parties.) The bridewealth of the paramount's great wife, usually the daughter of another paramount chief – Mqikela took his wife from Sarili of the Gcaleka – was of course paid by a levy on the people and would amount to perhaps one hundred head. Cattle thus tended to circulate upwards through the chiefdom in marriage transactions.

Yet the chiefs also had many sons, so that cattle were distributed frequently from the royal herds. In Pondoland, the system of marriage was exogamous.[17] There was not only a taboo against marriage within the same lineage, but also within the larger group of the clan, a cluster of lineages who acknowledged descent from a common ancestor. (New clans were formed possibly as a result of marriages agreed between members of two lineages within the clan.) The tendency was thus for bridewealth cattle to be widely dispersed in the chiefdom. In Sotho and Tswana societies, there was at least a stated preference for endogenous cousin marriages which, it has been suggested, tended to restrict the circulation of large bridewealth payments to royal groups. In Swaziland, endogenous marriage preference replaced exagamous practices, possibly so that the royal family could keep a tighter control over the distribution of cattle after the Mfecane. However, there is no evidence of such a change in Pondoland. The predominance of exogamous practices at all levels of the chiefdom probably made it difficult for the circulation of bridewealth goods to be restricted.

It was through loans and marriages that followings were built and homesteads extended. Indeed, the royal control over cattle after the Mfecane probably contributed significantly to the success with which Faku was able to establish royal homesteads which rapidly built up followings and became important subchiefdoms. Political authority cannot be immediately reduced to such relationships; it was diffused through concepts of rank, ritual authority and historic attachments. Yet there is no doubt that in a period when the social composition of the chiefdom was undergoing far-reaching changes, access to cattle could shift the balance of power. Further, by cementing a following, chiefs could exercise tributary rights, again probably features of pre-Mfecane society, which were paid in stock.[18] Perhaps central to chiefly conceptions of their rights to tribute were the death duties levied when homestead heads died. These varied from about one to ten head, depending on the wealth and status of the deceased. The duties of commoners in large immigrant chiefdoms and some of the major Mpondo subchiefdoms stayed with the respective local chiefs, but the paramount received the duties of deceased chiefs and of commoners in many of the Mpondo groupings. Rights over death duties essentially defined a chief's following, and disputes between chiefs over the extent of their authority often came to a head over claims to the duties.

Cattle also came to the chiefs in their judicial capacity. A beast was usually necessary to open proceedings in court, and fines for criminal offences, which were regarded as crimes against the 'state', rested with the authority that levied them. Many cases were decided within the subchieftaincies, but the paramount acted as a court of appeal and dealt with cases of conflict between chiefs. Although the Mpondo paramounts do not seem to have 'legislated' on the scale of the Tswana chiefs, the sphere of finable offences could be extended if the political balance in the chiefdom allowed.[19] The abolition of circumcision lodges is an example; fines for breaches of this rule continued to be levied throughout the nineteenth century, even after it had ceased to be so central to the paramounts' power. Witchcraft charges must also be located in the context of the relations of power in the chiefdom. Though witch beliefs had a far wider social significance, sources are agreed that they could be used to control accumulation by people who were not incumbent chiefs. If an accusation was sustained by the investigations of doctors – who tended to sound out public feeling in the rituals they performed – the property of the accused would be 'eaten up' and the stock driven to the Great Place. Chiefs also continued to levy settlement fees, usually a beast, on every immigrant who established a homestead in Pondoland. The levy of such tribute, which might follow a loan and service, signified the incorporation of the immigrant into a particular subchiefdom. It is not entirely clear whether such fees went direct to the paramount; as in the case of death duties, powerful subchiefs could probably authorise settlement and retain fees themselves.

The relationship between chiefs and people by the 1860s, then, was increasingly shaped around the way in which cattle were exacted and differentially distributed and by the implications of the circulation of stock for access to services, wives and followings. Chiefly rights were essentially conceived as being over groups of followers, although as the pattern of settlement took firmer root, a geographic concept of control, never absent, became more marked. Chiefs certainly did not exercise their power primarily by controlling access to specific pieces of land. Once a group had been accepted by the chief and had an area of settlement pointed out, the distribution of land for cultivation was largely left to individual homestead heads. As in Zululand, the ecology and variation in grass types in Pondoland was conducive to a pastoral system in which cattle were kraaled at night, milked daily and grazed for most of the year in the immediate vicinity of the homestead; the use of pasturage, while generally supervised through chiefs, would be decided on within the homestead.[20] Access to both arable land and pasturage was implied by the tributary relationship; though chiefs and their immediate supporters might secure the best sites and arbitrate in disputes, there is no evidence to suggest that commoners could be excluded from land. Chiefs did, however, exercise more direct control over communal resources such as the major forests.

As settlement became more dispersed and cattle holdings more decentralised, individual homesteads, the basic units of settlement in which all the people of Pondoland lived, increasingly became the nuclei of productive activities. Neither oral nor written sources dwell explicitly on the exact form of the homesteads in the pre-colonial period. Yet the picture of the society presented by early literate visitors is constructed around these physical manifestations of settlement which they first encountered, and the Mpondo traditions are suffused with assumptions about the relationships within them.[21] The impression given is of a basic similarity in all settlements; each was a collection of circular thatched huts, ranked in a semicircle around a single cattle kraal. Most were situated on hilltops and ridges, often a mile or more apart, with gardens on the slopes and in the valleys beneath them. Though homesteads varied in size and some areas were more intensively cultivated than others, chiefly settlements were not, in general, much more elaborate than those of commoners. After the period of close settlement, visitors remarked on the undistinguished nature of Faku's Great Place. Nor were the herds to be seen at chiefly homesteads much larger than those elsewhere. This apparent uniformity should not, of course, obscure the very real difference between settlement groups, predicated on the relationships described. Chiefly wealth was reflected in the number of their homesteads rather than their size, and herds were split up. Visitors were aware of such differences, for they commented on the large groups of people at the major chiefly homesteads: regiments of fighting men; groups of councillors and indunas.

18

Missionaries who first travelled to Faku's country around 1830 through the various chiefdoms nearer to the eastern frontier of the Cape were struck not only by the density of settlement around his Great Place, but by the size of Mpondo homesteads. On average, one mentioned, they were three times as large as those in the Xhosa chiefdoms. Each had between twenty and forty huts and housed perhaps up to one hundred people. Such large units may not have been the rule before the Mfecane, but neither were they merely a temporary response to a period of conflict, for they did not disintegrate when the population dispersed in the 1840s. Though homestead size perhaps became more varied, these large units remained the norm for much of the nineteenth century. At the core of each homestead was a group of agnatically related men, brothers and their sons, who would remain in the settlement well after their marriage, and perhaps for much of their life. In the early 1930s, old men could remember a time when up to twenty married men lived together; memories collected in the 1970s conjure up a similar picture.

The pattern of settlement was predominantly patrilocal: a woman would move into her husband's homestead after marriage, and the children would generally remain attached to this settlement unless the marriage broke up and the bridewealth cattle were reclaimed. As each man could potentially take more than one wife – the actual rates of polygyny at any particular time are unclear – the homesteads consisted of a cluster of extended families. Soon after a woman moved into the settlement, usually when she had borne her first child, a separate hut would be built for her. The huts were a physical expression of sub-units in polygynous families, usually called 'houses', consisting of a married woman and her children. Within each family, houses were ranked, and as each family emerged out of a previous house they too were ranked. The importance of such ranking is fully apparent in the traditions of both chiefs and commoners, for it played some part in establishing rights to property and succession. The position in the royal family was touched on in the section on placing and succession above (pp. 12–13). In commoner homesteads, primary rights to property and succession were vested in the house of the eldest son of the first wife married. Except for personal possessions and household equipment, women could not own or inherit property. In particular they were excluded from control over cattle.

The form of Mpondo homesteads in the second half of the nineteenth century must be located in the context of the wider political economy of the chiefdom and in an understanding of the way in which productive resources were managed. The continued need for defence, as much against internal enemies as against raiders from outside the chiefdom, no doubt played some part in keeping large settlements together. But perhaps more

19

central to the pattern of settlement was the increasing importance of cattle. Up to the 1860s, at least, most commoner homesteads were still attempting to build up a herd that would not only provide sufficient for immediate subsistence – soured milk and meat were essential food resources – but minimise the disruption from losses through disease and drought and through payments of dues and bridewealth. Fragmentation of homesteads implied a fragmentation of herds which was only possible for the large cattle-owners: an adequate base of breeding stock had to be maintained in one herd.

The locus of control over cattle within the homestead also probably contributed to their cohesion. After the period of close settlement, herds in commoner homesteads came initially from sources such as loans and bridewealth payments. It was through the homestead head, senior male of the senior house in the homestead, that such acquisitions were largely, though perhaps not exclusively, made. Customary rules in Pondoland suggest that the great house in the homesteads had a position of particular pre-eminence.[22] Like the Zulu, the Mpondo practised *ngena* (the levirate), which was not the rule in the Xhosa chiefdoms. In this way, the continuity of the great house was assured, as a brother could raise children in the absence of an heir. It seems too that rules of succession laid particular stress on the inheritance through the line of the great house, to the exclusion of brothers. Daughters of some of the minor houses would be assigned to the great house, thus providing differential access to bridewealth. The minor houses did have specific rights in certain types of property, and property would be distributed between, and bridewealth provided for, sons of other houses. But the relative power of the great house probably served to ensure that brothers and sons of other houses could not easily establish rights over a sufficient number of people and cattle to provide the basis for a separate settlement. This is not to suggest that new homesteads were not formed. The settlements re-established in the 1840s were nodes from which further expansion, either on new ridges or in separate homesteads close to the major settlement, took place.[23] But it was only when brothers and sons within established homesteads were able to secure control over resources, a process no doubt attended by conflict, that they could extract themselves from the more immediate control of the homestead head.

The logic of the pastoral economy was not the only influence shaping patterns of settlement and authority. For the homestead was increasingly also the unit within which cultivation and craft activities were organised. Except for the senior chiefs, homesteads were largely dependent on their own resources of labour for cultivation. The primary division of labour within commoner homesteads was by age and sex. As in all Nguni societies, women were forbidden to handle cattle, a reflection on male control over the goods central to bridewealth and reproduction of the family unit. Herding, milking and treatment of cattle fell to the men; as they progressed in age, their involvement with herds would increasingly become more managerial. Especially in the period of close settlement, men did participate in cultivation.[24] It was partly through their involvement that more intensive cultivation was possible. The sexual division of labour in Pondoland was probably not as strict as in Xhosa chiefdoms, but as cattle were reabsorbed male labour was increasingly withdrawn from cultivation. After the clearing of fields, cultivation, together with most household activities, was the province of the women. The division of labour was expressed in the system of land allotment: new lands would be broken when a married woman moved into the homestead, and she would take primary responsibility for a field. The restriction on the area cultivated was determined rather by the availability of labour than of land; thus more than one land could be worked by a woman. (In order to minimise risk from natural disaster and climatic conditions, a number of small scattered lands, rather than one big field, would be cultivated.) But at critical times in the agricultural cycle, particularly at harvest, the settlement as a whole would work on the fields. In the twentieth century, communal labour parties involving people from more than one homestead would be organised, but there is no clear evidence of such organisation, except on the chief's lands, in the mid-nineteenth century. Through the nineteenth century, maize vied with sorghum, the older crop, as the major staple, but sorghum was still of great importance by the end of the century.[25] It would have to be guarded from birds, usually by groups of children from the homestead, while ripening. Thus the capacity of the homesteads to maintain agricultural production depended on their ability to marshal not only individual women, but also groups of people at critical times in the agricultural cycle; again, this probably contributed to the maintenance of large settlements. Further, although there were specialist craftworkers, particularly those engaged in working metal (men) and clay (women), most homesteads prepared their own hides, skins, reeds, grasses and wood for building. A larger unit allowed a greater base for craft skills.

In stressing the importance of the homesteads, the linkages between settlement groups should not be underestimated. Though they were able to generate some of their own resources, the position of each homestead within the chiefdom as a whole was critically affected by its ability to secure certain necessities for production. Further, the extent of exchange between homesteads should not be underestimated. Not only were there a constant circulation of stock and a constant movement of people from homestead to homestead, there were also exchanges of goods. Reciprocity and hospitality were social norms, but, as in the case of external exchanges with other chiefdoms, there was a circulation of craft goods, tobacco, even grain through direct exchanges, beer drinks and feasts, and gifts. The ethic of communality should not disguise the fact that these could be unequal; homesteads with insufficient resources would be dependent on generosity in times of shortage. It was expected that chiefs would provide, but dependence implied service and support. The chiefs would also expect to be deferentially treated when they attended beer drinks or feasts at homesteads. It is particularly important to understand the internal dynamic of the relationships within the chiefdom and of the pattern of differentiation, if the effects of more extensive trade with the colonies, from the 1860s, are to be assessed.

2 Colonial traders, the cattle trade and new imports, 1860–94

Itinerant colonial traders first visited Pondoland in the 1820s and 1830s, after the Cape had abolished its policy of non-intercourse with the African chiefdoms, largely to exchange beads and cattle for ivory.[26] When the ivory trade fell off in the mid-1830s, the Mpondo had little to offer on colonial markets, and their limited demand for colonial trade goods could be satisfied by wagons passing through the chiefdom between the Cape and Natal and sporadic visits by ships to the mouth of the Mzimvubu river. The initial thrust of merchant expansion from the Cape into neighbouring African territories thus made little lasting impact on Pondoland. In the late 1840s, Natal-based merchants initiated regular coastal shipping, and a permanent trading population was established at Port St Johns on the Mzimvubu river. Much of their early business consisted in exporting timber and supplying the mission stations which had been established by the Methodists, first in Western Pondoland in 1830 and then at Palmerton, near Faku's new Great Place. Thomas Jenkins, appointed to Pondoland in 1838, had moved across the river with Faku and built up a second small community, many of them immigrants from areas which had been more thoroughly penetrated by colonial trade goods. Though Port St Johns' hinterland expanded in the 1850s and 1860s, it never became a major coastal entrepot. In the twenty years between 1857 and 1877, after which the port was annexed, the number of ships calling from Natal averaged four and never exceeded ten in a year.[27] Trade through St Johns was hampered by the bar at the river mouth and by the difficult wagon routes from the coast to the interior. But a more important factor in limiting the growth of the port was the specific character of the expanding trade links between Pondoland and Natal from the 1860s.

In that decade, the Mpondo started to barter cattle to traders from Natal on a large scale; Jenkins mentioned in 1866 that 'thousands of cattle' were sent out of the country annually.[28] Demand for draught animals in Natal soared during the commercial boom in the colony in the early 1860s, as all trade with the interior of South Africa depended on wagon transport. Herds in Natal had been severely affected by lung-sickness (bovine pleuropneumonia) from the mid-1850s, and an outside source of supply was essential. Mpondo oxen, once broken in, were regarded as amongst the best draught animals, and traders could make a substantial profit by bartering manufactured goods for oxen in Pondoland. Hides and horns were taken out of Pondoland in considerable quantities at the same time. While some hides were moved through St Johns, the cattle trade had to be conducted overland; traders would bring wagon loads of goods from Natal and collect pastoral products, as well as cattle, for the return journey. Because cattle were highly mobile and hides were light in relation to their value, the overland trade was not severely hampered by the absence of roads into Pondoland. Despite fluctuations in the cattle trade related to changing demand in Natal, disease and drought, cattle and hides remained the major exports from Pondoland until rinderpest killed off the herds in 1897.

Traders from Natal had to be on the spot if they were to compete successfully for cattle and hides; they needed access to grazing until sufficient animals were collected to justify the trip back to Pietermaritzburg, and needed covered storage for hides.[29] In the twenty years after 1860, perhaps fifty stations were established, more than half in the eastern part of the chiefdom. Many traders settled permanently on these sites, given by chiefs, where they could build huts, break fields and graze stock in much the same way as members of an established homestead. Faku had specifically agreed to allow free access by British traders in the treaty of 1844, and a separate undertaking was made to Natal in 1850. Though trading agreements were part of broader political negotiations, in which the integrity of Faku's polity was guaranteed by the colonial powers, there is no evidence to suggest that the paramount sought to prevent merchant penetration. Land was specifically reserved for, though not alienated to, the community at Port St Johns, and those seeking sites in the 1860s needed the express permission of both paramount and the local chief in whose area they settled. One trader, at least, claimed later that he had been sent to a specific spot by Faku. The paramount was able to derive considerable revenue from taxing trade. Fifteen or twenty pounds was levied on all ships that called, and by the 1870s the dues and gifts demanded from settled traders had been formalised into an annual five-pound licence fee. But the apparent willingness with which the chiefs accepted traders, as long as they could retain some basic control over their activities, must also be related to the changes described above that had been taking place in Pondoland over the previous few decades.

The beginnings of the cattle trade cannot be explained by the high demand for oxen in Natal alone. Traders had previously tried to barter goods for stock in Pondoland with little success. It was only when cattle numbers in Pondoland had grown sufficiently that the Mpondo started to part with animals on a large scale. Few cattle were obtained from external sources after the late 1850s, for Faku prevented the entry of colonial stock in order to stave off lung-sickness.[30] But by this time the herds were sustained by natural increase, and, commented a missionary bemoaning the 'worldly money getting spirit' that was in his judgement beginning to prevail, 'many have a large stock of cattle'.[31] Cattle diseases, lung-sickness in the 1860s and redwater in the early 1880s, did make their impact on Mpondo herds but were never sufficiently devastating to set trade back for long. Further, while disease and drought harmed the cattle trade, they helped the hide trade. Whether or not the alienation of cattle to traders was the result of any shift in the pattern of circulation of stock in the chiefdom, such as a general deflation in bridewealth levels or dues, is unclear. What is clear is that wealthier stockowners chose to divert to the traders some of the animals they would previously have used for loans and bridewealth. But it was not the leading chiefs alone who participated in the barter trade. The widely dispersed location of trading stations – they were established not only near the homesteads of leading chiefs, but also at the two mission stations, on important points along the wagon routes and near dense concentrations of population – suggests that many commoner homesteads were soon participating in trade. This is affirmed by a consideration of the nature of the goods which were obtained for cattle and hides, and the way in which they soon became fairly general in the country.

While the availability of stock for exchange goes some way to explaining the burgeoning of trade with the colonies, the alienation of cattle began at a time of urgent need for specific manufactured commodities. Aside from beads, copper wire and trinkets, which were used for decorative purposes, and certain labour-saving devices – tinder-boxes were a far easier means of making fire than sticks – it was largely blankets, firearms, horses and metal products, such as knives and agricultural implements, that the Mpondo sought. Blankets were perhaps the major import over the next thirty years. Faku had shown interest in acquiring them in the 1850s, and by the middle of the 1860s they were to be 'found in every hut'.[32] Cottons were relatively cheap; a pair could be exchanged for a hide, which was worth about three shillings on Natal markets. Woollens, at from three to five times the price, were at first luxury goods worn by chiefs and wealthier homestead heads as an index of their status. Imported textiles both diminished the time needed to prepare hides and skins and made more

24

hides available for export. They rapidly became the socially accepted article of dress for people at all levels of Mpondo society.

During the 1850s – before in some cases – the chiefdoms surrounding Pondoland began to use horses and firearms for military purposes. Whereas Mpondo numbers had previously guaranteed their military superiority, they too had to change their methods of combat if they were to secure the border areas to which they had expanded, protect their cattle against raids, and make their own raids effective. By the early 1860s, firearms and horses were being supplied by traders.[33] Their cost – in 1861 a gun could fetch six oxen – initially inhibited a rapid change in military technology. But around the time of Mqikela's accession, in 1867, the Mpondo both suffered a serious defeat at the hands of the better-armed Bhaca and found that the price of muzzle-loading rifles, shed by metropolitan armies switching to more effective breech-loaders, was diminishing rapidly. In the next few years, visitors to the Great Place saw large numbers of men, mounted and with firearms, when watching musters of the Mpondo armies. In the late 1870s, the Mpondo themselves switched to breech-loaders; they had now not only to defend themselves against neighbouring African chiefdoms, which had come under the control of the colonial powers, but to find a deterrent against colonial intervention. Some of the new rifles were obtained from chiefdoms which had been conquered by the colonial forces, but the traders, by now working illegally, still provided the most reliable source of supply, and there are many reports of gun-running into Pondoland, the last independent chiefdom between the Cape and Natal, in the early 1880s.

Imported hoes and picks, which could be exchanged for hides rather than for beasts, rapidly displaced the indigenous wooden, and sometimes metal, digging implements as the main agricultural implements when the cattle trade began.[34] Ploughs, for which an animal had to be exchanged, were not generally adopted till the late 1870s; an estimated one thousand were in use in 1879. This revolution in agricultural methods depended on access to draught oxen. Faku's sons had acquired draught oxen in the 1850s for use with a wagon, and teams were available to replace those stopped at the border in the 1860s, but it was only in the next couple of decades that the techniques of breaking in oxen became more general. Ox draught also opened the way to radical changes in the system of internal transport. Wagons, which were expensive and restricted to a limited number of routes in the broken environment of Pondoland, were acquired by only a few of the wealthier chiefs. It was the sledge, which could be locally made and required only two to four oxen, that by and large relieved women of their former role as porters carrying produce on their heads. The adoption of sledges and ploughs was intimately linked: the

25

sledge was used to transport the heavy implements to the fields, to collect the larger harvest that a ploughed land could produce, and to take produce to the trading stores.

Ploughs had been in use in the Eastern Cape, in Lesotho and in parts of Natal, as well as on mission stations in Pondoland, for some decades, and it is unlikely that the Mpondo were unaware of them. The specific times at which new agricultural implements were introduced must be related to periods of crisis in Pondoland itself. Drought visited the Transkeian region, though with varying severity, in a regular cycle every seven or eight years. In 1862 and 1863, and two cycles later in 1877, most areas of Pondoland suffered badly.[35] It was in the early 1860s that imported hoes, which enabled a greater range of soils, if not a much greater area of land, to be cultivated, were introduced. As the settlements spread through eastern Pondoland into inland regions with a lower rainfall, more versatile implements were advantageous. The drought probably hardened the ground and exacerbated the difficulties in breaking it, thus providing some urgency to innovation. The introduction of ploughs was a response to similar imperatives after the 1877 drought. By extending the area of land cultivated, grain stores exhausted in the drought could also be replenished. Both these droughts were followed by outbreaks of cattle disease. As in the period of close settlement, the loss of cattle seems to have called forth more intensive cultivation, though neither lung-sickness nor redwater made a major impact on Mpondo herds.

While natural disasters may help to explain the exact timing of innovation – the investment of surplus from pastoral production into cultivation – deeper structural changes in the patterns of production seem to have set the scene for innovation. It has been mentioned that hunting diminished in importance as a source of food, particularly in the upland areas, during the nineteenth century; the introduction of firearms hastened the extinction of all but small game in the larger forests. The upland areas were also poorer in the natural vegetation that still provided the basis for gathering as a supplement to the diet in the subtropical coastal belt; neither did the inland settlements have access to seafood. Lower and later rainfall in the spring (October/November in a summer rainfall area) coupled with winter frosts shortened the growing season away from the coastal belt and created pressure for more land to be cultivated at one time. There is also evidence to suggest that pasturages were coming under pressure. (No statistics on cattle numbers are available.) Despite regular exports of stock, Pondoland was still reported to be 'swarming with cattle' in the mid-1870s.[36] It is probable that cattle numbers had steadily increased through the previous few decades. Yet from the 1860s, when neighbouring polities, especially the Bhaca and Griqua, were able to restrict further

Mpondo expansion through their command of firepower, Pondoland's boundaries became more sharply defined.[37] Natal had annexed all the land north of the Mtamvuna river in 1866, while the Cape, arbitrating in border disputes, defined the line of settlement around the rest of the Mpondo chiefdom in 1872. Further areas for grazing had to be found within the boundaries of Pondoland. Both missionaries and officials felt that border disputes, and the aggression displayed by certain of the Mpondo border chiefs in the late 1870s, were a direct result of land short-age. In 1883, Mqikela explicitly expressed concern about the shortage of pasturage: 'already the cattle... are dying from sickness, poverty, etc., ow-ing to the want of sufficient ground to graze on'.[38] His statement should be treated with caution, as it was made during a dispute over land with the Cape – cattle deaths were probably due mainly to redwater – but his perception seems to accord with the impression of contemporary observers.

The weight of this evidence is increased by the fact that it was in the late 1870s and early 1880s that woolled sheep were brought into Pondo-land in significant numbers.[39] Africans nearer the Cape Colony and in Lesotho had adopted and bred sheep in large numbers for some decades. As Bundy illustrates, they were responsible for a considerable quantity of the wool exported through Eastern Cape ports from the middle decades of the nineteenth century. All the Nguni groups on the east coast had kept some small stock prior to the introduction of woolled sheep, but the number in Pondoland was probably limited because the damp coastal areas were not highly suited to such animals. Conversely, the drier up-lands provided a more congenial environment, and sheep and goats could also be grazed on land that was too steep, too bushy or too thinly covered by grass for cattle. It was indeed largely in the upland regions that woolled sheep were introduced; the shortage of suitable grazing for cattle seems to have been an important factor in the adoption of small stock, for these extended the range of pasturage that could be used in grazing.

This analysis of the penetration of Pondoland by traders, the beginnings of the barter trade and the adoption of new technology has intentionally played down the causative influence of a 'market response'. The broader political and military context necessitated the introduction of firearms; in the case of blankets, metal goods and tinder-boxes, considerable inputs of labour time could be saved; innovations in cultivation related to the changing balance between pastoral and agricultural activities and speci-fic periods of crises. The Mpondo were not producing for an abstract market, nor were the relationships within the society yet commoditised. Rather they were exchanging certain pastoral products for goods which had become available to them and which presented, for different people

27

in the society, specific advantages. The word 'surplus' has also been avoided because it introduces an absolute concept of what was necessary and unnecessary in the society. The Mpondo were not bartering 'surplus' cattle, though it may also be assumed that they were not selling off essential cows and breeding stock. They were, on the contrary, redirecting the pattern of circulation of stock. Chiefs, rather than seeking merely to enlarge their followings, were converting cattle into firearms. Commoners, rather than using all their wealth in cattle to increase the size of homesteads by marriage, were translating pastoral products into agricultural implements which could save labour time or allow cultivation to be extended. The concept of surplus can be misleading in this context.

But the changes taking place in the Mpondo system of production were becoming entrenched and irreversible. In order to maintain access to goods which were becoming essential for productive activities, and which they could not make themselves, the Mpondo had to exchange their produce. In the 1880s, therefore, some productive activities became more clearly oriented towards supplying external markets. The expansion of cultivation and introduction of woolled sheep, while initially a response to internal crises, also provided a more varied range of produce for exchange. Some rough indications of the relative proportion of different products sold can be obtained from the books of one of the leading traders in Eastern Pondoland at the time.[40] Pastoral products remained by far the most important exports: in ordinary years, about three-quarters of their value was from cattle, one-quarter from hides. But after 1880 an increasing amount of grain found its way to the traders, and through them to colonial markets. Some maize was shipped from Port St Johns in the early 1880s, and by 1885 grain grown in the midland and coastal regions of Pondoland was reaching Port Elizabeth, East London and Durban. Overland trade, initially restricted by the cost of transport – a wagon load of grain was worth very much less than a wagon load of hides – to nearby colonial military camps and towns, soon expanded, and by the late 1880s maize was reaching Pietermaritzburg. However, even the larger trading concerns seldom handled much more than 500 bags a year, worth perhaps the equivalent of fifty oxen on colonial markets, before annexation; the firm mentioned above, admittedly the largest in Eastern Pondoland, usually exported between 500 and 1000 head annually between 1886 and 1893. Tobacco, which had long been grown in the coastal parts of Pondoland and exchanged with inland chiefdoms, was also sold to the traders in substantial quantities from the 1870s, though much of the trade remained in the hands of producers and itinerant African middlemen. Mpondo tobacco became well known in colonial markets. Small quantities of wool were also sold to the traders, especially in Western Pondoland, as were pigs, poultry and eggs. From the early 1880s, some cash was being introduced into circulation in Pondoland in transactions between producers and traders.

The nature of the trade goods imported was influenced by and in turn had a significant effect on social relations and the locus of power within the chiefdom. It has been suggested that political authority increasingly devolved in the subchiefs after the mid-nineteenth century, a process which became more pronounced during Mqikela's reign (1867–87). Access to firearms was becoming a significant, but not determinant, factor in the struggle for power between chiefs. The fact that the paramount was not able to control the circulation of cattle in the subchieftaincies nor acquire a monopoly of arms from the traders opened the way for the more powerful chiefs to accumulate guns themselves. Firearms were one factor in the rise of Mhlangaso, son of Sitata, to prominence at the Great Place.[41] Not only did certain chiefs attempt to accumulate guns, they also set up centres for the manufacture of gunpowder from imported sulphur and saltpetre, the repair of rifles and the recycling of cartridges essential for breech-loaders. Of the five major gunpowder centres reported in 1881, only two were near Mqikela's Great Place, and the largest appears to have been under Mhlangaso's control.

If firearms were to be acquired on a significant scale, chiefs had to divert cattle from distribution to followers. Yet private accumulation did not displace differential redistribution. The chiefs do not seem to have maintained large central stores of arms; rather they distributed some of these to their followers instead of cattle. Blankets were also, on occasion, distributed, and imported spirits in particular, which traders sold from the 1870s, became an essential part of chiefly hospitality during meetings at the Great Place. Colonial observers attributed the decline of Mqikela's authority in the 1880s, particularly, to drink; he seems to have succumbed to spirits, but he certainly did not consume all the alcohol that came to the Great Place by way of purchase and gifts from traders himself. Chiefly distribution of trade goods did not, however, significantly displace the circulation of stock in the chiefdom. Further, it does not appear that commoner homesteads acquired trade goods primarily through the chiefs.

This was particularly the case with new agricultural implements.[42] The acquisition of ploughs hastened the atomisation of major productive activities to the level of the homesteads, the unit within which cultivation was organised. By extending the area under crops, homesteads were able to become more independent from the chiefs in their basic food resources. Nor were the chiefs able to levy dues in grain as they did in cattle. The individual homesteads, though they sometimes translated surplus grain into cattle, had far more immediate control over the products of cultivation. It is difficult to judge whether the chiefs were able to compensate for their decreasing control over production by intensifying the amount of tribute extracted from commoner homesteads. There is no clear evidence which suggests that new forms of tribute were levied, nor that firearms enabled the chiefs to place greater pressure on the homesteads for payment tribute. Colonial observers reported many witchcraft cases in Pondoland in the late 1870s and 1880s, and suggested that the incidence of accusations increased in the years immediately prior to annexation.[43] While such rumours may have had some basis – the chiefs had few other means by which to control accumulation in the area – their propagators were clearly attempting to whip up Colonial sentiment against the chiefs in preparation for annexation, and the evidence cannot be taken at face value. Thus the decline of chiefly control over the products generated within the homesteads, and over the circulation of cattle in the society – all processes evident before the advent of colonial traders – was hastened by the specific pattern of merchant penetration into Pondoland. Tributary relationships did not dissolve, but both chiefs and commoners now directed some of their cattle to the traders in exchange for manufactured commodities over which the individual homesteads retained control.

Imports also had important implications for the division of labour and organisation of production within the homesteads at every level of Mpondo society. Some local craft activities, particularly those connected with metal-working, declined. It would be misleading, however, to suggest that labour time expended in crafts diminished overall, for new crafts, such as the building of sledges and the production of leather thongs and yokes for draught, replaced some of the old. But craft work increasingly involved servicing imported commodities. Perhaps the most significant changes in the division of labour arose from the adoption of draught. As men alone could handle oxen, they became responsible for turning the ground with ploughs after seed had been broadcast on the fields. Similarly, they took over the transport work which involved the use of oxen. Homesteads were no longer entirely dependent on their access to women through marriage to maintain cultivation. Although the labour expended by women in the fields did not necessarily decrease with the introduction of ploughs, for more land had to be weeded, new implements and new techniques as much as larger production units were the means to expanding the area of land cultivated. The sources available do not allow for an adequate analysis of the effects of merchant penetration on the authority of the homestead heads. As there was no rapid reduction in the size of settlement units, it may be assumed that they were able at least partially to redefine their powers to cover the relationships of exchange with traders. But as cattle ownership and new technology became more widespread, the scene was set for a change in the form of settlement in Pondoland.

3 The Colonial state and the Mpondo chiefs, c. 1878–1905

The Natal government had, from the 1860s, shown interest in acquiring Port St Johns, and Pondoland itself, to protect the colony's trading interests and secure itself against border conflict.[44] But, having given up that part of his treaty state which he could not control in 1850, neither Faku nor his successor Mqikela had any interest in forfeiting land or their independence. Unilateral action by Natal was further inhibited by the Cape's concern to prevent any southward expansion by its sister British colony. In the 1870s, however, the Cape itself, the more powerful of the two colonies, began to extend its authority over the chiefdoms surrounding Pondoland. A resident was appointed in East Griqualand in 1873, and by 1878 magistrates had been placed in new administrative districts covering the whole of the area. This new wave of Colonial expansion beyond the Kei arose to some extent out of the Cape's desire to impose peace, secure its borders and protect its commerce. But at the root of the thrust beyond the Kei was the transformation of the political economy of the Colony following the development of diamond mining at Kimberley and the consequent boom in railway-building and commerce. Some colonial interests in the Cape and Natal, as well as the Colonial Office in Britain, responded to these changes by seeking to create a confederation in South Africa under imperial hegemony which would absorb both the Boer republics and the remaining independent African states. Bartle Frere, Cape Governor and High Commissioner sent to implement plans for confederation, was an ardent proponent of imperial expansion. His appointment coincided with the coming to power in 1878 of a Cape government which favoured a similar policy.

Pondoland was a peripheral problem for those executing imperial strategy.[45] There was no great incentive for them to annex the area, a step which might provoke another costly war. However, they were intent on controlling the ports along South Africa's coastline and blocking access by other foreign powers to the subcontinent. Although it was recognised that Port St Johns was not a major point of entry for firearms – most of the gun-running was conducted overland – Frere was concerned about the lack of Colonial control over goods coming into both Pondoland and the recently annexed Transkeian chiefdoms by this route. The customs duties which could be levied at the port provided an added attraction. When Mqikela refused to sell the port, not for the first time, in 1878, he was 'deposed' by Frere and the strip of land at the Mzimvubu mouth was purchased from the western Mpondo chief Nqwiliso, who was more cautious in the face of Cape expansionism. Colonial expansion into the areas around Pondoland also provided an opportunity for some of the chiefs on

31

the borders of Pondoland, who were subject to Mpondo raids and refused to recognise Mqikela's authority, to switch their allegiance. The Xesibe chief had been asking for a Colonial magistrate since 1873; in 1878, his country was taken over. At the same time, a British resident was appointed in Pondoland.

These unilateral Colonial encroachments had serious repercussions for the Mpondo paramountcy. The deposition itself hardly affected the balance of power within Pondoland, but Mqikela lost the £100 annual payment made by the Cape after the treaty of 1844. He also lost the levy made on each ship calling at St Johns and the licence fees from the traders settled there. He claimed control over Xesibeland and had given concessions on minerals and land in the area reputed to bring in £150 a year. Not only was his income much reduced at a time when firearms were urgently needed and a paid secretary had been taken on, but his independent access to trade goods was curtailed. These new forms of income had become particularly important to the paramount as centralised control over production and trade diminished in the later part of the nineteenth century. It was this attempt by some of the Mpondo chiefs to transform the nature of the Mpondo state that brought them into conflict with the Colony.

The paramount stopped short of opposing Colonial incursions by force. Though there was clearly sympathy with the revolts against Colonial authority in neighbouring East Griqualand in 1880 and a Mpondo force was mobilised on the border, little direct support was lent to the rebellious chiefs.[46] Rather the Mpondo attempted to accumulate firearms to counter further Colonial expansion and to explore diplomatic channels in order to secure a reversal of Cape policy. It was Mhlangaso, ambitious in his own right and determined to defend Mpondo independence, who emerged to take control of the councils of the Great Place and direct Mpondo policy. He secured the help of some of the largest local traders, whose interests were also threatened by the imposition of Cape customs dues and controls over the firearms trade. They were particularly keen to secure favoured access to the leading chiefs, still by far the largest cattle-owners, because of the trading depression in the early 1880s. The strategy developed was to appeal to the imperial authorities behind the backs of the Colonial government. When this had failed by 1884, Mhlangaso and his allies took more direct action against the Cape. He proclaimed a levy of fifty pounds on each wagon load of goods entering Pondoland from St Johns, thereby cutting the port off from its hinterland; lesser tariffs were imposed on overland routes. Plans were set in motion, with the aid of a trader who had previously been involved in the coastal trade, to establish an independent port on the Pondoland coastline. In 1885, Mhlangaso treated with

German agents and promised a land concession in exchange for aid against the Colony.

The Cape and imperial governments responded rapidly to this challenge.[47] An imperial protectorate was proclaimed over the whole coastline of Pondoland. The Cape refused to allow any shipping between its ports and the new Port Grosvenor; Natal was soon induced to support this prohibition. Colonial officials, aided by the Methodist missionary Hargreaves, exploited internal divisions in Pondoland – some of the chiefs had become concerned about the aggressive policy pursued by Mhlangaso – to secure a settlement in favour of the Colony without resort to arms. They met with some measure of success, not least because Mhlangaso was perceived to be aggrandising himself at the expense of other chiefs in Pondoland. When a major Mpondo army, reported to be 15,000 strong, was mobilised in 1886, the Cape responded by collecting together a large force of levies to aid its contingent of Mounted Riflemen. Faced with the possibility of a war which they could not win, the Mpondo chiefs agreed to submit to all Cape demands. The annexation of St Johns and Xesibeland was accepted, and a strip of land through which the major road from the Cape to Natal passed was sold. The roads were thrown open, the new port was closed, and a guarantee was given that no ships, save those cleared at Colonial ports, would have access to the Mpondo coastline. Substantial cash compensation was paid by the Cape, but the settlement severely limited the income that could be derived by the paramount as trade expanded. Mhlangaso's attempts to transform the Mpondo state and extend chiefly powers over merchant activity were finally blocked.

Mhlangaso did not immediately give up his attempts to construct an alliance against the Colony.[48] But his influence at the Great Place was rapidly undermined after Mqikela's death in 1887. Mqikela's great wife, Masarili, daughter of the Gcaleka paramount, had not borne a son. A number of contenders from amongst the supports to the great house were overlooked in favour of Sigcau, son of a low-ranking wife or, according to some traditions, of an unmarried woman, who was adopted by Masarili into the great house. It is clear that Sigcau was chosen as a strong man, a representative of the chiefs opposed to Mhlangaso. By 1889, Sigcau, at the head of an alliance which favoured conciliation with the Cape, emerged dominant at the Great Place. Mhlangaso, reluctant to accept subordinate status, chose to test Sigcau's power, and after two years of mounting tension, civil war broke out in 1891. Though the paramount's forces were by far the larger, Mhlangaso was able to retain the loyalty of his substantial personal following, and he won the support of Patekile, the powerful chief of the imiZizi on the Natal border, whose relationship with the paramountcy had long been strained. The well-armed 'rebels' could not win the war, but neither could Sigcau dislodge them from their defensive strongholds. Fighting continued until early 1894, when the Cape annexed Pondoland after a major, though not entirely decisive, battle between the two chiefs.

The civil war in Pondoland was a struggle for power between a new paramount and the dominant councillor of the old, a struggle over policy towards the colonial powers.[49] But there were other, related elements under-lying the conflict. Mhlangaso envisaged a very much expanded role for the chieftaincy. He was in favour of 'progressive' policies: a rapid increase in trade with tariffs as the basis of state revenue; concessions; and mining and transport development within Pondoland under the political authority of the chiefs. His policy was not greatly different from that of the Boer leaders in the Transvaal. Many of the lesser chiefs, reflecting popular opinion, were perturbed not only by the fact that his strategy increased the possibility of armed conflict with the Cape and consequent loss of land and stock, but also because such changes threatened to undermine their remaining authority. It was the paramountcy which would reap immediate benefit from new sources of income, while land would be alienated and the basis for communal access to resources disturbed. Mhlangaso was accused of 'selling' the country and alienating resources for his own benefit. These questions were debated explicitly at mass meetings at the Great Place after Mqikela's death and remained important points of tension in Mpondo politics over the next half century.

Sigcau accepted the limitations placed on his power by the Colony. However, the paramountcy as an institution was now increasingly dependent on new sources of revenue, all the more so after the benefits to be derived from the expansion of trade had been removed. His reign coincided with the period in which well-capitalised concessionaires and speculators, stimulated by the excitement of gold discoveries in the Transvaal, sought opportunities to invest throughout southern Africa.[50] Concessions were the only immediately available method by which the paramount's revenues could be expanded, and in the years between 1889 and 1894 Sigcau granted mineral, railway and land rights to one company in return for £6,000 in down payments and £1,900 annually. (Payments were made, but no works started before annexation.) He still collected trading licences and received payments from the Cape government for St Johns under the settlement of 1886. His position was thus not radically different from the concept of the chieftaincy held by Mhlangaso although Sigcau pursued the interests of the paramountcy far less aggressively.

It was the dispute over trade, tariffs and the powers of the Mpondo paramount that led to direct Colonial intervention in Pondoland in the 1880s. The Cape was not prepared to countenance a rival authority within its sphere of influence which drew revenue from trade and invited in foreign powers. But whatever the outstanding issues, an independent African chiefdom between the Cape and Natal was an anomaly in the 1890s. Annexation had only been delayed because the Colony was reluctant to go to war and could secure its major demands by exerting other forms of pressure.[51] Cecil Rhodes, representative of mining interests in the Colony and leading expansionist, came to power as Prime Minister in 1890. When he diverted his eyes from their northward gaze and began to busy himself with 'native affairs' in the Cape in 1894, he decided on immediate action. Renewed interest in the area on the part of Natal and chronic civil conflict in Pondoland provided immediate pretexts. The Chief Magistrates in the Transkeian Territories believed that the Mpondo would not fight unless they were forced. Both Sigcau and Nqwiliso, chief of Western Pondoland, were induced to accept the Colonial takeover.

Colonial rhetoric in justification of this 'peaceful transfer from a barbarous to a civilised government', as Rhodes called it, centred on the 'murder, rapine and spoliation practised by the chiefs'.[52] Annexation would not only save the people from the chiefs, it would also remove a dangerous focus of opposition to Colonial rule. This ideology reflected the intended transfer of power from one ruling group to another and the increasing orientation of the taxes, produce and labour of the homesteads to the colonies rather than to the chiefs. In this context, it is particularly important to understand the position of the Mpondo chiefs in the couple of decades before annexation, for they were the immediate targets of Colonial policy after annexation. The paramount's new sources of revenue were rapidly removed. Licence fees and control over traders were taken over by the Colonial state, concessions disallowed, rights to control access to major natural resources such as minerals and forests removed, and the importation of ammunition and liquor prohibited. In return, Sigcau received an annual payment of £1,000 – Nqwiliso in Western Pondoland was given £700 – which included moneys due for St Johns. Though the retainer was significantly larger than those granted to other Transkeian chiefs and underlined the importance attached by the Colonial authorities to the Mpondo chiefs, it would not make up for lost revenue, nor would it increase in the future. The threat of withdrawal also gave the administration an effective means to keep the chiefs under control.

The administrative system enforced in Pondoland had been developed over the previous few decades in other parts of the Transkeian Territories taken over by the Cape.[53] At its apex were the two Chief Magistrates – the posts were amalgamated in 1902 – in Umtata and Kokstad. They had considerable independent authority but referred major decisions to the Native Affairs Department, headed by a permanent secretary, in Cape Town. (The portfolio of 'Native Affairs' in the Cape Cabinet was usually held in conjunction with other posts.) The Transkeian area was divided into districts, each under the control of a magistrate who served as both a judicial and administrative officer. Districts were divided into locations – between about twenty and forty – under government-appointed and paid headmen. Though small detachments of police were stationed at each magisterial headquarters and the Cape Mounted Riflemen were on hand in the event of serious disturbances, the magistrates relied largely on the headmen to keep control. Colonial rule was financed by a ten-shilling hut tax. Married men paid this sum annually for each of their wives, who were considered to have separate huts. The system was designed to minimise the powers of the chiefs.

Sigcau had little alternative but to accept the terms imposed by the Colony, which were favourable in comparison with those obtained by other Transkeian chiefs. However, he did not accept the limitations placed on his power without a fight. In an attempt to win concessions from the Colony, he argued, in the next few years, that the administration was not honouring pledges it had made in 1894. His unease about the imposition of magisterial rule found a focus in the Colony's refusal to punish those who had rebelled against him before annexation.[54] The Colonial forces had moved into Pondoland before terms could be agreed between Mhlangaso and Sigcau. The new administration was prepared to recognise that Sigcau had won the war, and the paramount understood that Mhlangaso and four of his chiefly supporters would be exiled; that Patekile, chief of the rebel imiZizi, would be fined 200 head of cattle; and that Mhlangaso's followers, crowded into their defensive strongholds, would be dispersed throughout the chiefdom after submitting to the paramount and paying small fines. These were the kind of measures that the paramount would attempt to enforce after internal conflict in the chiefdom; by refusing to enforce them, the administration was underlining the fact that Sigcau was no longer an independent chief.

Mhlangaso was exiled, but Patekile delayed paying the full fine, and some of Mhlangaso's followers attempted to remain in their settlements. The administration would not use force on behalf of the paramount nor allow Sigcau to impose his own methods of coercion. When the first attempt to register huts for taxation was made in 1895, a large number of Mpondo came armed to a meeting with one of the newly appointed magistrates. Sigcau, accused of instigating the 'disturbance', claimed that he accepted the principle of a hut tax but would not sanction its collection until Mhlangaso's followers had been dispersed. By registering them in a block, the administration would be recognising that they could stay and thus, the paramount felt, provide his enemies with the opportunity to re-group against him. As the disagreement could not be settled by negotia-tion, Rhodes, who handled the crisis personally, eventually ordered Sigcau's arrest. In order to legalise Sigcau's detention, Rhodes rapidly passed enabling legislation. Sigcau's councillors in turn organised a collection of cattle to pay the legal expenses of challenging the Prime Minister and succeeded in having the proclamation invalidated after a much-publicised series of court cases. Sigcau was released and became the hub of rumours that an armed uprising was planned. He succeeded in hampering the implementation of Colonial rule for a year, but his tactics brought no concessions, and by the middle of 1896 he again adopted a more conciliatory stance. Rhodes and his successor, Sprigg, again made it clear that they would confiscate land and cattle in the event of a rebel-lion. Sigcau was rumoured to be sympathetic to rebels in neighbouring East Griqualand in 1897, but he gave them no active support.

Five districts were demarcated in Pondoland immediately after annexa-tion; some were found to be too large and the number was soon increased to seven: Lusikisiki, Flagstaff, Bizana and Tabankulu to the east of the Mzimvubu; Libode, Ngqeleni and Port St Johns to the west. Of those in Eastern Pondoland, Lusikisiki, with the paramount's Great Place at its centre, was the largest; Flagstaff included the areas under the authority of a number of leading Mpondo subchiefs, including Mhlangaso's former strongholds, while immigrant chiefs predominated in Bizana and Taban-kulu. The task of demarcating locations, an important step in relocating power at the level of the headmen, was delayed by Sigcau's resistance and the coming of rinderpest, but resumed in 1897.[55] Most chiefs were appoint-ed as headmen. However, the geographical area under their authority in the Colonial system was limited to one location even if they had controlled much larger areas of land beforehand. Some were allowed to nominate headmen in the other locations into which their former chiefdoms were divided. Sigcau, arguing that he was chief of the whole of Pondoland, refused to accept the large personal location offered to him. It was divided into seven locations, the paramount nominating the headmen. In loca-tions where a number of petty chiefs or commoner leaders lived, the administration had to elevate one of their number and give him support until his authority was accepted. Such men, who owned their position to the Colonial state to a far greater degree than the leading chiefs, could provide an important basis of support for Colonial rule.

The exercise of delimiting boundaries and appointing headmen stimu-lated a number of serious disputes. The state could favour more sympathetic chiefs and limit the authority of those who displayed reluctance to bear the burden of Colonial rule. In particular, officials discriminated against the paramount. Sigcau rapidly realised that if he was to protect his position he would have to play by the administration's rules. He thus attempted to secure the nomination of sympathetic headmen wherever possible. He claimed the right to appoint headmen in the whole of Mhlangaso's former chiefdom, on the grounds that it had been forfeited by rebellion, and sought to place his great house, with his son and presumed successor, Marelane, in the heart of the area.[56] While officials allowed homesteads to be built for the great house in what became Nthlenzi location, Flagstaff, they would not allow Sigcau to appoint the headmen in this location, nor in the neighbouring areas formerly under Mhlangaso. The issue was complicated by the fact that some of the rebels, who had fled during the civil war, began to return, having neither submitted nor paid fines to the paramount. In 1899, Sigcau took matters into his own hands and sent indunas to bully the rebels out, initiated witchcraft accusations and personally manhandled one of Mhlangaso's followers. The administration again refused to concede any of Sigcau's demands and convicted him for assault. The paramount was eventually allowed to nominate the headman in Nthlenzi location itself after the initial appointee fell foul of his local magistrate, but not in the rest of Mhlangaso's area. Some officials felt that none of Sigcau's nominees should be appointed outside of the seven locations surrounding the Great Place at Qaukeni, as 'experience had shown that men recommended by him for Government work did more work for him than for the authorities'.[57]

Though the headmen in the Transkeian Territories were not actually responsible for the collection of taxes, and received no portion of the tax, they were required to see that the people of their location came to the office to pay. They played some role in supervising an increasing range of state regulations over stray stock and cattle disease, minor forests and noxious weeds, census counts, immigrants and schools, to mention but a few. They also became increasingly important in the system of land allocation. For their services they received annual retainers of between £6 in the case of a recently appointed commoner and £40 in the case of a high-ranking chief. By the turn of the century, the headmen had not become nearly so central in the administration of the Pondoland districts as they were in some other parts of the Territories. Magistrates still consulted with chiefs on important matters and were aware that the support of the chiefs was important if administrative action in connection with, for example, inoculation against rinderpest and the dipping of sheep was to be successful. But the position of headmen provided scope for incumbents to build a local power base out of their intermediary position between the state and the people. If the chiefs could not control headmen, the latter could compete for power with hereditary rulers and expect some support from the state. And a shift in the balance of power between chiefs and those headmen who were not chiefs had implications for chiefly control over customary dues as well as the new intermediary functions. Such dues became all the more important to the leading chiefs as they had lost control of communal labour on any scale, had become less pivotal in the relationships surrounding the circulation of stock, and, in the case of the paramount, had lost access to revenue from traders and concessionaires. Whereas chiefly politics had increasingly centred on trade and firearms in the period before annexation, competition for control over headmen and dues again became more central. The paramount's income from such sources may have been declining in the late nineteenth century, but death duties, immigration fees, court fines and property 'eaten up' after witchcraft accusations still brought in hundreds of cattle. These were not only still of some importance for securing followers, but also in trade; in cash terms, at the turn of the century, one hundred animals were worth over £1,000. The payment of dues was also an important element in the symbolic recognition of chieftaincy by commoners.

Officials adopted the policy that customs which were not directly inimical to 'civilised government' should be allowed. Witchcraft was not sanctioned, but the chiefs were allowed to collect customary payments as long as they did not use force. Officials believed that 'our system of administration in its broad effects gradually destroys adherence to native customs'.[58] The people had, in any case, a prior creditor in the shape of the administration, nor were all any longer so reliant on the chiefs for the wherewithal to live. Indeed, where evidence is available on the collection of tribute payments, it suggests that the chiefs lost ground rapidly. In 1901, Langasiki, chief of the Ngutyana in Bizana district, claimed that he was owed thirty beasts for death duties by his people. Without them he maintained he 'would have no food to eat' or, as the magistrate clarified, 'no revenue to support him in his proper state and dignity as chief'.[59] When Langasiki ignored the magistrate's warning and took dues by force, as he would have done before annexation, he was immediately cautioned, and the stock and cash seized were returned. The magistrates were well aware that they did not always hear of disputes and that dues were 'frequently collected by force, though there is usually no proof of this, as the people are afraid to report their chiefs'. But Sigcau was also warned when complaints were received about the activities of his indunas, and he stood to lose very much more in the shape of death duties than Langasiki. If such cases were reported, it was often through local headmen who were not sympathetic to the chiefs. Sigcau and other leading chiefs also appear to

39

have lost control over the settlement fees of the many immigrants who came into Pondoland after annexation.[60] Though officials promised at annexation that Pondoland would not be flooded with aliens, neither they nor the chiefs could fully control the flow of people into the relatively sparsely populated Pondoland districts from the overcrowded locations of the Ciskei, southern Transkei and southern Natal. When magistrates did learn that strangers had moved into their districts without permission, they usually found that it caused less trouble to allow them to stay, particularly if the local headman was favoured by the magistrate. It was to the headmen that immigrants would go to obtain sites and pay fees.

No chiefly courts were recognised after annexation, and all criminal cases were supposed to be tried in the magistrates' courts, for crimes were now against the Colonial state rather than the chiefs. But except where the small local police contingents expressly sought out offenders, the magistrates relied on headmen to report breaches of the law. Officials reported on a number of occasions that many headmen did their best 'to keep their followers away from the office' and that 'crime was hushed up and settled privately in Native style'.[61] As one magistrate realised, it was probably for this reason that crime was 'conspicuous by its absence' in the years after annexation. It is likely that certain headmen were able to expand the area of their authority to cover some criminal cases that would previously have gone to chiefly courts. The expense of taking civil cases to the magistrates was prohibitive. Lawyers had to be paid, as well as court and messenger fees; litigants could not necessarily expect any different form of justice, as the magistrates applied 'native law and custom' in cases between non-Christian Africans. It was, for the most part, civil cases involving colonials and Christians that came to the courts in the early years after annexation. For the rest, the state was content to let chiefs and headmen arbitrate.

During the decade after annexation, then, the paramount lost not only income from traders and concessionaires, but found that the customary dues received were whittled away. The administration attempted to locate power at the level of the headmen and to make the headmen directly responsible to magistrates rather than the chiefs. The pace of change was not rapid, and the paramount in particular retained considerable authority in Pondoland. But the balance of power was shifting to headmen and to certain of the chiefs who chose a more clearly co-operative role. Although Sigcau was more cautious after the Nthlenzi episode in 1899 and supported Colonial measures in a variety of spheres, his early attempts to retain power made officials all the more determined to make an example of him. Annexation reinforced and hastened political changes that had been evident in the late decades of the nineteenth century and finally closed off the possibility of any extension of chiefly power based on new sources of wealth. State intervention did contribute further to freeing the homesteads from tributary controls exercised by the chiefs. But while the diminution of tributary constraints contributed to release new forces of production in Pondoland, the homesteads faced new demands which locked them further into the broader Colonial economy.

2
Crops, cattle and the origins of labour migrancy, 1894–1911

1 Production, exchange and the entrenchment of economic dependence

At the time Pondoland was annexed, Cape 'native policy' was in flux. The opening of the Witwatersrand goldfields in the mid-1880s and further development of a capitalist mining sector in the subcontinent had, as Bundy and Trapido have suggested, important repercussions for the African peasantry of the Cape.[1] Demand for labour in the mines increased rapidly. Large new markets in the interior quickened the pulse of commerce in the Colonial ports and pulled the Cape out of the economic depression of the early 1880s. Labour was also required in the coastal towns and farms of the Colony. The influence of those Colonial interests which favoured the retention of an African peasantry began to wane; that of those who saw the future of the African population as labourers in capitalist enterprises waxed.

Rhodes brought the issues facing the administration in the Territories into sharp focus in a speech delivered at Kokstad, shortly after he had visited Pondoland to finalise the terms of annexation.

> We have now on this side of the Kei 600,000 Natives, and we must leave the land for them. The Natives [will] no longer be destroyed by tribal wars and their increase [will] become a very serious matter. We can only hope that we shall be able to deal with them and show them that there is dignity in labour and that we pay the highest price for labour of any country in which the manual work is performed by natives.[2]

His priority, the mobilisation of a labour supply, was manifest. At the same time he was adamant that no more land should be taken from the African population in the Territories, that they should live separately in 'native reserves' and 'not be mixed with the white man at all'.[3] It was partly for this reason that he was unsympathetic to the concessions in Pondoland.

42

Rhodes's thinking was crystallised in the Glen Grey Act, passed in the same year that Pondoland was annexed, which both drew on existing developments in policy and presaged the new future for the African areas.[4] The Act, a compromise between various factions in Cape politics, had three major provisions: a change in the nature of land tenure, local District Councils in the African areas and a labour tax. Communal tenure was to be replaced by a system of individual tenure under which title would be given to plots of land which could be neither alienated nor accumulated. While underpinning a stable rural population, individual tenure would in time drive more people on to the labour market. Control of land distribution would be taken out of the hands of the chiefs and headmen. The labour tax, to be levied on those who could not show that they had been out to work, would 'give some gentle stimulus to these people to make them go on working'.[5] A Government Native Labour Agency was to be established to supervise the large new labour force which the Act sought to mobilise. The Councils were the first step on the road to separate political institutions for the African population. Mindful of the threat that voters from the Transkeian Territories could swamp the established electorate of the Colony, the Cape legislature had already increased its franchise qualifications in 1887 and 1892. The District Councils, to be funded by an additional tax of ten shillings on each married man, would, under the guidance of the magistrates, take charge of local development and thus remove this expense from the central government.

The Act was initially implemented in the four Fingoland districts of the southern Transkei, but officials hoped that it would soon be extended throughout the Territories. Its measures, however, stimulated widespread opposition from a broad cross-section of the African population.[6] Partly because of this opposition and partly because of administrative difficulties, the labour tax was dropped and individual tenure became optional – each district could decide for or against the scheme. The effects of natural disasters, land shortage and the operation of the market proved enough to mobilise labour in the next decade, and direct state intervention became less urgent. By contrast, strenuous efforts were made to implement the council system after the South African War (1899–1902). Despite continued protests, District Councils were imposed in most parts of the Territories by 1906, and representatives from the districts were incorporated into a Transkeian Territories General Council. The Mpondo chiefs, however, remained doubtful of the advantages of the council system, and the Chief Magistrate of the Territories accepted that 'the Pondos were not yet ripe for it'.[7] Councils were only introduced in Western and Eastern Pondoland in 1911 and 1927 respectively. The Glen Grey Act thus had little effect on the people of Pondoland, and no immediate attempt was made to restructure land-holding or the older Colonial administrative system in the area.

Indeed, Colonial rule initially stimulated rather than constrained rural production, especially of crops. Except for small areas around the magisterial centres, the land in Pondoland remained in African hands under communal tenure. If grazing land was still under pressure, a situation soon to be changed by rinderpest, there was no shortage of space for homesteads and arable plots.

> As regards Pondoland [commented an official in 1897] the population is very sparse and with the exception of a few favoured localities where the soil is rich the country could easily sustain twice the number of persons it now carries. In fact when travelling one is struck by the small number of kraals in sight as compared with those in the other [African] Territories, and there will be no difficulty in locating the Pondos for another generation or two.[8]

The hut tax had been imposed, and, as it had to be paid in cash, every family had now to find an annual income. It was a tax conceived in earlier decades when the primary aims of the Colonial state had been to raise revenue and stimulate the general process of commoditisation in the African areas, rather than specifically to mobilise a labour force. As a rate on the number of wives or huts, it was an indirect tax on production. But as a flat rate it did not discriminate against larger producers and indirectly encouraged the adoption of new technology which reduced dependence on female labour for the extension of cultivation. It was usually collected after the harvest months of June and July. Commoner families were also less subject to demands for tribute and dues by the chiefs, and the constraints on accumulation by commoners probably diminished. Furthermore, annexation had the effect of opening larger markets, especially for grain, to producers in Pondoland.

Magisterial headquarters were established on the transport routes at points where sufficient wood and water were available for the anticipated village settlements. Some, such as Libode and Flagstaff, grew around existing trading stations. Lusikisiki, on the other hand, was chosen because of its strategic location; it was near the Great Place and, as an official pointed out, 'between the Pondos and the forests'.[9] The headquarters were roughly equidistant from one another, about one day's ride on horseback apart, so that none was too isolated in case of trouble. Within a decade after annexation they had drawn a sizeable and mixed population. The magistrates soon started courts and their inevitable accompaniments, lock-ups. Court and prison officials were assigned to them, along with clerical staff, small police contingents and a few officers from other

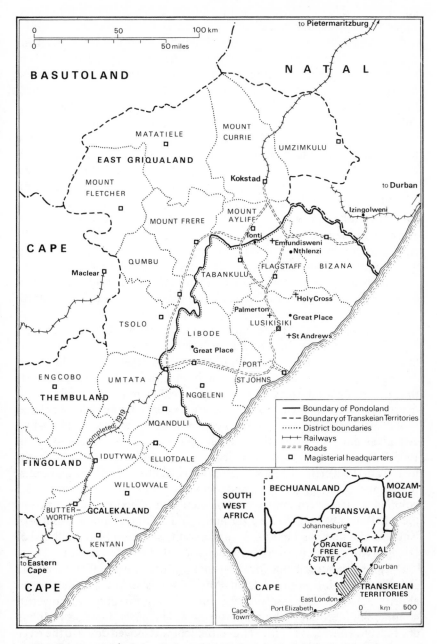

2 Sketch map of Pondoland after 1910: Colonial administrative boundaries and place names.

government departments. Detachments of between fifty and one hundred Cape Mounted Riflemen were maintained at some centres for a few years; with them arrived canteen-keepers. Small hotels sprang up to cater for the more transient elements in the European population. Craftsmen were needed as permanent buildings began to be erected; smiths were essential for colonial riders. (The Mpondo did not shoe their horses.) Traders, transport riders and butchers arrived to supply these communities. The villages also catered for the surrounding African population. A few specialist labour recruiters set up business. Eating houses provided sustenance for those coming into town to pay taxes, attend on the magistrate, purchase goods or contract for work outside Pondoland. European and Coloured families, at least, employed servants. Only Port St Johns with 778 inhabitants was classified as an urban community when the census count was taken in 1911.[10] Lusikisiki, the most important administrative centre, and Flagstaff and Bizana, with the greatest concentration of traders and recruiters, probably grew to almost half the size. Although some of the settled village inhabitants had access to garden plots and to the commonage which was reserved around the magisterial headquarters, few could produce sufficient for their subsistence. The villages did, therefore, provide new markets for produce from the districts.

The network of dispersed trading stations remained intact. Traders organised themselves into local associations and were able to win significant concessions from the administration. By 1904, officials began to enforce a rule that each station should be at least five miles from the next, thus providing established traders with a local monopoly.[11] While not all the rural sites were taken, those that remained tended to be in more isolated spots; new village stores largely accounted for the increase in trading establishments from something under 100 prior to annexation to 119 in 1905.[12] Pressure from the traders led to the exclusion of Indian businessmen from the Territories; it was also partly due to their efforts that transport links between stations and between Pondoland and the major colonial centres were improved. The metalling of major roads was completed. Railways had reached termini in East Griqualand and southern Natal, and a new road linking Bizana and the southern Natal railhead of Izingolweni was built, partly with newly available prison labour.

Despite pressures from local business interests and officials, all the schemes involving railways from Port St Johns to the interior proved abortive. A large new harbour was considered a threat by the powerful commercial interests in the established colonial ports. But Port St Johns did receive a new lease of life. The settlement was moved down to the river mouth itself; a jetty, warehouse and new roads on either side of the river bank linked by a pontoon ferry were built. The volume of shipping through the port increased dramatically.[13] Even after the 1886 agreement, seldom more than 20 boats called annually; in 1898, the number had climbed to 164. Cape merchants could now compete with those in Natal for Pondoland markets. The value of goods forwarded by this route increased from a few thousand pounds annually to over £113,000 worth of imports and £45,000 of exports by the same year. Pondoland had become more accessible both by land and sea routes; at the same time, markets outside Pondoland could be reached more easily.

In the first few years after annexation, such advantages were of little aid to producers, for Pondoland was struck by a devastating series of natural disasters which were completely unrelated, at least in the official mind, to the new political order. In 1894 and 1895, 'drought unprecedented within memory' returned; there was a general shortage of food, and grain had to be imported.[14] The situation was exacerbated between 1894 and 1896 by a series of locust plagues. The magistrate of Ngqeleni, in one of his first annual reports, claimed that 'locusts in myriads' had invaded the district and 'crops which were a foot high were eaten off the ground'. These reverses, while they hampered cultivation and resulted in a small increase in labour migrancy, had no serious long-term effects. By 1897, the magistrate in Flagstaff could report that a good harvest had been reaped in 1896. In the next year there were more general reports of 'abundant crops' and exports. However, as cultivation began to recover, rinderpest, the virulent cattle disease which had swept through much of subsaharan Africa in the previous few years, decimated the herds.

Neither the Colonial government nor the Mpondo themselves were unmindful of the damage that the disease could cause; when it reached the borders of the Cape Colony early in 1897, preventive measures were taken. The Cape closed its borders to cattle movements, built fences to keep cattle from Natal and Basutoland outside the Territories, and cleared belts around these barriers. Cordons around Pondoland were 'almost entirely maintained by the voluntary guards of the Pondos', and 'at the special request of Sigcau, a cordon was also established along the Mzimvubu river to divide East and West Pondoland'.[15] Such measures had been used against exotic diseases prior to annexation. In neighbouring East Griqualand, rinderpest fuelled rural 'disturbances' which arose initially out of conflict between white landowners and the surrounding African population. The latter saw the disease as part of an attempt by the settler population and the Colonial government to undermine their position on the land. Throughout the Territories, there was opposition to the system of inoculation based on 'culture kraals' in which animals were infected to produce serum. Although there were rumours of resistance in Pondoland, Sigcau 'the owner of several thousand head of cattle fell in with the idea of inoculating'. Little inoculation was in fact done in Pondoland, by no means a priority area for the much-overstretched Colonial veterinary services. In any case, rinderpest proved uncontrollable. Pondoland was one of the last areas infected, probably because of the efforts made to isolate herds, but between August and December 1897 most of the cattle died. The Chief Magistrate estimated losses in the Territories at 80 per cent; statistics of the cattle numbers both before and after rinderpest are insufficiently accurate to confirm this figure (Table 5). One trader in Flagstaff district, who had inoculated diligently, lost all but nine of the forty-one animals he had on hand.[16] The course of the disease was erratic; few homesteads escaped, but, while some lost all, some were left with at least the nucleus of a herd.

Whatever the exact losses, the disease was clearly a serious blow to the rural population. The cattle trade was killed at a stroke. Some traders bought up animals for very low prices while the disease raged, in the hope that they could immunise and resell them, but once rinderpest had passed those who still had animals hung on to them.[17] Although hides from diseased animals were supposed to be buried, along with the carcasses, in order to prevent further infection, many did find their way to the traders. Sixty thousand hides reached Port St Johns by December 1897, but the temporary boom in the hide trade was short-lived.[18] The Mpondo had been deprived of their two key exports. Rinderpest had even deeper implications for an economy so closely tied to cattle. Not only were milk and meat short and loans and ceremonies involving the passage of stock restricted, but cultivation, which was increasingly dependent on the use of draught, was severely hampered. Another starvation threatened, for although many families had cash from hides, rinderpest disrupted the system of transport and drove costs of wagon carriage upwards, thus restricting imports of grain.

The resilience of the rural economy was such, however, that recovery was rapid.[19] But in the process of recovery the shape of the rural economy underwent further change. Unlike lung-sickness and redwater, rinderpest did not become endemic. Demand for cattle drove prices up to heights of over £15 a head, but the Mpondo soon began to import.[20] While a few homesteads had sufficient cash or produce to exchange for stock, many men had to migrate out of Pondoland to work, often for the first time, in order to restore the herds; the number of men obtaining labour passes increased from under 2,000 before the disease to over 4,000 in 1898. As grazing was very lush, the animals remaining, and those purchased, increased rapidly, and within a few years many homesteads again had sufficient oxen for ploughing. As in the nineteenth century, cattle losses stimulated more intensive cultivation. More ploughs were purchased – by 1904, according to the census, there were over 8,000 in Pondoland – and the area of land cultivated was greatly extended. Crops were now increasingly important both for subsistence and as a source of cash income with which to pay taxes and purchase commodities.

Not only had transport facilities improved in the years after annexation, but the demand for crops outside Pondoland also soared. Production on many European farms was severely disrupted during the South African War at a time when the colonial powers had to feed large contingents of troops. Africans in other parts of the Territories, who were already beginning to feel the pinch of land shortage, were not in so favourable a position to respond to this demand. In fact, parts of the Transkei were struck by a series of droughts between 1901 and 1904 which had a far less serious effect on Pondoland. Markets for Mpondo grain therefore opened within the Territories as well. The availability of large quantities of produce attracted considerable numbers of itinerant European and African traders and speculators, whose activities supplemented those of the established traders. Prices paid for grain rose in the first decade of the century, sometimes to over ten shillings a bag.

It is true that the magistrates, from whom most of the information about production at this time comes, had reason to emphasise the benefits of Colonial rule, of which, they considered, hard work in the fields was one. Yet they generally considered the Mpondo 'backward' with 'no desire for advancement', and their reports are made despite their general opinion of their charges. In 1901 the magistrate of Lusikisiki recorded that 'thousands of bags of mealies and Kaffir-corn [sorghum] were harvested, most of which were exported to the Colony and other territories where grain is scarce and dear'.[21] 'I estimate', wrote the official at Flagstaff in 1902, 'that the Traders in this district bought up some nine thousand bags of mealies and Kaffir corn from last year's crops and they are now selling to outside buyers who have come into the district from Thembuland and Transkei'.[22] Two years later, the magistrate at Bizana could say with confidence that 'in an ordinary season, this district exports many thousand bags of grain'.[23] According to the census of 1904, more sorghum was produced in Libode than in any other district not only in the Transkeian Territories, but in the Cape Colony as a whole, while Ngqeleni had the largest harvest of maize.[24] Such figures are highly suspect, for they are based on estimates. However, enumerators in the various Transkeian districts used similar methods of estimation, and many of the census officers, usually magistrates, had had experience of other districts. Their returns do suggest that Mpondo crops made a better impression on them than those elsewhere.

Rough calculations from estimates made at the time suggest that traders were purchasing about a fifth, perhaps a quarter, of the grain produced in Pondoland. (Yields and exports varied greatly from year to year.)

Average homestead production was probably well over twenty bags (200 lb each), perhaps closer to forty; sales at average prices could have brought homesteads over £3 a year. All that was needed to produce this comparatively small surplus was a plough, and most families needed income from crops to compensate for their loss of income from pastoral products. If there were indeed around 8,000 ploughs by 1904, for a population which totalled around 200,000, ploughs must have been available to almost every homestead, and observations suggest that this was the case (Table 1). Although a minority of families clearly produced more, and others less, than the average, the extension of crop production appears to have been a fairly general phenomenon. For the most part, producers concentrated on the staple grain crops, maize and sorghum. However, it was particularly maize, which had a shorter growing season, a higher yield per unit of land planted, and stored better, which was planted more extensively. While production of sorghum remained fairly stable in the first decade of the century, estimates suggest that production of maize almost doubled (Table 7). Though traders did purchase sorghum, maize was of far greater importance as an export crop. By and large, producers used their own maize seed, which had been acclimatised in Pondoland over a long period. Some new crops were introduced: coffee, cotton, bananas and citrus on the coast; peaches and wheat, grown as a winter crop, inland. None of these were marketed on any scale, and cash cropping of tropical plants did not take root.[25] Most successful of the new crops was oats, grown for horse fodder, which was always in demand at the magisterial towns. Recently arrived immigrant families led the way in diversifying cropping patterns.

The sudden loss of cattle also increased Mpondo receptivity to small stock.[26] Sheep and goats provided a source of meat, even milk, as well as an alternative to cattle in bridewealth transactions. Wool gave a new source of income to many homesteads, which was particularly valuable, as it could carry them over lean periods in the annual productive cycle; shearing times were in October/November, some months after crops had been exchanged, and in March/April, before the next harvest. Woolled sheep were purchased from traders – at prices of under £1 they were far more easily accessible than cattle – but in 1900 and 1901 'great numbers of sheep and goats from Transkei and Thembuland were exchanged in Pondoland' by African people who had little else with which to pay for Mpondo grain.[27] Estimates, again suspect, suggest that the number of woolled sheep in the area quadrupled to about 200,000 by 1909, while the number of goats doubled to around the same figure (Table 6). Small stock were incorporated in coastal districts as well as in upland areas; they were no longer being used merely to exploit grazing unsuitable for cattle.

Officials specifically encouraged the adoption of small stock, and the Scab Proclamation, which enforced dipping to combat the disease, was extended to Pondoland in 1903. While the proclamation excited some opposition, as it had in other colonial districts amongst both African and settler stockowners, the chiefs in Pondoland were amenable to the construction of tanks, and the work of the sheep inspectors was not seriously hampered.

Grain exports probably did compensate, to a large degree, for the loss of income from pastoral products in the first decade of the twentieth century. In the best seasons, perhaps 40,000 bags were sold to traders; at from five to ten shillings a bag these fetched close to the amount that the few thousand cattle, at around £5 a head, exported annually fetched before rinderpest. Similarly, wool exports, at least from the upland areas, to some extent compensated for the loss of hides. Most homesteads, however, remained dependent in this decade on migrant labour to restock; labour pass figures, after climbing to around 10,000 annually in the drought of 1904, remained stable for the rest of the decade, partly because cattle numbers rose so sharply (Table 2). By the end of the decade, the cattle population had probably reached its pre-rinderpest level, and well before this time hides and cattle were again being sold to the traders (Table 5). Disease regulations made cattle movements to the Cape impossible and to Natal increasingly difficult; as will become clear in the following section, much of the buying and selling of cattle through traders was conducted within Pondoland itself. All in all, then, the population of Pondoland had more to offer on colonial markets than ever before and was largely self-sufficient in foodstuffs. The magistrate at St Johns was probably justified in commenting, in 1909, that 'the natives as a whole are becoming richer in this district'.[28] What he did not say was that the producers were now dependent on continued imports and colonial markets; nor that new forms of production rendered rural producers highly vulnerable to natural conditions as well as to fluctuating prices.

Whereas sufficient could be produced for export in good years, bad years had a more devastating effect on crop production – few irrigated their lands – than they had on the pastoral economy. Imports of grain proved necessary not only immediately prior to rinderpest, but again during the next cycle of drought in 1903 and in specific districts hit by unpredictable local droughts on other occasions. Further, once production on European farms began to recover after the South African War and indeed expand rapidly in the latter part of the decade under stimulation from the reconstruction governments in the Transvaal and Orange Free State, markets for African grain become more limited.[29] More-developed white and yellow varieties of maize began to set the standard in the most impor-

51

tant markets. The magistrate of Mount Frere, on the borders of Pondoland, summed up the situation in 1909.

> The vast strides which the Mealie Export Trade has made in the past two or three years, and the great quantity of superior mealies which are now produced in the Transvaal, Natal and other parts of South Africa, has practically ousted the Kaffir Mealie from the market which it formerly possessed, and, if the present condition continues, – in my opinion it is likely to become more acute – the Trader will decline to buy mealies from the native, or purchase only in very limited quantities.[30]

Competition in external markets, coupled with the increased dependence of traders in Pondoland on finding buyers for grain within the Transkeian Territories, resulted in more violent price fluctuations.[31] Although Pondoland was, in general, less susceptible to drought than many other parts of the Territories, the cycle of rainfall tended to affect the whole of the area between the Drakensberg and the sea. A good year in Pondoland was likely to be a good year in the region as a whole, and, in an unregulated market, there was always the danger of a glut. Prices offered by the traders could drop to below five shillings a bag in comparison to the more usual price of between six and eight shillings. Traders could be more selective about the type of grain they purchased and the way in which they paid producers. In the years immediately before annexation, they had begun to pay cash for produce. When markets outside Pondoland became more accessible after annexation and producers demanded cash for their grain in order to pay taxes, cash payments became common. Towards the end of the first decade of the century, however, and in subsequent decades, traders became more and more reluctant to offer cash, for they could not easily recoup their expenditure on external markets. Instead, they gave 'good fors', usually metal tokens which allowed producers to purchase goods only at the store to which they had sold their grain. The system enabled traders to tie the local population to their stores.

Producers could store more grain during times of glut in the hope that demand and prices would improve in the next season. However, grain stored in underground pits tended to become musty and discoloured, and was of little use for sale outside Pondoland.[32] Traders were reluctant to purchase it at all. Gluts therefore tended to result in increased consumption – the quantity of grain consumed was to some extent elastic – marked by the frequent beer parties that so often aroused the ire of officials. The dangers of overproduction seem to have inhibited further extension of cultivation by the end of the first decade of the century. 'In good seasons', the magistrate of Ngqeleni remarked in 1910, 'the prices realised barely pay for the cost of production.'[33] At the same time, the growth in stock numbers reduced dependence, at least in some homesteads, on grain for both consumption and sale. When markets could not be found outside Pondoland, traders had little alternative but to store more of the grain they bought in anticipation of a bad season in Pondoland or of the periods of shortage in the annual agricultural cycle, when they could sell grain back to the homesteads. Buying and reselling had begun in the later decades of the nineteenth century. After purchasing about 400 bags of grain in the good season of 1893, one trader sold most of it back within Pondoland during the drought of 1895.[34] During the early years of the twentieth century, the availability of markets for grain outside Pondoland and the lack of demand within had curtailed the development of this practice. But from the end of the first decade of the century, buying and selling became widespread. Traders could make large profits from storing and reselling grain, as they had a monopoly of the market around their stations. Whereas they would pay up to ten shillings a bag for grain in bad years, and less than five shillings in good years, they charged up to £2 during times of starvation and often over fifteen shillings when demand was slow.[35]

The necessity of repurchasing grain was, to a large extent, forced on the African population. During bad seasons, as has been suggested, production in some homesteads failed to meet subsistence requirements. Even after good seasons, however, some families had to sell more grain than they could afford. They needed a cash income to pay taxes levied after the harvest, and as prices for grain dropped in good years, they would have to sell more than in bad years to realise the same income. They would then have to rely on cash from other produce, such as wool or tobacco, or on wages, to repurchase maize. The position was complicated by the problems of storage. Pit storage, a technique which had been general for some centuries along the east coast of South Africa, safeguarded grain against infestation by weevils.[36] But if seepage was to be prevented, the pits had to be dug in special soils and sealed carefully by a flat stone lined by dung. In areas where no suitable soils were available it served little purpose to dig pits; information from oral sources suggests that by no means all families used this system of storage.[37] Indeed, Hunter's map of a hillside in Pondoland in the early 1930s suggests that all the pits were concentrated in one area and that only about a quarter of the homesteads in the settlement had pits.[38] Even when pits were used, there was always a chance that the grain would become waterlogged. Some homesteads preferred to transfer the risks involved in storage to the traders, for it was better to face the prospect of having to repurchase grain at high prices than to

53

have neither cash from sales nor stored grain. Traders initially stored grain underground themselves. In fact, the high prices they charged in resale resulted in part from their attempts to cover themselves against the risk of grain being spoilt. But from the turn of the century the better-capitalised traders began to invest in large overground storage tanks. A few producers did the same, but the expense involved was prohibitive for most. There is little doubt that the majority of families tried to put aside sufficient grain to meet their needs till the next harvest and, where possible, reserves. (Pit-stored grain could, if kept dry, be used two or three years later.) Yet it was not always possible for them to do so.

The phenomenon of resale was also indicative of differential production. Those homesteads which had to purchase grain were not always those which had sold it after the harvest. Magistrates pointed to paupers who could not find the cash to pay their hut tax after rinderpest.[39] While many families were able to reaccumulate cattle in the next decade, some still remained short of draught and could not participate in the general extension of cultivation. Such families could no longer rely on help from surrounding homesteads or from the chiefs; wealthier producers often sold rather than distributed their surplus. Poorer families were therefore likely to become indebted to traders, debt that would be compounded in each bad season.[40] The traders were not averse to extending credit, for it further entrenched their monopoly. Traders also acted as money-lenders, an activity that was only partly controlled by the Usury Act of 1908, which limited interest rates on cash loans. When reporting on the operation of this piece of legislation in 1911, magistrates revealed that they were not enforcing its provisions strictly.[41] Though usurious rates of interest on cash loans became less common, traders steered around the provisions of the Act by disguising loans as cash payments for pledges of cattle that were not yet available. The cash advanced for the animals could be less than half their market value. Indebtedness was not widespread in Pondoland in the first decade of the century, as it was in other parts of the Territories. The disadvantages to producers of an uncontrolled market had only begun to be felt. But in the next few decades it became a more general feature of the relationship between traders and producers. Debt cemented the dependence of Mpondo homesteads on wage labour.

2 Cattle advances and the origins of labour migrancy from Pondoland: traders, the mining industry and the state

Labour migrancy came late to Pondoland. During the 1870s and 1880s, when recruiters were 'opening up' surrounding Transkeian areas, missionaries and officials commented on the near impossibility of finding anyone in Pondoland who was prepared to leave the area for paid employ-ment.[42] Few Mpondo went to the diamond mines in Kimberley, the major employers of African workers in this period, and although some members of the small mission communities crossed the Mtamvuna to work in Natal, there was no significant movement to the neighbouring colony until the late 1890s. As has been illustrated, the simultaneous invasion of locusts and labour agents after annexation, coupled with the imposition of taxes and the serious drought of the preceding years, contributed to drive a relatively small percentage of the population into a spell of wage labour; rinderpest pushed the numbers up significantly (Table 2). Although some migrants, especially from Bizana, worked in Natal in the 1890s, most went to the Rand.[43] During the South African War, when the gold mines shut down, the rate of migrancy declined for a few years and the majority of workers switched to Natal. From 1903–4, when the coastal colonies were hit by a severe depression and wages for Cape workers on the Rand rose significantly, migrants from Pondoland returned to the gold mines; for the rest of the decade, well over 80 per cent of Mpondo migrants worked underground on the Rand.

By the turn of the century, the inhabitants of some South African chief-doms, which if anything were more remote from the labour centres than the Mpondo, had been involved in wage labour for over half a century.[44] Every other part of the Transkeian Territories was sending out a higher proportion of its male population (Table 4). The crux of Mpondo econom-ic independence, as has been illustrated, was their wealth in cattle. With these, they could purchase the commodities they needed; they had not found it necessary to go to Kimberley to work for firearms. The Mpondo chiefs, who retained their political independence for so much longer than those in most other parts of the country, were, unlike the Pedi chiefs, either unable or unwilling to send their men to the labour centres. They had effectively kept recruiters out of the country until the 1890s. Though some families had become indebted to traders by the turn of the century, and were forced to send migrants out to square their debts and pay their taxes, it was primarily the necessity to reaccumulate cattle that drove most early migrants from Pondoland to the labour centres.

When migrancy from Pondoland began, it took a peculiar form. At the turn of the century, a worker leaving the Transkeian Territories had some degree of choice as to how he entered employment. On the one hand, he could leave 'voluntarily', arrange his own pass and transport, find suitable employment at the labour centre of his choice, pay his own expenses in doing so, and have his wage paid out to him as he worked. On the other, he could 'join' with a labour agent in the Territories, 'touch pen' to a contract which specified his employer before he left home, and everything would be arranged for him, including an advance to cover travelling expenses and some or all of the wage. There were a variety of combinations of voluntary and contract migrancy, but whereas workers from most other parts of the Transkeian Territories preferred not to commit themselves to a contract before leaving home, most Mpondo workers were content to do so. In 1908, for example, over 80 per cent of migrants leaving Pondoland went through agents, but only 13 per cent of those leaving East Griqualand, 25 per cent leaving Thembuland and 42 per cent leaving Gcalekaland and Fingoland made this choice.[45] In some Eastern Pondoland districts the number leaving through agents exceeded 95 per cent.

It was essential for a worker to go to an agent if he wanted any advance on his wages, and most migrants from Pondoland took a very specific kind of advance.

> The natives of Pondoland, like the natives in the adjacent districts of Natal, were accustomed to go out to work on the 'cattle system', i.e. a native contracted to work for an employer for a certain period for nominal wages on condition that he should receive one or more head of cattle, which was generally issued to his family in advance.[46]

The origins of the system are obscure. Stock had often been paid to workers on farms, but an organised system of cattle advances for migrants on the mines was thought, at least by contemporary observers, to be unique to southern Natal and parts of the Transkeian Territories. The system appears to have come into operation soon after recruiting began in Pondoland and reached its height during the first decade of the twentieth century. There is no regular record of how many Mpondo migrants took cattle advances at this time. In 1907, proponents of the system claimed that about half did so, although magisterial reports suggest that the proportion was considerably higher.[47] Many more took advances of goods or cash.

Labour recruitment at this time was largely in the hands of the mining industry itself or of specialist labour contractors. The Government Labour Agent, appointed by the Rhodes ministry after the Glen Grey Act, succeeded in making only a marginal dent in the dominance of private-sector recruiters.[48] Employers and contractors usually used local agents to mobilise labour; in Pondoland, most of the agents were established traders. The latter provided a network of recruiting points throughout the area and were keen to augment their cash income with the capitation fees offered. Traders and the specialist agents who based themselves in the magisterial towns in turn employed runners, often African or Coloured men, who actually went from homestead to homestead persuading Mpondo families of the attractions of an advance. The runners received a commission for each worker that they channelled to an agent. It was not only the capitation fee, usually twenty to thirty shillings a worker, but sometimes more, that led the traders to take to recruiting. A system of advances was also the best method of ensuring that local business would benefit from wages earned outside Pondoland. Cash advances – the money would later be paid by the employer to the recruiter – increased turnover in the trading stores. Advances of goods over a period of time were even more profitable, as interest could be charged on the debt and the profit margin for goods given on credit was usually higher than on goods sold for cash or exchanged for produce. But cattle advances, for reasons that will be explained, opened the way to even higher gains for the traders.

The traders were in the best position to organise a supply of cattle from which to offer advances. Many ran herds of cattle themselves, which they grazed on their stations or on the commonages. Although they also suffered severe losses during rinderpest, they purchased cattle from outside the area in order to supplement the natural increase of their herds. As the number of cattle in Pondoland began to increase in the first decade of the century, they also renewed the local cattle trade, and because of the very high prices they offered for animals, those Mpondo homesteads with sufficient stock or in need of cash income began to sell. A beast could fetch over £15 at the turn of the century, the equivalent of at least thirty bags of grain, which few homesteads could produce in surplus crops. Even so, the local supply of cattle was never sufficient to meet the demand under the advance system, and by the end of the first decade of the century syndicates with substantial capital had been formed to organise and finance the purchase of stock from outside Pondoland and distribution to agents and traders within the area.[49]

Prospective migrants, sent in by a runner or on their own initiative, would have to visit the trading stations if they wanted an advance. In many cases, the actual cash wage for the job was not mentioned in the negotiations over the contract.

> We found [wrote two officials appointed to investigate the system in 1906] that the arrangements about the cattle had in all cases been made between the Pondo and some trader, the latter pointing out an animal and asking the native if he would work so many months for it to which the native readily agreed. In no transaction, so far as we have been able to ascertain, was a money value placed upon any animal as between trader and native.[50]

The cash wage was paid by the employer directly to the trader. It was possible for a worker to complete a contract without seeing cash at all, although in 1907 the Transvaal authorities stipulated that a minimum of ten shillings had to be paid out to workers on the Rand every month.[51]

The migrant would return to his homestead with the animal and often stayed at home for some months before going out to work. When he did depart, his family would keep the animal, but ownership would not usually pass until the trader had received the full cash wage from the employer. Recruiters specified this in the contracts in order to protect themselves, for if the migrant did not complete his contract, employers might refuse to pay the cash wage. If an advance beast died before ownership had passed, the trader was not usually bound to replace it. A migrant could find that he had worked through his contract, as one complained to an official, 'for a hide'.[52] As an animal was indivisible, it was all or nothing. Cattle imported from the interior into Pondoland were highly susceptible to redwater and lung-sickness, diseases that were more prevalent on the coast, and some did in fact die.

The traders were well protected, at least on paper, against losses in the advance system. At the same time, they made sure that their profits covered all contingencies. The value of cattle advances relative to the value of the cash wage advanced varied considerably from contract to contract.[53] Six months' work for a beast became a fairly standard rate. 'They went to the gold mines', an informant recalled, 'and worked six months for a beast. It did not matter if you were earning [the value of] £30 there, you would only get one beast for working six months.'[54] But some traders and contractors demanded more; some took less. If the worker went to the gold mines on a standard advance contract, the trader stood to get up to £18 for a single animal, as the basic underground pay for Cape workers by the middle of the first decade of the century was £3 a month. (The term 'month', as used in the contracts, referred to thirty shifts, which would take well over a month to complete.)

Traders who bred stock themselves and advanced beasts from their herds could make a very large cash profit, as their overheads were low. If they had to purchase stock from outside, where the cost of scrub cattle was lower than in Pondoland, they could probably realise half the value of the cash wage as profit. If they had to purchase from within Pondoland itself, their margins would be cut, as they sometimes had to pay prices approaching £15 until about 1904 and 1905. However, after this time, when the period of acute shortage had passed, cattle prices in Pondoland began to drop, and by 1908 the traders themselves admitted that £7 or £8 was a good price for an animal bought locally.[55] By this time, cattle could be got for £5 or less outside Pondoland. Yet the terms of the advance contracts remained relatively stable. One source suggests that in 1910, when another virulent cattle disease, East Coast fever, was raging in Natal and the areas around Pondoland, syndicates bought up cattle for next to nothing in areas where the disease had struck and moved them to Pondoland, which was still clean, for disposal at inflated prices under the advance system.[56]

Although there is no doubt that profits could be high, the business was not without its risks. In an area where redwater and lung-sickness were rife, and in an era of uncontrollable cattle diseases such as rinderpest and East Coast fever, traders and agents could face large and sudden losses while handling cattle. They also ran the risk of finding that a worker had deserted before completing his contract. While they may have been entitled to reclaim animals under the contract, recovery could be impossible if the family had sold or hidden the beast or if it had died. Recruiters designed the system to transfer as much of the risk as possible on to the migrants and their families, but still felt it necessary to keep their margin of profit high so that losses could be absorbed. At least one trader in Western Pondoland, and probably others, also reserved part of the cash advances he made as risk money which he did not pay back to the worker when the contract was completed.[57]

In 1902, when the gold mines recommenced production after the South African War, they were faced with an acute shortage of labour and turned their attention to the Transkeian Territories in order to win back and augment their former supply. While they relied to some extent on independent labour contractors and recruiting firms, the mining houses established their own recruiting organisation, the Witwatersrand Native Labour Association (WNLA), which had its roots in a similar body set up before the war. The Cape Regional Manager of WNLA had little in the way of permanent staff and was forced, as in the case of most other firms, to rely on the traders.[58] His chief agent persuaded him that there was very little chance of winning Mpondo workers for the gold mines unless cattle advances were offered. Despite reservations, WNLA committed itself to the system in 1904. It agreed to pay traders at a rate of £2 a month for each advance contract. The workers would receive 10s. a month on the Rand in addition to their advance. The remaining 10s. of the £3 wage was reserved by WNLA to start a fund which would cover losses incurred in the operation of the system. In effect, Mpondo workers were being paid at below the rates paid to voluntary workers from the Cape in return for the benefit of receiving cattle advances. The traders were fully protected from claims by WNLA for.the return of the cash paid to them, and WNLA sought to cover itself by stipulating in the contracts that 'the cattle should be returned to the Association in the event of the native's death or desertion before the agreement was completed'.

In the first half of 1904, 358 workers were sent to the mines through the WNLA scheme; in the second half of that year, 1,083; and in the first half of 1905, 1,560. Advances were initially limited to the cattle equivalent of £20, but this soon went by the board. The traders, who were anxious to commit WNLA as far as possible, for the scheme gave them an immediate cash income, started to offer much higher advances and longer contracts. The Secretary of WNLA, on his side, felt that the success of the scheme in mobilising workers offset the problems that large advances might cause. He even went so far as to try and have the regulation limiting contract periods in the Transvaal to an initial twelve months waived.[59] One migrant was advanced cattle to the value of £76, a sum which would have taken about four years to work off. In the first half of 1904, the total value of advances of £26 and over (implying contracts of at least 390 shifts or nearly one and a half years) amounted to £142. In the next six months the sum rose to £2,951, and in the first half of 1905, to £17,264. These amounts did not, of course, represent the total cash value of advances made to Mpondo workers by WNLA.

Payment of such large advances would not have led to serious problems in a situation where the work force was totally controlled. But despite pass laws, compounds and police, many Mpondo workers found it possible to desert; as their wage was at home in the shape of cattle, they had little to lose but the advance itself and a great deal to gain. Some, in fact, never left home. Some deserted on the journey to the Rand and walked home. Once on the Rand, migrants could purchase forged passes from a distribution network that appears to have been organised by the African clerks on the Rand, and could use these to return by train to the stations nearest Pondoland.[60] Extra passes, obtained by friends posing as voluntary workers under false names, could also be sent from home. WNLA called on the local traders, who had made the advances in the first place, to help in reclaiming cattle, but many refused to do so unless they were paid extra cash for their services. The fund established to provide for such a contingency had been discontinued early in 1906, when it was still in the black, and the advantage of cheap labour from Pondoland had been given directly over to the mines employing workers with advances. Though the losses faced – at least £6,000 and probably more – were not ruinous for an organisation of WNLA's size, it was clear that the system had to be stopped. Carried away in its eagerness to mobilise labour, the WNLA had devised a system which it could not control and had been, in effect, duped by the traders and those Mpondo workers who had deserted successfully. In the same year, WNLA, beset by internal conflicts, had for other reasons suspended its operations in South Africa.

Cattle advances did not die with the WNLA scheme; if anything, they became more widespread after 1906. A number of independent recruiting firms, in addition to the agents sent to Pondoland to recruit for individual mining companies, continued to operate the system extensively.[61] These firms protected themselves more carefully in the contracts by placing greater responsibility on the traders. However, the reverses suffered by WNLA were not without repercussions. Some of the leading mining houses decided that steps had to be taken to abolish advances completely. The Chamber of Mines had long been anxious to eliminate middlemen and labour touts, as they considered that such people, by taking a profit out of recruiting, increased the costs of labour to the mines. Cattle advances in particular made control over recruiters and workers difficult; they led to irregularities and desertions, and were far too unpredictable. As a result, when H. Taberer, formerly an official in the Transvaal Native Affairs Department, was sent to the Territories in 1908 as sole recruiter for such leading houses as Eckstein, Rand Mines and Consolidated Gold-fields, he refused to operate the advance system.[62] By this time, the position in relation to the labour supply had changed. The importation of Chinese workers had eased the labour shortage and, in the meantime, the supply of African workers had increased. Between 1904 and 1909, the number of Cape Africans working underground soared from under 4,000 to nearly 50,000: from 5.2 per cent of the total labour force to over 25 per cent.[63] While the mining houses were still concerned to secure more African workers to replace the Chinese, whose departure was imminent, some were now prepared to insist on their own terms.

Although the efforts to establish a state recruiting organisation in the Cape Colony had been abandoned before the turn of the century, the Colonial government was by no means unconcerned with regulating the activities of the private sector. In 1899, a Cape proclamation stipulated that all those seeking to procure workers from the Transvaal Territories for work elsewhere had to apply to the local magistrate for a Labour Agents Licence costing £5, and also provide evidence that they were backed by a surety.[64] From 1902, runners also had to be in possession of a licence, which cost five shillings, and were allowed to work for one agent only. The licences had to be renewed annually, and they could be withdrawn at the discretion of officials; the government, therefore, had some power to ensure that its regulations were implemented. The Colonial government was, however, totally committed to labour mobilisation, and magistrates were directly used to encourage migration and assist in recruiting.[65] Especially during the South African War, magistrates were deeply involved in recruiting and organising labour supplies to various sectors of the Cape economy and to military installations. Regulations over recruiting, as Schreiner made clear in his speech to the 1899 Cape

Native Labour Agents Bill, while they aimed at eliminating malpractices and giving some protection to the mines and the migrants, were primarily designed to maintain a future labour supply. 'It was of the greatest importance', he said, 'that this should go on without such circumstances as would make the native labourer hesitate to go forth where labour was required, and to earn money and bring back money to this colony to make this colony wealthy.'[66] Any regulation of the recruiting business had to take into account the necessity of maintaining supply, and as there had to be some profit for private sector agents if they were to continue their efforts, interference had to be circumspect.

Desertions, forgeries, unsound contracts and the complaints and legal proceedings that arose from advance contracts soon made them into an important issue for the Cape Native Affairs Department. Magistrates had not been unaware of the system prior to the difficulties experienced by WNLA in 1906, as many of the contracts were attested by them. Though some thought that the system led to abuse, advances were not illegal. When officials were appointed to investigate complaints arising out of the WNLA contracts, they hesitated to suggest the abolition of a system so successful in mobilising labour and advised only cosmetic changes.[67] Their recommendations had little or no effect on the working of the system, although the 1899 Agents Act, which demanded higher licence payments and higher sureties from recruiters, was extended to the Territories in 1907. Administrative problems, pressure from the mining houses, and the changing position in regard to the supply of labour brought about a reversal of official attitudes in 1908, and circulars requesting that the magistrates phase out advances were issued.[68] The Pondoland traders were up in arms. Though some complained that the risks involved in the system were so great that it was hardly worth their while continuing it, their response to its abolition suggests that such claims were merely designed to pull the wool over official eyes. They persuaded the Chief Magistrate that the workers were not getting an unfavourable deal; their concessions and threats won the day.

Their victory was, however, short-lived. From 1907, the Chamber of Mines and the Cape and Transvaal governments co-operated closely to control migrancy. Burton, Cape Minister of Native Affairs, and Merriman, Prime Minister, agreed with Taberer and the Chamber about the evils of advances. After a visit by Burton to the Territories and a labour conference in Cape Town in 1909, action was taken.[69] Cattle advances were first abolished in all but the Pondoland districts; then, in June 1910, in Pondoland itself.[70] The immediate pretext was the risk of spreading East Coast fever to Pondoland and the Cape through the many cattle movements that the system necessitated. A sudden loss of cattle, the Chief Magistrate felt, might lead to wholesale desertions.

All advances of over £5, in whatever form, were abolished at the same time. The victory of the Chamber of Mines was entrenched in the Native Labour Regulation Act, passed by the Union parliament in 1911, which further restricted advances to £2. It signified the position of dominance in the country achieved by the mining industry, which had succeeded in shaping the system of recruiting from Pondoland and elsewhere to its own ends. Local trading interests had been defeated, and the abolition of advances was not without implications for rural homesteads. In order to understand the effects of wage labour and state intervention on the homesteads, the analysis must be focussed on their position in the early years of migrancy from Pondoland.

3 Advances, homestead structure and differentiation

The specific system of migrancy that developed in Pondoland cannot be attributed to coercion on the part of the state, chiefs or recruiters, on the one hand, nor to ignorance on the part of migrants on the other. Though officials did their best to assist recruiters, there is no evidence to suggest that they used physical coercion; their attitudes to advances were ambivalent, and magistrates were certainly prepared to give passes to voluntary workers. Sigcau was willing to assist recruiters – in return he received 'a horse and other presents' from WNLA – and headmen were used as runners.[71] But the chiefs no longer had substantial controls over labour within Pondoland and appear to have played a persuasive role. In fact, one of Sigcau's efforts proved counterproductive because he was thought to be 'selling the Pondos for his benefit'. The traders could force indebted families to send out a migrant. But the very fact that the great majority of migrants were in a position to take cattle advances shows that they were still free of this type of bond. Traders and chiefs did have greater access to knowledge about conditions outside Pondoland, and there are suggestions in the evidence that they attempted to exploit their monopoly of information. One worker who complained about the terms of his contract asserted that he 'was induced to enter into this agreement by reason of having been told that there was no money in Johannesburg'.[72] However, it is unlikely that the Mpondo had no idea of the cash value of cattle – which they had been selling to traders for some decades – and information about wages would have soon filtered back into rural society.

To men like Burton, the cattle system appeared to be superexploitative; migrants were not receiving the full cash value of their wage, and this type of recruiting opened the way 'to endless abuses and *verneukerij* [swindling, trickery]'.[73] Yet the mining industry recognised that the system was the best method of mobilising a formerly recalcitrant rural population, and officials confirmed that the Mpondo would only go out for advances.

63

Traders, throughout their struggle to defend advances, claimed that they had the support of the people. While such assertions should be viewed with caution, for traders had much at stake and were in a good position to convince outsiders of what rural people thought without fear of contradiction, there is little doubt that their claim had some foundation. Nor was the preference of migrants based merely on the 'fondness of Natives for stock and their inability to resist anything offered on credit', as suggested by one official.[74]

One advantage in the system, for those prepared to take the risk, was the possibility of desertion. There is no doubt that some men took large advances, just as some took multiple advances, and either disappeared without working at all or failed to complete their contracts. The magistrates had moved into Pondoland only shortly before migrancy began and were not sufficiently in control to find and try every offender. Colonial courts were reluctant to bring criminal charges in cases which were essentially considered to be breaches of civil contracts. Though many traders defended the system strongly, they also railed at their inability to indemnify themselves against such risks. 'The Pondos', wrote a despairing Natal recruiter who received migrants from Pondoland to a trader in Bizana, 'will never show you mercy and in dealings, well you can tell me, they will do you down every time if they can. As you well know, false names, and false passes is [*sic*] the rule of the day in Natal.'[75] Their agitation for enforcement of criminal law and punishment against migrants who broke contract confirms that they did not always have sufficient means to recoup their losses from absconders. However, even in periods when desertion was at its peak, such as under the WNLA scheme in 1905–6, the proportion of unfulfilled contracts was probably no higher than 15 per cent of the total. The possibility of desertion cannot alone explain cattle advances.

Indeed, the advantages of the system for the rural population should be sought in the degree of control it enabled rural homesteads to exert over their migrants. An analysis of advances throws considerable light on the position of, and tensions in, the homesteads in the early twentieth century. Most of the early migrants from Pondoland were young men; by the end of the nineteenth century, hunting and military activities which had called on their labour in the earlier part of the century were no longer of great importance in Pondoland. Male labour had been absorbed largely in the pastoral economy. However, the actual task of herding, at least when the cattle remained in the more immediate vicinity of the homestead, usually fell to youths in their teens; those moving towards marriage would increasingly become involved in supervisory functions over herding and milking. Further, the sudden loss of cattle at the time of rinderpest no doubt diminished the immediate need for male labour in day-to-day pastoral activities. It is true that the use of oxen drew young men more deeply into certain phases of the agricultural cycle. The extension of the amount of land cultivated may also have increased demand for male labour in communal labour parties assembled at times of weeding and harvest. However, male labour was essential in cultivation only for very limited periods of the year, and in general the homesteads were still sufficiently large to spare the labour time of one or two young men without any great disruption to cultivation. The monthly figures of migration in the first decade of the century tend to confirm this point, for they reveal no very clear seasonal pattern in migration (Table 3). At this time, migrants do not seem to have timed their departure to meet with the demands for male labour in cultivation at planting and harvest. Indeed, contracts were often so long that men could not hope to return in under a year. Demographic changes in the late nineteenth century may have reinforced the tendency described. It seems that population growth from more rapid natural increase rather than immigration in the last few decades of the nineteenth century may have increased the proportion of youths in the homesteads by the turn of the century. (It would similarly have affected the female population, with possible implications for the amount of labour available for cultivation.) Unfortunately, the demographic evidence is not sufficiently clear to confirm this point.

The feature of early migrancy from Pondoland, then, was that large rural settlement groups sent out young men to sell their labour in order to augment the resources of the homesteads. The critical problem for those who remained at home was to ensure that the earnings of their youthful migrants did in fact benefit the homestead.

> The parent of a young man who 'joins' wishes to ensure that his wages shall come back to his kraal, and the young man himself likes to know that his earnings are safe as too many of them have experienced the cuteness of various 'sharks' that look out for the natives returning from the mines and rob them by some device or another of their earnings.[76]

There were both gangs and shops between Johannesburg and the Pondoland recruiting centres that were adept at separating migrants from their wages. But even more difficult to avoid were the temptations of the city.

> It is the unanimous opinion of traders and all who come into close contact with the native people at their homes [wrote one traders' representative] that most of the boys who go out to work return with little or no money. Their money has been frittered away on tin

65

boxes, concertinas, tawdry jewellery, sjamboks and suchlike things. It is no uncommon thing to hear them talk of illicit liquor sellers and prostitutes who have enticed their money from them.[77]

'Tawdry jewellery' was of little use to a family trying to survive in the years after rinderpest. The advance was therefore the best means for the family to remain in control of the worker's wage while he was away and to ensure that the spell of labour would benefit the homestead. Cash left at home, goods bought on credit over a period of time, or, best of all, a beast in the cattle kraal would guarantee this completely.

Advances had a further advantage for the homesteads. They helped to ensure that the migrant himself also came home. With little or no income in town, a worker had no means by which to establish himself outside the world of the mine compound where his basic needs of accommodation and food were, albeit inadequately, provided. He could do little in the way of sampling urban pleasures and acquiring urban tastes. The lack of financial resources pulled him back to rural society as effectively as limited contracts and pass laws pushed him. Aside from emotional considerations, the people at home had to defend themselves against the loss of a member of the homestead who had value both as a rural worker and as a future migrant. They did not want him to abscond and 'increase the ranks of criminal gangs' in Johannesburg.[78]

After rinderpest, when many homesteads were short of cattle, an advance system was particularly beneficial. It was far more sensible to place an advance beast in the kraal before the migrant left home than to wait, perhaps for more than a year, till he returned with cash. A cow in the kraal could make the difference between having a little milk and having none; an ox, the difference between being able to make up a span, or help a neighbour do so, and having insufficient cattle for draught. A cow could drop a calf in the period of a worker's absence and the advance would be doubled; it was better to secure the interest sooner rather than later, and the potential rate of interest was high. Cattle could then be exchanged, if necessary, with traders for high prices to acquire cash, food or commodities. Nor was it only for their productive and reproductive capacity that cattle were urgently needed. At a time when cultivation was being extended so rapidly, homesteads needed to secure their control over women. After the next major cattle disease (East Coast fever) some evidence suggests that fathers, in order to rebuild herds quickly, were demanding more rapid bridewealth payments.[79] Their ultimate sanction was the withdrawal of their daughters from the husbands' homesteads. There were certainly constraints on such action, but it was not exceptional.[80] In the post-rinderpest period, when competition for both cattle and female labour increased, there was probably great urgency for migrants to accumulate cattle for bridewealth, both to make initial payments and to prevent intervention by fathers. The rapidity with which cattle could be moved into the homesteads under the advance system offset the risks involved not only immediately after rinderpest, but also as cattle stocks began to increase. An official suggested that by the end of the first decade of the century the Mpondo were becoming more discriminating about the type of stock they took as advances.[81] It seems that at the turn of the century families took oxen so as to fulfil bridewealth obligations and accumulate draught, while later in the decade they specifically demanded young breeding stock.

Cattle, rather than cash advances, which could later be used to purchase cattle perhaps on terms more favourable than those offered in the cattle advance contracts, gave a further advantage to the families. For rights to cattle within the homesteads were clearly defined. In the case of unmarried migrants, who could not exercise independent rights of ownership over cattle, the advance system ensured that fathers retained complete control over their sons' wages. Young men could certainly own consumer items in their own right, and possibly kept some portion of cash advances for their own use. An advance of cattle excluded this possibility. 'The inducement of cattle at the present time', mentioned an official in 1906, 'is that it prevents boys from spending their wage directly they receive it.'[82] A cattle advance was the final insurance against the wage being wasted on commodities which could not reproduce themselves. It guaranteed both immediate conversion of earning power into stock and family control over wages. The fact that cattle advances were not so widely used outside Pondoland at the time was probably related to the smaller size of homesteads and more commoditised relationships in other parts of the Territories.

It would be a mistake to seek approval on the part of Mpondo homesteads for every phase and detail of the cattle system. The terms of the advance were, in the first instance, decided on by traders and agents who had a virtual monopoly of advance recruiting, and if migrants and their families could not be forced to take advances, they had sometimes to accept unfavourable contracts if they did want them. It may be that more migrants wanted cash advances, but the traders may have been reluctant to provide these, for they were not so profitable. In any case, many of the smaller traders probably found it more difficult to raise large sums of cash in the early years of recruiting. Migrants did sometimes object when they found that the wages they were receiving were, in effect, lower than those paid to workers on different types of contracts who were doing the same job.[83] They also objected, and deserted, when they learnt that their cattle had died and had not been replaced. But despite the sometimes un-favourable terms offered in advance contracts, both Mpondo families and the traders had an interest in defending the system against the policies of the mining industry. The specific interests of the Mpondo homesteads were not, however, taken into account by the state in its decisions about the abolition of advances. Cape ministers regarded the system as unfair and felt that the new schemes of deferred pay and remittances, paid after the work had been done, offered sufficient protection to both rural home-steads and rural traders.

Advances, particularly cattle advances, were a means by which the Mpondo homesteads could resist the downward spiral of impoverish-ment, increased expenditure on consumer goods and, ironically, prole-tarianisation. The cattle earned by migrants were, for many families, the means to agricultural recovery. Few could purchase cattle outright from the sale of crops or small stock, as prices after rinderpest were so inflated. Moreover, an adequate herd was a prerequisite for the extension of cul-tivation; there was little chance of a homestead being able to produce any surplus crop, much less sufficient to purchase stock, before it had actually acquired enough oxen for ploughing and transport. The system of migrancy preferred by the majority of Mpondo families enabled them to extend cultivation at the same time as the rate of migrancy increased. Migrancy from Pondoland was not initially predicated on the develop-ment of stratification; any homestead subject to losses from rinderpest may have needed to send out workers in order to restock. Yet the system of cattle advances was bound into, and reinforced, existing patterns of dif-ferentiation. The demand for cattle in Pondoland after rinderpest coupled with the high cash values attached to stock in advance contracts tended to keep the price of stock in Pondoland high. As the traders once men-tioned when arguing for the system, high prices benefited those home-steads which were in a position to sell animals during the first decade of the century.[84] The sons of such families were more likely to be able to escape migrancy once an adequate herd had been rebuilt. Families which were more dependent on their sons' earnings were, in effect, subsidising the price of cattle for the wealthier homesteads.

The advance system also hastened the commercialisation of cattle ex-changes within Pondoland. As those with cattle to sell could realise high prices and needed some cash income, there was less incentive for them to distribute cattle through loans. Families without cattle were less likely to be able to raise loans, even when the number of cattle among the wealth-ier had increased. Cattle were now circulating within Pondoland on a substantial scale through the medium of the traders. Such changes in the pattern of circulation were not entirely to the disadvantage of those with fewer animals. They could now accumulate the nucleus of a herd without having to enter into the relationships of service and dependence which had characterised stock distribution in pre-colonial times. They could also retain all the increase of the cattle they obtained from the traders. The cost they had to face was increased dependency on wage labour, although, at least in the first decade of the century, this did not necessarily entail permanent proletarianisation, for, as their herds increased, their sons could escape further trips.

Commercial exchanges were not always mediated through the agency of the traders. There is evidence to suggest that loaning relationships between households became transformed. Africans as well as traders were involved in money-lending, that is, in providing cash in return for pledges of cattle.[85] Cattle were also bought and sold outright between homesteads. How far such cash and credit transactions replaced the older system of loans is unclear. But the gradual transformation of loaning systems must have served to lock some families yet further into the system of migrancy. Such changes tended to reinforce the processes of differentiation based on the ability to produce a surplus crop. Those with more cattle were, after all, in a better position to extend cultivation. Although rinderpest did not discriminate between rich and poor, and probably did reshuffle the hierarchy of stockowners in Pondoland, there is little doubt that some were in a better position to reaccumulate a herd than others. The chiefs and headmen, the largest stockowners prior to rinderpest, could still command some income from dues, fines and differential bridewealth payments.[86] The homesteads of the chiefs and wealthier commoners tended to be larger: they could most easily afford to send sons out, if necessary, and generally were in the best position to extend production with family labour. Chiefs also had access to some communal labour in their fields. They, together with some of the immigrant population, who tended to invest more in cultivation and implements than in stock and were more receptive to new crops, were almost certainly the largest crop-producers in Pondoland.[87]

3

Rural production and the South African state, 1911–1930

1 Drought, East Coast fever and the crisis of 1912

By 1911, the year after Union, the economic position of most families in Pondoland was by no means desperate. The herds of cattle had been re-built, and the cattle population, at close on 280,000, was probably as high as before rinderpest (Table 5). There were more small stock in the area than ever before (Table 6). If the extension of cultivation had been constrained by lack of markets and rendered less urgent by the recovery of the herds, the homesteads still probably produced as much grain as they had immediately after the turn of the century. 'Every kraal possesses its plough', affirmed a magistrate in 1911 – the number returned in the census of that year exceeded 14,000 – and most could produce sufficient for subsistence in good and average years.[1] Despite an apparent increase in population from under 200,000 to over 230,000 in the first decade of the century, land was not yet as short as in the rest of the Territories (Table 1). Pressure on arable plots began to show in a few locations, but in general the magistrates still thought that their districts were 'by no means densely occupied' nor 'crowded' and 'thickly populated'.[2] Immigrants from other Cape districts continued to find space in which to settle. Whereas roughly 9 to 10 per cent of the male population left Pondoland to work in 1911, the average for other Transkeian districts was around 18 per cent (Table 4). Yet the homesteads were now locked into the larger capitalist economy. Their position of dependence was to be highlighted by a new series of natural disasters and the measures taken to combat them.

In 1911, drought, following its regular cycle, returned to Pondoland.[3] The harvests in that year and the next were poor, and little grain could be stored. As the ploughing season of October 1912 approached, demand for grain from the traders rose sharply not only because many families were already short of food, but because the rains were still inadequate and yet another harvest failure was anticipated. At the same time, East Coast fever, a cattle disease which equalled rinderpest in its destructive capacity, reached Pondoland and severely hampered ploughing. Traders, who had begun to import maize soon after the 1912 harvest, seriously underestimated demand. When they tried to increase the scale of imports in October, they found that movements of produce were being hampered by the shortage of draught oxen consequent on East Coast fever. With their cattle dying around them, it became clear that the people in Pondoland faced a serious famine.

East Coast fever, which progressed more slowly through southern Africa than rinderpest, had long been expected in the Cape. As early as 1904, when the disease had spread into Rhodesia and parts of the Transvaal, Colonial veterinary officials were discussing preventive measures.[4] It was known that, unlike rinderpest, the fever was not directly contagious but could only be transmitted by certain types of ticks once they were infected. The disease could therefore be controlled if the herds were isolated and sprayed or dipped so that the ticks would be killed. Anxious to prevent another disaster on the scale of rinderpest, the Colonial government began to build dipping tanks in the Territories in 1906. Stringent controls on the movement of cattle were proclaimed during the next few years.[5] Again the preventive measures were inadequate; dipping had hardly begun in Pondoland by 1910, when the disease crossed the Transkeian border from Natal. Within a few years East Coast fever had spread throughout the Territories.[6] Losses in Pondoland and other coastal districts, where the disease-carrying ticks were most prevalent and the dipping programme most backward, were particularly serious. An official estimate made in 1914 suggests that only 76,000 head, or 27 per cent of the cattle enumerated in the 1911 census, survived (Table 5). In the same year, a head count in Lusikisiki and Flagstaff gave total figures of little over 17,500 cattle in these districts, or about 20 per cent of the 1911 figures.[7] A trader in Flagstaff lost all but 16 of his 205 cattle in the nine months from June 1912 to March 1913.[8] East Coast fever was not as sudden as rinderpest, but the losses were as great. It made its greatest inroads in Pondoland during the latter months of 1912, precisely the time when the drought was most keenly felt. Further, the drought in Pondoland was more serious than in other Transkeian areas, a reversal of the usual pattern.

Imports of grain were not only limited by the shortage of oxen – teams could be found in Natal, where the disease was under control, and East Griqualand, where it made less impact – but also by restrictions on the movement of cattle. Though the railway through southern Natal had advanced to within six or seven miles of the Pondoland border, veterinary officials were reluctant to allow oxen to pass through the intervening farms and locations. There was no overall shortage of grain in the country

71

as a whole. Fifty million pounds (250,000 bags), grown largely on European farms, were apparently available for sale in South Africa in 1912. Further, grain could be imported from overseas if necessary. The crisis facing Pondoland was largely the result of problems of distribution rather than supply. Other isolated areas such as northern Zululand – the drought threatened many parts of South Africa at the end of 1912 – were also highly vulnerable.[9]

The ban on cattle movements was not absolute. Officials were prepared to allow a few immune or 'salted' teams to travel along selected routes. However, demand for haulage was so great that the costs soared.[10] Rates on the short routes between Natal railheads and Pondoland increased from under two shillings a bag to between eight and ten shillings. Some traders invested in mules, which could move about freely, but the cost of a team, at around £200, was very much higher than of a team of oxen. Mules were also more expensive to feed, as they could not survive on the pasturage, itself reduced by drought. The use of equine transport did little to alleviate the difficulties of distribution or reduce costs. At the same time, general drought conditions in the country drove up the price of grain; in October and November, people in Pondoland had to pay between forty and fifty-five shillings for what little maize they could find. The pressure of rising prices soon began to tell on poorer home-steads.

The Mpondo did not suffer in silence. In November, Marelane, the paramount chief of Eastern Pondoland, sent a deputation to the Chief Magistrate in Umtata to 'represent the condition of famine'.

> No such famine had been known in the history of the country. Last season the people had reaped no crops, – their prayers for rain had been in vain ... The people were sharing what grain they had with one another. Those who had gave a bucket to those who had not. Marelane had got a few buckets to help his people but he could do but little. The dawn of each day saw the price of grain [rise] higher and now it was selling at £2 and £2/10/– a bag. The proceeds of the hides of dead cattle were exhausted and other means of ob-taining money were insufficient.[11]

The position in Western Pondoland was equally serious.

Representations were not limited to information about the famine; deputations also suggested methods by which it could be alleviated. As the traders themselves could do little, and some were suspected by the African population of capitalising on the shortage, the Mpondo specifi-cally called for state intervention. They requested first that the state take over the distribution of grain at a controlled price.

We are starving here at Mtombe so we ask the government to send us bags of mealies that will charge £1–00. We are selling bags of mealies to shopkeepers for 5/– now they charge us £2–00.

We are unable to pay £2. Our cattle are dead and we are bound to pay hut tax, that is why we send our grievances to the government because we look him upon [*sic*] as our father.[12]

Secondly, they asked that restrictions on cattle movements to the rail-heads be lifted so that the Mpondo themselves could arrange transport with the few remaining cattle. They also demanded that the £2 limit on advances be waived. Men were prepared to go out to work, but they found it difficult to purchase even one bag of grain before leaving while advances were so restricted.

Local officials were already well aware of the situation.[13] Missionary opinion also pushed for government intervention, and the story was taken up by the national press, which spread (untrue) rumours that traders had been attacked and murdered in Pondoland. One correspondent stressed that '10,000 starving Kafirs means trouble before long', a point which must have struck home in the official mind.[14] While magistrates tried to contradict alarmist reports, they did not and could not hide the crisis from their superiors. Yet whatever the response of the officials who had to meet the situation at a local level, they had little power to intervene themselves. The Native Affairs Department as a whole lacked the facilities to organise transport, had little say in determining the nature of East Coast fever regulations, and could not unilaterally amend the legislation governing labour advances. Any intervention had to be authorised by the central government acting through other departments.

A basic principle of 'native policy' in the Cape, which was carried over into Union, was that the African areas should, as far as possible, be self-supporting. The Colonial government had been reluctant to establish any precedent of relief during times of shortage except in very limited amounts to a few paupers.[15] Officials felt that if they were to distribute grain in Pondoland at less than £1 a bag, the state would have to shoulder very large losses. Some did suspect that traders were using the shortage to drive up prices. There were suggestions that Natal traders and farmers were refusing to clear grain from the railheads, thus blocking further deliveries, until prices rose even higher.[16] It was also rumoured that Transkeian traders had tried to create an artificial shortage in order to force the government to extend railway lines into the Territories. However, officials allowed themselves to be persuaded by an active lobby of leading traders that all but a few speculators were as much the victims of high grain and transport prices as the African population. There was, in fact, some truth in their argument. By November, it was costing traders as much as thirty shillings a bag to land grain at their stations. While they were certainly taking profit from the sale of grain, their mark-up of ten to fifteen shillings was not very much higher than in ordinary years. Indeed, the speculation in grain was probably taking place amongst dealers outside the Territories rather than amongst local traders alone. The government was offered grain below such prices during the crisis, but officials were aware that the costs of setting up an alternative distribution network would be prohibitive. The traders, who were opposed to a system of distribution which could undercut them, therefore received a sympathetic hearing despite some official suspicion about their motives. The Cabinet decided that no direct relief would be given until it was certain that the crisis was beyond the resources of private enterprise.

The government was, however, prepared to ease the shortage of transport so that the existing network of trading stations could meet demand. Veterinary officials, under the Department of Agriculture, reluctantly agreed to relax restrictions on the movement of cattle within Pondoland itself. They also allowed some traffic between the railheads and the borders of Pondoland. The South African Railways and Harbours and the Native Affairs Department provided additional equine draught and 'salted' ox teams to ply these routes at commercial prices. Deliveries to the railheads were speeded up as grain was cleared more rapidly. Government vessels were used to increase the supply through Port St Johns. (A suggestion that Port Grosvenor be reopened was not acted on.) These measures were not implemented without mishap: deliveries through St Johns were delayed by the sand bar, and one vessel was grounded. The costs of transport soon rose again, and the state was not prepared to subsidise it.[17] Communications between the various newly established Union departments were often difficult and the broader policies governing aid not always clear. However, state intervention, although it made little impact on prices, did help to bring more grain into Pondoland.

Traders, for obvious reasons, and some local officials joined the African population in demanding an increase in advances. But the proposal met with strong opposition from the mines, which had but recently succeeded in abolishing them. The Chamber intervened at Cabinet level to prevent any reversal of policy and was supported by S. N. Pritchard, Director of Native Labour, an official whose major task at the time was to organise the supply of migrants to the mines.[18] Other senior officials in the Native Affairs Department did not represent mining interests so directly; Pritchard became less adamant after he visited the Territories himself. By November, a compromise was reached. The advance given before departure would remain at £2, but workers would be given a further £3 as soon as they arrived on the Rand, which they could send home immediately.

In December, the rains eventually came, and some land could be ploughed with the remaining oxen. The demand for grain fell slightly, for though the rains did not immediately ease the position of those who were already short, families were no longer so desperate to lay in stocks against yet another lean season. Imported grain was more readily available, as was the cash, from advances, with which to purchase it. Although some deaths resulted from the famine – infants were particularly susceptible because of the lack of milk – the immediate danger of widespread starvation had passed.[19] However, the crisis of 1912 revealed the vulnerability of the rural population, and it drove more migrants on to the labour market, thereby entrenching the dependence on earnings: the number of men leaving Pondoland increased to over 16,000 by 1912 and probably rose higher in the next year (Table 5).

The crisis also served to define the parameters within which the state was prepared to act. It emerged clearly that the central government saw the solution to the problems facing the rural population primarily in terms of increased rates of labour migrancy. During the later months of 1912, the Department of Native Affairs in Pretoria was inundated with requests from a variety of sources, including farmers and other public departments, for labour. These were all rejected, and Transkeian migrants, under the watchful eye of the Director of Native Labour, were largely channelled to the gold mines. The official response reflected the increasing position of dominance of the mining industry in the state. Yet local officials were far more sensitive to the demands emanating from the rural areas; on some points at least, the representations of the traders and the African population coincided. Magisterial concern to maintain order and to avert serious hardship and starvation was sufficient to activate some central government departments. During the next major drought, that of 1919–20, following the Spanish influenza epidemic in which over 5 per cent of the population of Lusikisiki died, the state acted in a similar way.[20] Transport facilities were provided for imports, and the activities of speculators in grain were watched closely. On this occasion, motorised transport, which was not restricted by East Coast fever regulations, was used in the southern Transkei; the drought in Pondoland was not so severe as to call for extensive intervention. Although the basic legislation governing advances was not altered, despite pressure from the rural population, the limit was again raised to £5 for short periods in 1916 and in 1919.[21] Officials and traders were alerted to the danger of famine in the rural areas. A system of crop reporting and an annual agricultural census, started throughout the country in the second decade of the century, helped to provide prior warning of shortages.[22]

While the government was prepared to act in an emergency, it declined to intervene in the relationship between traders and producers. Throughout the decade after 1912, there were demands from the General Councils in the Territories for an end to speculation in staples and for payment to producers in cash rather than 'good fors', but these fell on deaf ears.[23] The administration never allowed its resources to be used for purchase of grain or price subsidies, and even refused to accept the suggestion that General Council funds be spent on grain in an emergency. The structure of local trading remained intact. In only a couple of respects did officials try to reduce the monopoly of local trading firms. Some major concerns began to purchase numerous stores. In 1917, the administration articulated an informal regulation of refusing to grant licences to the same firm for stations within twenty miles of each other.[24] The idea was that 'every trading station should have a competing station as a neighbour'. The regulation was designed to protect smaller traders, who had initially agitated against concentration, as much as the peasantry. It was, however, difficult to enforce. Firms adopted the practice of establishing tied stations owned by individual traders but financed and exclusively supplied by one merchant house. In 1922, a proclamation was passed limiting the number of cattle that traders could graze on the commonage outside their stations. They, like the larger African stockowners around them, had begun to loan cattle on some scale not least because of the difficulties created by East Coast fever regulations, which limited their ability to export stock. But neither of these measures made a significant impact on the bonds which traders were able to develop over many rural homesteads.

2 East Coast fever regulations and stock-keeping in Pondoland

Whereas rinderpest had disappeared soon after its initial ravages, East Coast fever remained endemic once the ticks in any area had been infected. Veterinary officials felt that a district could only be declared 'clean' once it was completely free of the disease and all the cattle were being dipped regularly. The government was not prepared to finance dipping tanks itself; in most of the Transkeian districts, General Council funds were used for this purpose. The threat of East Coast fever had, in fact, been one reason for the urgency attached by the administration to the implementation of the council system, and dipping expenses drained the General Councils of much of their resources. In Eastern Pondoland, where the council system had not been introduced, funds for dipping tanks were short. An extra five-shilling tax was levied from 1915, again in the face of considerable opposition, and it was only by about 1920 that regular dipping of the large majority of cattle could be enforced.[25] There were sporadic outbreaks of the disease during the intervening years. After the drought of 1912, the regulations restricting cattle movements were tightened in order to prevent inter-district movements in Pondoland without a special permit.

Under an Act of 1911 and subsequent regulations, permits for cattle removals were granted in special cases by the magistrates, who, up to 1915, had to receive prior authorisation from the Department of Agriculture.[26] Applications were usually granted if it could be shown that cattle were from clean areas and had been quarantined for a period in isolation from other animals. As the Mpondo could not isolate their herds effectively in a communal grazing system, few could get permits. Officials allowed some movement of stock into Pondoland from surrounding districts but would permit little traffic in the other direction. They made an exception in the case of transport riders with immune teams, who were generally free to ply their trade in and out of Pondoland as long as they did not leave their oxen in Pondoland for over three months.[27] The record of permits granted by the magistrate of Lusikisiki suggests that exemptions for inter-district movements were initially given largely to European traders and butchers. Marelane, the paramount chief, was given permission to move bridewealth cattle on the grounds that his was an exceptional case; he had his own dipping tank and his herds were, by and large, grazed on separate pastures.[28]

In the years immediately after East Coast fever, the cattle population in Pondoland remained low. It was not impossible to import stock, but fewer came into the area than after rinderpest. Young cattle continued to succumb to the disease, and only those which had become immune were assured of survival. However, the pastures were again rich, and once a good base of immune breeding stock had been established after dipping began to take effect, cattle numbers increased rapidly. (Dipping also helped to stave off other tick-borne diseases, such as redwater, which had remained endemic.) By 1918, the cattle population had increased from around 70,000 to a little over 100,000 (Table 5). During the next two years the figures leaped to 146,000 despite the minor drought; by 1925, the number of cattle doubled again to over 300,000 and probably exceeded the pre-East Coast fever total. The figures are based on dipping statistics, which were totalled twice annually in each district, and they may reflect, at least till the early 1920s, a rapid increase in the number of cattle being dipped rather than the actual number of cattle. But such rates of increase – over 20 per cent a year between 1918 and 1923 – were not impossible in optimum conditions.

77

As the demand for cattle for restocking in the Transkeian Territories was high during the 1910s, the price of cattle kept well above £5 a head. But when cattle numbers began to increase, local demand fell off and prices declined, for the traders could only sell cattle within the area. In districts well away from the coast, where the losses during East Coast fever were not as severe as in Pondoland, prices were already beginning to fall before 1920.[29] In Pondoland, the price remained stable for a few more years; yet by the mid-1920s stockowners could not even realise £5 for a good ox. Towards the end of the decade, cattle prices reached their lowest level since the depression of the early 1880s and perhaps since the beginnings of the stock trade in Pondoland. Hunter found that the average price in the early 1930s was around £3 a beast.[30] One man who was buying stock in Lusikisiki a couple of years later remembered even lower prices. 'Prices were very low – £1, £2; £2/10/– was the price of a big ox. Sometimes you would buy a cow for £2 and the owner would say "No, don't separate the calf, it must stay with its mother". You gave him another five shillings.'[31]

Those who owned sufficient stock to sell animals were well aware that their difficulties were a direct consequence of the restrictions on cattle movements. In 1914, the limitations on export were an important issue of conflict in East Griqualand; the Transkeian Territories General Council made representations to have the regulations relaxed as early as 1915.[32] In the face of declining prices, the pressure to allow export increased. Yet the administration remained adamant that East Coast fever should be thoroughly stamped out, for it threatened not only herds in the Transkei, but in the country as a whole. Only in 1919 did the local magistrates begin to join the call for a change in policy.[33] They were persuaded that the people would not be able to purchase grain in the drought of that year unless they could obtain reasonable prices for their stock. By that year, a railway had been built through the southern and central Transkei to Umtata, the major administrative and business centre of the Territories. The Department of Agriculture therefore decided to meet the representations of magistrates with minor concessions. They would allow immune stock, branded as such, to go forward in sealed trucks by 'fast special trains' to the quarantine sections of the Johannesburg abattoir, where good slaughter animals could fetch as much as £25. Despite the high prices offered, traders made little use of the offer, as the conditions were 'so stringent as to make the concession practically useless'.[34] Officials lost their sense of urgency about relaxing restrictions after the drought, and as late as 1930 the Member of Parliament for Thembuland, representing both traders and those literate wealthier Africans who qualified for the vote, told the House of Assembly that 'in the Transkei they had more than half the cattle of the Cape Province, yet in view of the repressive legislation which had been introduced their cattle were value-less unless dead when the hide could be sold'.[35]

Judging from the number of cases involving breaches of the regulations, they could not be rigidly and universally enforced; but officials certainly attempted to keep close control over cattle movements, with important and complex results for the way in which stock circulated within Pondo-land. Despite the new patterns of circulation that had developed with the cattle advance system after rinderpest, loaning practices, though perhaps changed in form, had by no means died out. One chief in Eastern Pondoland was 'so rich in cattle [before East Coast fever] that a very large proportion of the people in his country had cattle from him on loan'.[36] The regulations now made it difficult for loaned cattle in other districts to be reclaimed. 'It was their custom to have cattle in different parts of the country', mentioned a leading councillor to the western Mpondo paramount arguing for a relaxation in regulations in 1916; 'as the law was now a man could not get his cattle from Mount Frere or Elliotdale to pay his debts with.'[37] The restrictions gave some security to families who had taken animals and were desperate to keep what they had left after the devastation of the disease. 'Now a new custom was spring-ing up', the councillor continued, 'and it was often found that people to whom one had farmed one's stock for a long time ... made difficulties about returning cattle when they were sent for.' This breakdown in loan-ing relationships, to some extent made possible by the cattle regulations, was probably a specific feature of the post-East Coast fever period. Families fought to retain control over what stock they had in their kraals and to escape obligations, perhaps even for cattle that had died. It fuelled the perception of leading chiefs that stock theft was on the increase, although the straitened circumstances of the rural population also gave rise to more direct forms of theft. The response of the chiefs, for whom theft was a major issue, was to demand harsher punishment for stock-theft and increased surveillance by the state.[38]

East Coast fever had again reduced the herds indiscriminately, and the enforcement of restrictions favoured those commoner families who had cattle on loan. Moreover, as the cattle numbers began to grow in the 1920s and sale to traders was inhibited by low prices, there was little alter-native for the wealthier stockowners but to distribute their cattle within Pondoland. On the one hand, they could still loan cattle, which at least gave them the opportunity to claim back in future years; the regulations did not affect movements within a district, and by the 1920s movements between Pondoland districts, though not outside of them, were becoming easier. Although it is impossible to prove, it seems that there was a distinct shift from the commercial patterns of circulation through traders which characterised the first decade of the century back to loaning practices once the scramble for cattle immediately after 1912–13 had subsided. On the other hand, the wealthier stockowners could sell animals, not to the traders, but direct to other homesteads. Many of those interviewed recalled that they had been able to purchase cattle direct from other Africans in the 1920s and 1930s.

Moreover, the fact that cattle had declined so rapidly in price gave poorer families, and those who were attempting to establish independent homesteads, the opportunity to accumulate. As Wilson has shown, the wages received by migrant labourers on the Rand remained static, or even declined, in real terms between 1910 and 1930 when compared against the price of commodities.[39] However, the fact that the value of wages increased in relation to the price of cattle, at least in Pondoland, has generally been overlooked. Whereas many migrants had been forced to purchase grain and commodities with their wages immediately after East Coast fever and in 1916 and 1919, crop production recovered by the 1920s, and wages were again invested very largely in stock. Cattle were cheaper, and they still had many of the same advantages as after rinderpest. Grazing lands were still open to all those who paid taxes. As settlement units began to decrease in size at the same time as the population was increasing, there was a steady demand for cattle as each new homestead sought to accumulate and maintain adequate herds for ploughing and milking.[40] Migrants who started their working life in these decades confirmed in interviews that their major investment had been in cattle and that they had been able to form the nucleus of a herd because cattle were so cheap. With sale outside Pondoland impossible, and with more homesteads attempting to establish a working herd, it is not surprising that the cattle population increased so rapidly. By 1930, there were over half a million cattle in Pondoland. Hunter found that homesteads in one part of Western Pondoland had an adequate supply of milk for most of the year in the 1930s;[41] draught was fairly generally available.

Between 1911 and 1930, the number of woolled sheep in Pondoland increased from about 200,000 to over 500,000 (Table 6). As after rinderpest, sheep were used to compensate for cattle losses, but they became of even greater importance in providing cash income in these decades. The price for wool in the Territories dropped as low as a penny a pound when the market collapsed for a few years during the First World War, but recovered to remain fairly stable at between sixpence and one shilling a pound until the depression of the early 1930s.[42] While cattle and crops were difficult to market, wool could always fetch a good cash price. Sheep became particularly important for wealthier families, who were trying to make a cash income from their produce. The sheep in Pondoland were generally of low quality and yielded perhaps only four pounds of wool a year.[43] Especially in bad years, when cash income was urgently needed, the Mpondo tended to shear too early and too often, thereby reducing the value of the wool.[44] However, scab had to some extent been controlled by dipping, and a family with a flock of about a hundred sheep, which was not particularly large by the standards of the time, could realise at least £10 a year. This amount was equivalent to the price of at least three or four head of cattle, or three months' wages in the goldfields, yet it could be earned without diminishing the size of the flock or reducing the labour available to the homestead. In fact, sheep demanded far less labour per capita than cattle; they were particularly suitable in a situation where the size of the productive unit was declining. As one man put it, 'I had cattle so I wanted sheep; I did not want to keep a lot of cattle as there was nobody to look after them.'[45] Sheep were also unaffected by the restrictions on the movement of stock. They now shared, and competed for, the best grazing with cattle.

It seems that the goat population increased rapidly in the years immediately after the major cattle diseases, but once the cattle population began to recover, the number of goats stabilised and began to decline (Table 6). Few of the goats in Pondoland were angoras, and though some income could be realised from their skins, they could not be sheared. They were more directly used than sheep to replace cattle for meat, ceremonies, bridewealth and even milk. Once the cattle herds recovered, goats became of more marginal significance to the larger stockowners, although they remained an important part of the resources of poorer homesteads which could not accumulate adequate herds.

State regulations imposed after East Coast fever undoubtedly contributed to the increase in the herds and flocks. In the 1920s, Pondoland was relatively free from the major tick-borne diseases which had plagued the area during the previous half century. Diseases such as anthrax and lung-sickness occasionally manifested themselves but never caused significant losses. The eradication of scab had provided the basis for increasing exports of wool. By 1930, there were almost certainly more stock, large and small, in Pondoland than at any time in the previous century. Yet the increase in the number of animals did little to free the Mpondo from their dependence on migrant labour or provide them with a cash income. Although wool and hides could be sold on external markets, the stock had little cash value. Even when sale was possible it was necessary to sell many more animals to realise the same return.

State intervention had further costs: the quality of animals probably began to deteriorate.[46] The original strains of cattle kept in Pondoland, so well suited to local conditions and which adapted well to draught, had been mongrelised by constant imports of mixed and scrub cattle from other parts of the country. While these new crosses may in turn have adapted to conditions in Pondoland, it seems that the imports were often of low quality. In one report on the Territories, it was argued that dipping, which increased the chances of survival for weaker animals, had led to an overall deterioration in the standard of cattle kept.[47] Those families which were trying to build up their herds were reluctant to slaughter weaker animals with any regularity. It is therefore possible that the average yield of milk decreased and the average number of oxen needed to pull the ploughs and sledges increased.

It cannot easily be proved that the stock actually deteriorated in quality, but the increase in stock numbers did affect grazing resources. Some of the inland parts of Pondoland with thinner grass cover, steeper ground and a lower rainfall, which tended to come in storms in the space of a few months every year, began to show signs of erosion in the late 1920s. Even in these parts of the Tabankulu, Flagstaff and Libode districts, erosion was not nearly as serious as in parts of the southern and western Transkei, where, according to the Native Economic Commission of 1932, 'desert' conditions prevailed.[48] Yet the drying up of watercourses, the washing away of topsoil, and the thinner grass cover contributed to a general deterioration in the condition of animals. The coastal districts with a higher rainfall spread out through the year – Lusikisiki, Port St Johns and most of Bizana and Ngqeleni – largely escaped actual erosion. But sweetveld grasses, which were most nutritious especially in the winter months, were subject to overgrazing. They were gradually replaced by sourveld types, particularly the Ngongoni veld (*Aristida junciformis*), in parts of Bizana, Lusikisiki and Flagstaff, which, while it was edible in the spring and summer months, became rank and tough in winter.[49] Restrictions on cattle movements also made it more difficult to take cattle to the coastal pasturages in winter. The decline in winter grazing resources on the open veld, however, was to some extent offset by the greater amount of maize stubble left in the fields after harvest, a result of the general extension of cultivation. There is no evidence to suggest that fodder was specifically grown for cattle. Whereas the annual rate of increase in the herds in Pondoland had been about 20 per cent between 1918 and 1923, it dropped to around 12 per cent in the next four years and to little over 7 per cent between 1928 and 1930 (Table 5). In the 1930s, the cattle population began to decline. At the same time, the percentage of animals lost during the winter droughts increased markedly. The sheep population also reached its maximum level around 1930 and then began to decline. Stock numbers evened out partly because the pasturage, given the system of stock-keeping could no longer support more animals. There were, however, other reasons.

Officials were by no means unaware of erosion; even before the turn of the century some articulated their concern about the dangers of over-stocking.[50] Towards the end of the 1920s, this issue became of central importance to those more directly concerned with agriculture in the Territories. They, and the anthropologists who studied the Transkeian peoples, tended to ascribe overstocking to 'traditional' attitudes towards cattle.[51] By this they meant the reluctance to sell and the survival of such 'uneconomic' customs as bridewealth and loans. They felt that 'tradition-alists' took little interest in the quality of their stock and that the status of an African man depended largely on the quantity of stock he owned. They failed to appreciate the position of stockowners. Wealthier families could not realise good prices; poorer families had to accumulate draught and milking animals. Loans became of renewed importance, and bride-wealth served, in an era of mass migrancy, to ensure that workers' wages returned to rural society. The Mpondo had clearly not been reluctant to sell some of their cattle before the turn of the century, a fact which does not seem to have come to the attention of officials and observers. The reluctance to sell cattle was a specific feature of the 1920s and early 1930s, a consequence of state intervention and the changes in family structure which accompanied mass migrancy. It may be, however, that officials were recording, at this time, changing attitudes towards stock in a trans-formed structural situation.

The remedies advocated differed. The Director of the Transkeian Department of Agriculture, which was established under the General Council in 1924, argued that while cattle should be reduced and goats 'which had very little economic value ... eliminated', sheep should be encouraged.[52] He felt that many parts of the Territories which were pre-viously considered unsuitable for sheep, which needed shorter grass, had become suitable because of overgrazing; sheep also provided a quicker cash return. Both sheep and cattle should be improved by careful breed-ing with selected sires. On the other hand, a study sponsored by the Chamber of Mines argued that sheep had been the ruin of the Territories, that the official policy to encourage them had been mistaken, and that cattle-keeping should be encouraged instead.[53] The Director of Agricul-ture's solution must be set in the context of the idea of a 'farmer class', which was already beginning to take form in the minds of local officials. Sheep ownership was far more unequal in the Territories than cattle ownership by this time; his policy favoured wealthier families, while the reduction of goats and cattle would tell against poorer families. The policy suggested by Fox and Back, on the other hand, was directly aimed against families who were accumulating on the basis of wool and, they felt, destroying the grazing for cattle; such processes contributed to the impoverishment of the majority of families in the Transkei and threatened the health of migrants by undermining the general level of rural production. They advised that widespread access to cattle, essential in rural cultivation, would assure at least a basic rural subsistence to most families without affecting the labour supply. It was an argument which fitted neatly with the interest of the Chamber of Mines in underpinning the migrant labour system.

By the early 1930s, few steps had been taken in either direction. In the next few years, first local officials and soon national policy-makers began to agree that a major programme of 'betterment' should be the basis of any more radical intervention by the state in the 'reserve' areas. But, under constant pressure from stockowners in the Territories, the state did relax East Coast fever restrictions in the early 1930s. The threat of overstocking and falling prices for other produce as the depression began to affect the Territories, coupled with the fact that East Coast fever had at last been largely eradicated, persuaded officials that urgent action was necessary; not only were traders and stock speculators allowed to move cattle to markets outside Pondoland, but the Transkeian Department of Agriculture itself organised sales.[54] Prices fluctuated wildly for a couple of years, but by 1934 they were moving upwards. In 1933 the magistrate of Lusikisiki estimated that 5,000–6,000 head were taken out of that district alone. In the next year the number sold in the district had risen to around 10,000. This overwhelming response somewhat surprised officials; and it led them to believe that attitudes to cattle were changing very rapidly.

> They are at last learning that in their cattle they have an economic asset. The bounds of custom and of the quasi-religious sanctions surrounding the cattle cult are gradually loosening, and this is the more significant in view of the fact that the Pondos are probably the most conservative tribe in these Territories.[55]

The magistrate felt that sales rather than deaths accounted for the evening out of the stock population in his district. In fact, although the volume of sales was sustained for a few years, the rapidity of response to the reopening of markets for cattle was probably related on the one hand to the urgent need for cash during the aftermath of the depression and on the other to the accumulation of surplus stock amongst at least certain families during the previous decade. But the evidence of the early 1930s confirms the argument presented here that an understanding of the relationship between the Mpondo and their cattle demands a different approach from that informed by theories of the 'cattle complex'.

3 Cash cropping and agricultural improvement

It has been suggested that a monolithic view of the South African state is an inadequate basis on which to explain the nature of intervention in areas such as Pondoland. The central government set the parameters of policy, and local officials enforced its enactments. However, although the independence of the Transkeian magistracy was constrained, especially after Union, it was not completely undermined. The Territories were governed largely by proclamations framed in terms of Acts of the central legislature. But records of local officials show clearly that they played an important role in shaping the form of proclamations, deciding when they were to be extended and how they were administered. In the twentieth century, they even had their own informal decision-making body in the shape of an annual magisterial conference at which they aired their problems, reached common decisions and made recommendations to the Secretary of Native Affairs. They were also able to use their position in more informal ways, in shaping the style of colonial rule in the Territories.

There were significantly different sets of pressures operating on local officials and the central government. After Union, government departments became increasingly sensitive to the demands of the dominant elements in the newly forged South African state, and in particular to mining and agrarian capital. The Native Affairs Department became more centrally concerned with regulating and distributing African labour to various capitalist enterprises in the region. This is not to suggest that the state was merely the arm of specific interests and had no independent authority beyond them. The way in which it attempted to regulate labour was to ensure the possibility of continued accumulation. Similarly, the enforcement of East Coast fever regulations and dipping throughout the country was essentially geared to securing the long-term future of pastoral production without regard to the immediate interest of either white or black stockowners. (The regulations did tend to favour better-capitalised stock farmers who used fences and fodder.)

Transkeian officials inherited a paternalist and in some respects 'liberal' tradition of administration, which, although changing as industrialisation progressed, was to some extent kept alive by their position in the rural areas. They retained their interest in some of the ideas that made up the late-nineteenth-century view of progress for the African population: 'civilisation' and Christianity, education, agricultural progress. They were also far more open, in the milieu of the magisterial villages, to the force of missionary and trader opinion. But perhaps most important in shaping the response of local administrators was their position in relation to the people who fell under their charge. It was they who had to

85

remain sensitive to, and manipulate, the local political balance in order to maintain control; they had to weather recurrent rural crises with none but the most general policy directives to guide them; they also listened to the many representations and deputations from the rural population. And in the Territories they had a further duty which introduced an element of ambiguity into their position: administering the councils which were largely responsible for initiating and funding local development. The magistrates sat in both District and General Councils, participated in debates, advised on and sometimes initiated motions, and relayed those passed to the central government. While this gave them the opportunity to influence the formation of African representations to the state, their functions demanded that they were not solely instruments of the state. Their first loyalty was to the government, but their responsibilities were, admittedly to a limited degree, divided.

African representatives on the Councils were for the most part chiefs, headmen and wealthier, more highly educated members of the rural communities. One of their early demands in the Transkeian Territories General Council, to which most districts besides those in Pondoland sent representatives by 1906, was that some of the funds at their disposal be spent on agricultural improvement schemes. The Transkeian magistrates took up their requests with enthusiasm, and it was largely they who shaped the way that the schemes developed. As early as 1904, an experimental farm was established in the Tsolo district partly in order to train African apprentices.[56] In 1912, an agricultural course was offered to African students, aimed at producing 'a man, who, when he left the school, would be able to farm on more up-to-date lines, and influence the people around him by his example'.[57] Shortly before, officials had initiated a scheme, inspired by the agricultural extension programme developed in Ireland, in which trained demonstrators were sent into the field to work plots. The Union Department of Agriculture provided some help by supplying, and paying, young graduates of the European agricultural schools as demonstrators. But it soon became clear that they were unsuitable for work in the Territories, and after 1915 they were gradually replaced by Africans trained at Tsolo. These the Department of Agriculture would not pay, nor did they make further contributions. As the General Council budget was small, and much stretched to cover dipping, education and other expenses, there were still only ten African extension workers by 1920. However, in the next decade the programme expanded rapidly. In 1925, the Councils were freed from their partial responsibility for funding education in the Territories. During the same year, the whole system of taxation in the Territories was changed; parliament introduced a £1 poll tax on every adult male, some of the proceeds of which went into a National Development Fund topped up by the state on a rough pound-for-pound basis. More was now available from General Council resources, and a limited amount from the Fund was channelled to the Council programme; expenditure on extension work had doubled to roughly £24,000 in 1925 and in the next few years doubled again.[58] A Department of Agriculture under a European director was established; the supervisory bureaucracy, all European, expanded; a touring demonstration caravan was put on the road; and an agricultural journal in Xhosa and English, *Umcebisi Womlimi Nomfuyi* (Advisor to the Cultivator and Stock-Keeper), was launched. Two new agricultural schools were opened, one at Teko in Butterworth and one, in 1930, near Flagstaff in Eastern Pondoland. By 1930 there were one hundred demonstrators in the field.

Each demonstrator was equipped with a set of ox-drawn implements: a plough, harrow, cultivator and planter. His primary task was to show how they could be used to advantage: that better ploughs than the cheap, fragile 'seventy-fives' would cut the soil more deeply; that two ploughings were better than one; that harrowing would improve results. They advocated the use of hillside ploughs with reversible shares on steep lands so that the land could be more easily ploughed along the contour, rather than up and down the hills as was the usual practice. They tried to introduce winter ploughing so that the frosts could help to break up the soil prior to the rains and weeds would find it more difficult to take root. They discouraged broadcast sowing, demonstrating instead that if crops were planted in rows, seed could be saved, each plant given more space to grow, and ox-drawn cultivators used. They castrated rams and caponised cockerels to increase the supply of meat and eradicate poor-quality stock. Most demonstration work concentrated on improving production of existing crops, although in the 1910s cotton was encouraged. Some efforts were made to provide selected breeding stock either for sale or to sire animals brought to the schools, and by the 1930s imported exotic strains were being introduced.

As the Western Pondoland General Council, formed in 1911, remained separate from the TTGC, and as Eastern Pondoland remained outside the Council system until 1927, the area received demonstrators, except for those working on cotton projects, some time after other Transkeian districts. But in 1922 officials decided that Pondoland should not be left behind, and by 1926 there was a demonstrator in each district of the area.[59] (At the time there were two in each of the other Transkeian districts.) Their impact in the period under discussion here was fairly limited. They were few in number and could work in only one location – there were over 200 locations in Pondoland – at a time. Their efforts tended

87

to be monopolised by local headmen, for the produce from the demonstrators' plots went to the men who had granted the plots. The bulk of the rural population was highly suspicious of what they felt might be a new form of state intervention: demonstrators not only questioned local methods, but agricultural officials soon raised the question of stock limitation. The demonstrators' success in producing better-than-average crops was not always sufficient to stimulate imitation. A set of implements cost well over £20; their use presumed adequate draught throughout the year. Winter fallowing interfered with grazing patterns and, by removing the stubble and weed cover, increased susceptibility to erosion. Investment of more cash in agriculture did not necessarily bring commensurate returns, especially when it was difficult to market crops for cash. Oral evidence suggests, however, that some progressive and wealthier cultivators adopted the demonstrators' teachings wholeheartedly and were able to grow very much in excess of their household needs.[60] Others introduced one or more of the suggested improvements or purchased new implements. But the schemes did little to ease the dependence of most homesteads on income from wage labour.

As noted above, one of the cash crops encouraged by officials in the early decades of the century was cotton. The fate of the crop in the Territories serves to illustrate the divergence between central government and local officials, as well as the more general problems facing rural cultivators. Cotton had been tried in the subtropical belt on the east coast of southern Africa on a number of occasions in the nineteenth century; further inland near Pondoland, Adam Kok, the Griqua captain, had raised a successful crop for a number of years.[61] But by the turn of the century there was no sustained production of cotton in the Territories. In 1906, a further call by the British Cotton Growers' Association for Empire supplies was taken up by an Eastern Cape merchant house, which put pressure on the Transkeian administration to establish an experimental farm and help in distributing free seed through the District Councils; an African newspaper carried articles explaining where seed could be obtained and how it should be planted.[62] The Chief Magistrate, at first lukewarm to such proposals, which would entail expenditure, found his hand forced by the enthusiasm in the coastal districts, in some cases encouraged by local magistrates. Within a year, there were applications from aspirant growers throughout the Territories, including a chief in Pondoland. The central Department of Agriculture was persuaded to help, and by 1910 an experimental farm had been established. Extension officers started work shortly afterwards. A trader whose station included rich alluvial lands along the Mngazi river, in which the Mpondo had settled in the early nineteenth century, also planted cotton with departmental help. The results on these carefully controlled plots were highly successful; yields compared favourably with those in established cotton-producing areas of the world.[63]

The problem of finding markets for the small quantities initially grown was solved by a merchant house which offered to buy any quantity of raw cotton, at reasonable prices, in order to stimulate production. Some was sent to England, where it was well received. Reports during the preceding few years suggest that a number of African growers tried the crop and that other traders became excited about its future. But the initial euphoria soon passed. Both traders and African cultivators reported that their cotton had been destroyed by insects. This was clearly the major difficulty in cotton production, but one producer complained that he had too little land for the crop; another that his plants were eaten by goats and sheep, as they could not be properly fenced. Most found that their cotton was too spoilt or dirty to be of much value even at the relatively favourable terms offered by the merchants. Some of those who had not dropped out after one or two failures were forced after the crisis of 1912 to concentrate on food production. Further, the chiefs, after their early enthusiasm, seem to have turned against the experiment. They were reluctant to allow any land to be fenced, for this both affected winter grazing patterns and threatened their control over communal land. They were increasingly sensitive to the danger of losing land to Europeans, the likely consequence, they suspected, of a successful cash-cropping enterprise.[64] When one headman in Port St Johns was given land by the local magistrate to plant cotton in 1915, he openly disobeyed by planting maize instead.[65]

Financial cutbacks during the First World War necessitated the removal of the most successful extension workers, and merchants, now deprived of access to overseas markets, found it too expensive to continue their offer.[66] By 1915, there were still two African and three European producers in Port St Johns, but they could no longer find a market for their crop. When the central government, which had other priorities, refused the local magistrate's request for a system of advances to producers, he was forced to purchase the crop himself. After the war, demonstration work started again, and a gin was purchased for one of the agricultural schools in the Territories.[67] Some interest was regenerated, and local traders and newspapers remained excited about the possibility of extensive cultivation till the mid-1920s. However, only substantial state aid to combat insect pests and create a marketing structure could have provided the basis for sustained production. The Councils had insufficient funds, and neither local officials nor traders could mobilise support from the central government. By this time, export crops were regarded as the preserve of large-scale capitalist farmers who received the great bulk of the financial and research resources of the state. No efforts were made to encourage cash-cropping of bananas and citrus in the coastal districts of Pondoland; except in the enclave of European-owned land at Port St Johns, these were grown largely for household consumption.

If cotton production failed partly because of the lack of interest on the part of the state, another non-edible product, tobacco, succumbed to more direct state intervention to support large-scale producers.[68] The market for the Mpondo crop, considered the best of the varieties grown in the Territories, was limited by the expansion of production on European farms in the Transvaal and southern Cape during the first two decades of the century. But Mpondo tobacco was still used by Africans in the rural areas, by migrant labourers in the cities and even by some rural European consumers. Tobacco was sold locally by growers themselves, or hawked further afield by African middlemen. Traders still bought substantial quantities and often paid close to a shilling, or even more, for a pound of carefully prepared roll tobacco in times of shortage. As in the case of maize, overproduction in good years sometimes resulted in a glut and low prices, because of the restricted market. Producers had to be extremely wary of increasing their output, for the curing and rolling of leaves was a time-consuming task. But production was not so constrained by pressure on the homesteads to produce food crops, for although some growers began to plant large fields, much tobacco was still grown on small garden plots. Many families in the coastal districts, especially those with less stock, depended on tobacco for cash to meet taxes.

While the First World War cut off markets for cotton, it boosted demand for Pondoland tobacco. In February 1917, the South African army ordered 30,000 lb of African-grown tobacco for the troops of the South African Native Labour Contingent in France.[69] It was to the Chief Magistrate of the Territories that the Director of Supplies turned, and the Chief Magistrate immediately activated the Pondoland traders, who were known to have the largest and best-quality stocks. The traders, having driven up the price, supplied over 10,000 lb at an average of 1s.2d. within a month. A few thousand pounds more were found in other districts. Towards the end of the year, a new order was placed, and by March 1918, when it was eventually cancelled, about 5,000 lb had been forwarded and a further 12,000 lb was on hand. This evidence suggests that production of tobacco for the market in Pondoland was fairly limited, although the suddenness of the orders took both traders and producers by surprise. A few years later, officials estimated annual production in Pondoland at about 300,000 lb, most of it grown in Port St Johns, Lusikisiki and Ngqeleni.[70] In 1921, a leading trader in Ngqeleni estimated that the stores in his district alone had 220,000 lb on hand, an amount worth at least £5,000 to producers.[71] If these figures are correct, output was certainly larger than the amount supplied to the army, though it did not rival the millions of pounds being produced by European farmers even before the war. However, the trader in Ngqeleni, at least, had reason to exaggerate the importance of the crop.

European tobacco farmers began, in the second decade of the century, to advocate an excise duty on tobacco grown in the country in order to stabilise prices. Parliament, attentive to their demands and keen to raise revenue from tobacco, passed a Tobacco Excise Act in 1921.[72] Its aim was to restrict the purchase of tobacco to licensed dealers who would forward the crop to manufacturers, the latter paying the excise duty; some of the excise would be used by the state to purchase crops at fixed prices, but only from registered co-operatives. Those selling unmanufactured tobacco direct to the public would be subject to a shilling a pound excise so that they could not undercut the major producers.

Transkeian producers were not organised into co-operatives, nor was their tobacco suitable for manufacture into cigars and cigarettes. Whether best-quality rolled or loose leaves, their tobacco had already been sun-cured when it reached the traders and was used for snuff or pipes. All those who dealt in it would, therefore, be subject to the excise, which threatened to double the price of African tobacco at a stroke. Traders felt the Act was 'greatly injuring a native industry which should be encouraged rather than discouraged', and local officials argued that it would be impossible to collect the excise, that it was unfair, and that it would deprive families of cash to pay taxes, especially as the market for stock and grain was so depressed.[73]

Despite threats by the Department of Excise, little attempt was made to enforce the tax, but the uncertainty created was sufficient to scare traders out of the African tobacco market. Sales between Africans were soon exempted, as was the African crop as a whole after Hertzog's government came to power in 1924. But some longer-term damage appears to have been done; in 1933, agricultural officers in the Territories were still lamenting the decline of tobacco production and suggesting that something be done to distribute seed so that growers could exploit the market among migrant labourers in the cities. Marketing along African networks continued, and production had probably declined only marginally by the 1930s.[74] But the excise created uncertainty at a time when the amount grown in Pondoland was increasing and when African producers were in any case finding their market threatened by tobacco grown and processed on a large scale and sold with heavy advertising. In later decades, it was dagga, also long grown and smoked in Pondoland, that became of more importance in providing a cash income than tobacco.

Local officials had lent their support to both cotton and tobacco cultivation. However, at a time when state resources were being mobilised to protect and develop large-scale capitalist agriculture, African producers were at best neglected by the central government, or were at worst the victims of such measures as the Excise Act. Loans from the central Land Bank, established in 1912, were not available to Africans. They did not benefit from state attempts to stabilise markets – in the 1930s, African-grown maize was similarly affected by an excise duty – and little was done to improve transport infrastructure in the reserves. As has been suggested in the section on cotton, however, the development of cash cropping was not inhibited by the action of the state alone.[75] And conflict within the African population over the trajectory of development in the Territories is further illustrated in the response to schemes for rural industrialisation.

On this issue the sensitivity of local officials to African opinion led them to take a different position. During the decade after Union, there was a significant growth in the number of import-substituting manufacturing industries in South Africa. Industrial growth was largely confined to the major urban centres, the Witwatersrand and the ports, where both infrastructure and markets were available. However, amid the general excitement about industrial development, a number of schemes were floated in the Transkeian Territories.[76] Most involved the primary processing of natural raw materials that were to be found in the area: fibrous leaves of strelitzia (wild banana) plants, aloes and *ilala* palms could be used for rope and sack manufacture; milk from euphorbia trees and gum from acacias should be collected for rubber production. Only one idea canvassed from 1914, which envisaged the manufacture of paper from the long, sour 'dobo' grass, prevalent in the coastal districts of Pondoland, received serious consideration, particularly because of the shortage of paper in the country during the First World War.[77]

The central issue facing both the administration and the rural population was that any enterprise based on private capital would imply alienation of resources that were regarded as communal. It was for this reason that officials first vetoed the proposal; they had already ruled against commercial exploitation of thatch grass by headmen in East Griqualand. It was for this reason, also, that a modified proposal which envisaged the purchase of grass from rural families, rather than the alienation of rights to grass in any area to a private firm, met with opposition in Pondoland. Chiefs and headmen in Western Pondoland felt that natural resources were becoming too scarce, that stockowners would suffer and only

92

some poorer families would benefit in the short term, and that there would be conflict between those wishing to sell grass and those wishing to use it for domestic purposes. The regent in Western Pondoland summed up his position in 1915.

> The grass helps people. We live on it. When one loses his way he goes to the dobbo [*sic*] for shelter. When we put up a new hut we first put up a *pempe* [thatch shelter]. We use the grass for thatching. It is good food for stock. We can't spare the grass; other districts have none to spare.[78]

Marelane, paramount in Eastern Pondoland, to whom energetic entrepreneurs devoted some attention, was less adamantly opposed. The coastal grasslands were particularly rich and underutilised after East Coast fever; grass could be cut without affecting spring grazing, and both grass itself and the products made with it were sometimes sold in Pondoland. Not only would the paramount derive income, as in the days of concessions, but it would provide ready cash for poorer families struggling after drought and cattle disease. He alone of the chiefs consulted was interested in the scheme so long as it could be controlled and the 'rights, comfort and contentedness of the Native inhabitants were not interfered with'.

The enthusiasm of entrepreneurs and local traders kept the scheme alive for a few years. 'Just at present', the Member of Parliament for Thembuland argued, 'any method of disposing of grass assets other than putting them into unsaleable and unexportable cattle seems to me to smack of sanity.'[79] The central Native Affairs Department became particularly encouraging when a Swedish company investigated the possibility of investment. But local officials remained wary of the precedents that might be set and were unwilling to act against what they believed to be the thrust of African opinion. By 1918 the scheme had been dropped; the original applicants withdrew, technical problems in processing the grass were raised, and the urgency of finding a new source of raw materials for paper had diminished. The response to the proposal reflected the general policy that was being elaborated in regard to rural resources. Demarcated forests remained under the control of the state. A few sawmills, run by traders, were allowed near densely afforested areas, but in general timber was used by government departments and only windfalls sold to traders or the Africans. Smaller areas of forest, under the control of headmen, were left to provide for homestead fuel and timber needs. Whether state policy would have been reversed if any significant mineral deposits had been found in the Territories is unclear. Prospecting licences were granted, but all the attempts to work the copper and nickel deposits on the borders of Pondoland in Mount Ayliff district met with failure. When the *Territorial News* reported in 1919 that a 'new era in the industrial life of the Natives' was opening, they referred to a craft show organised in Umtata in that year.[80] Rural industries came to mean the production of craft goods, an activity which did receive some encouragement in the schools and at shows. But plans for basket, hat and mat 'factories' were never realised. It was only from the 1940s, when the political economy of the country was changing rapidly, that the state began to take some interest in industrial decentralisation as part of a broader segregationist and later apartheid policy.[81]

The effects of state intervention, and the lack of intervention, in Pondoland in the early decades of the twentieth century were complex. The processes described in this chapter cannot be said to constitute an overarching attempt to destroy the basis of rural production in the area. East Coast fever regulations did have the effect of protecting markets for the European farmers who could meet with their requirements; the tobacco excise was also geared to the interests of larger producers. Little was done by the central government to encourage new cash crops in the Territories. However, staple crops remained largely unaffected by immediate state measures; as migrancy had become entrenched without further state action, there was little imperative reason to intervene further in production. The state acted to provide the conditions in which continued accumulation in the capitalist economy could take place, with often unpredictable and ambiguous results for the rural population. The state must be disaggregated if the particular pattern of intervention is to be understood. Local officials sometimes pursued initiatives which, if not diametrically opposed to the thrust of state policy, were not supported by the central governments. Further, it has been argued that the position in Pondoland cannot be understood purely in terms of state action or of the operation of markets. In the next section, the response of rural producers and the position of the homesteads is assessed in more detail. In Chapter 4, the specific pattern of local political relations and their effects on the pattern of production are discussed.

4 Migrancy, homestead structure and staple crop production

By the 1920s, producers in Pondoland had been blocked from access to external markets for their grain and stock and were intent on protecting their natural resources for communal purposes. Cash-cropping experiments had, for the most part, failed. Most families had to rely to some extent on income from wages to meet cash needs or accumulate sufficient to maintain rural production. Rates of migrancy from Pondoland, as has been suggested, increased substantially after the crisis of 1912. Although no annual figures of the labour passes issued are available after that date, occasional statistics suggest that they did not again decrease. By 1921, according to the census of that year, nearly 19,000 men from Pondoland were at the labour centres; by 1936, around 30,000 (Table 2). The percentage of men absent rose from about 9 in 1911 to 13.5 in 1921 and to 17 in 1936 (Table 4). In 1911, roughly 25 per cent of men between fifteen and forty-five were absent; by 1936, around 45 per cent.[82] Migrancy rates remained lower in Pondoland than in other parts of the Territories, but in these decades migrancy became an experience general to most sections of Mpondo society. As men did not migrate in every year of their lives, it can be assumed that the large majority of homesteads – there were exceptions – had migrants.[83]

Yet while labour migrancy became entrenched, no further attempt was made to restructure relations on the land in Pondoland before the 1930s. The triumph of segregationist land policy in the Union as a whole had the effect of maintaining the *status quo*: Pondoland remained reserved for African occupation under communal tenure.[84] Production of staple crops was thus not deeply affected by state action. The changes in patterns of cropping over the first few decades of the century must be examined against the complex interaction of migrancy, control of property in the homesteads, and the organisation of labour in local productive units.

The cattle system, which had enabled families to control the wages of their migrant members, did not die out entirely after it was abolished by the state in 1911. Mackenzie's, a firm which had specialised in cattle advances, continued to offer them in the next two decades.[85] They supplied the Robinson group of mines, which did not share the Chamber's point of view on the issue. Mackenzie's recruiters, including some of the leading Pondoland traders, disguised the advance contract by introducing third parties and promissory notes into the transaction, and defended their activities with some success in a series of court cases. Moreover, the 1911 Act regulated recruiting only for mines and works. Less highly capitalised agricultural enterprises, which were competing against mines and towns for a labour force, did not find the same advantages in close controls over the way in which labour was mobilised. When their supply of indentured Indian workers was cut off after Union, sugar farmers in Natal turned to the Territories to win a migrant labour force.[86] As they were able to offer advances, they succeeded in finding a considerable supply from Pondoland, despite the low wages offered. In 1921, parliament legislated to abolish advances in recruiting for all sectors of the economy, partly at the instigation of the Chamber, which was concerned

95

about the competition from the agricultural sector. Although the cattle advance system survived in a variety of disguised forms for at least another decade, and migrants co-operated with recruiters to hide it from the view of officials, it became less general and increasingly insignificant as a means of control over wages by rural families. The mines did provide alternative systems of repatriating earnings through remittances and deferred pay. But deferred pay in particular, which was the most popular method of repatriatìon, did not provide the family with the same hold over wages. Migrants themselves collected the pay in cash when they came home.

Even when cattle advances were operating, but especially after they had been abandoned, it seems that tensions over the control of the migrants' wages within the family began to increase. Young men still often wanted to purchase cattle when possible with their earnings; the question was who would control the cattle. Monica Hunter observed the result of such conflicts in the early 1930s, when the process of change was probably well advanced. 'Formerly an *umzi* [homestead] was under the thumb of the father', an informant told her; 'now it is under the thumb of the son.'[87] The magistrate of Lusikisiki noted 'the general tendency towards individualisation' and 'the desire of the young men and women to control and dispose of their own personal earnings irrespective of parental control or custom or house responsibility'.[88] One man interviewed in the 1970s suggested that migrancy initiated changes in ideas about the control over resources within the family. Before labour migrancy 'the cattle belonged to the homestead head because there was no-one working'.[89]

These tensions over the control of wages had particular importance in relation to patterns of marriage.[90] Male members of the homestead could now obtain at least part of their bridewealth without depending on their fathers, homestead heads or wider networks linking their male kin and local chiefs. Sons could even pay bridewealth for their fathers. According to the available evidence, bridewealth transactions in precolonial times had predominantly been arranged between the homesteads of the intended spouses. Hunter noted in the early 1930s that such arranged marriages were now only a minority of those contracted. It has been suggested in the context of other African communities in southern Africa that bridewealth tended to inflate as migrancy became established.[91] In southern Mozambique, at least, 'elders' attempted to control the wages of migrants by forcing them to pay higher bridewealth in order to secure access to wives. The evidence from Pondoland does not suggest that bridewealth inflated substantially, although the position was complicated by the constant changes in the value of cattle, the measure by which

96

bridewealth was valued, in relation to other commodities. Immediately after rinderpest and East Coast fever it seems that bridewealth, if anything, deflated because cattle values inflated. Records of civil cases in Lusikisiki, admittedly an inadequate source on which to base conclusive arguments, suggest that bridewealth levels for commoners remained at about five to ten head, or their equivalent, till the 1920s. As the price of cattle declined in the 1920s and early 1930s, a magistrate mentioned that cattle had become so devalued that parents were demanding horses and sheep instead. Such switches, however, seem to have maintained the real value of bridewealth at a fairly constant level. There certainly were a number of marriages in which no bridewealth was paid or which were only regularised in customary law well after the marriage; Christian marriages were also available, although not widely entered into. Eventually payment of bridewealth remained the norm, and this in itself, aside from the question of inflation, served to bring wages back to rural society.

Aside from having more independent access to wives, men could also accumulate the nucleus of a herd through purchase without entering into the same obligations of service and dependence. The homesteads also began to play a less central role in the allocation of land; as plots and homestead sites became more scarce, location headmen became increasingly important in supervising allocation to new homesteads.[92] There was no longer any need to remain in large homesteads for defensive purposes. Further, new technology, access to draught and a wage enabled smaller units to survive. The result of such changes was that brothers and sons established their own homesteads at an earlier stage and the average size of homesteads declined, a process underlined by declining rates of polygamy. The decline in homestead size was uneven, and it cannot be plotted on the basis of statistical returns relating to hut tax, for all married men, whether they lived in their own homesteads or not, were registered as hut-tax payers. Wealthier homestead heads, with more resources to offer their male kin, could probably delay the process for longer than poorer; on the other hand, sons of the latter may have found some advantage in maintaining larger productive units. By the 1930s, it was certainly not unusual for three-generational families and even brothers to live together. Yet information from Hunter's book and from interviews suggests that large homesteads probably now comprised at most fifteen to twenty people and that the average size was considerably smaller.[93]

Under Mpondo family law, which was enforced by the magistrates' courts, homestead heads were ultimately responsible for the civil liabilities, fines and taxes of the members of their settlement group.[94] This obligation was the converse of the homestead head's control over resources within the unit. Indeed, this was one of the reasons why homestead heads had fought to maintain control over wages. In 1913–15, for example, the administration's attempts to enforce a dipping tax on all adult males, instead of hut-tax payers alone, met with strong popular opposition, for it implied that young men could be sued individually for their liabilities. But as homestead heads began in fact to lose control over wages, their responsibility for civil liabilities became a burden. By the early 1920s, there were suggestions being made in Western Pondoland that the great house should no longer be liable for members of minor houses. Homestead heads did not therefore always oppose the separation of younger men in the family, as this freed them from responsibilities they were no longer in a position to bear. Further, as arable land in some areas became more scarce, it was necessary for the homestead to be split if the family as a whole was to secure access to more plots. The disintegration of large homesteads was not a process without ambiguities.

Migrancy now became incorporated into the process of homestead segmentation and reproduction. Workers would migrate to earn bride-wealth. After marrying and establishing their own homesteads, many continued to work in order to build their herds, purchase agricultural implements and accumulate other commodities. A man who migrated between about 1920 and 1942 recalled:

> I ran away from school during East Coast Fever and am illiterate. I was married before I went to the mines [c. 1920]. Joyi [his father's eldest brother] paid the bridewealth, seven head in one day. That was not the end: I paid twelve head for the first and nine for the second, whose bridewealth I paid myself. Things were hard so I went to the mines. I found out from friends which were the good compounds. We did not have machines at first but after getting them the money was better. That is how I got enough money to build a kraal, and that got me my second wife. I went twelve times and finished before I was old – only a literate man would remember the exact date [c. 1942]. I had a second wife when I finished. I bought cattle, cattle. They were cheap. Clothes were cheap. When I was putting up my kraal I got some [cattle] belonging to my late father. I bought a plough, I had six oxen for it and there were more too. I also had enough milk.[95]

The position of the migrant within the family changed radically. He became both wage-earner and homestead head, a joint role which was not unknown, but less common, in the earlier phases of migrancy. This was probably already the dominant pattern of migrancy in many other parts of the Transkeian Territories at the turn of the century, and may have been the reason for the relative unpopularity of advance systems outside of Pondoland at the time. State regulations contributed to the disappearance of advances in Pondoland and thereby hastened the changes in homestead structure. In turn, these changes rendered the system unnecessary.

The decline in the size of the rural productive unit necessitated further changes in the organisation of rural cultivation, of which the most striking reflection was the virtual disappearance of sorghum as a staple crop. Maize had displaced the older crop in the late nineteenth century and early twentieth century when cultivation was extended and grain was marketed on a large scale. But while estimates made at the turn of the century suggest that the output of sorghum still totalled at least half the output of maize, by the 1930s it was only planted in small quantities in dryer upland districts (Table 7). Most informants agreed that they had stopped planting the crop, which had an open cob, because it was eaten by birds before the harvest.[96] It is possible that the feeding habits of birds changed during the early decades of the twentieth century; natural vegetation diminished as forests and bushlands were cleared for grazing, arable plots and firewood. Some species may have adapted themselves to feeding on crops and may even have become more numerous once the adaption had been made. However, informants made it clear that sorghum had always been threatened by birds while it was ripening unless it was guarded. This task fell to the children of the homestead; a temporary shelter or platform would be constructed in the sorghum fields where groups of children would spend most of their daylight hours scaring birds away. As the size of the productive unit became smaller, there were fewer children available to each family for day-to-day work in the fields; a number of informants confirmed that they had stopped growing the crop because they could no longer find the labour to guard it. The gradual spread of school education probably contributed to the shortage of labour in some homesteads.[97] Once the quantity of sorghum planted began to decline, each remaining field became even more susceptible to devastation by birds. Maize cobs, on the other hand, were protected against birds by their fibrous husks.

The disappearance of sorghum opened the way to more far-reaching adaptions in the system of cropping. In pre-colonial times, vegetables and grain, at least in the coastal districts, had usually been planted separately. Pumpkins, beans and sweet potatoes were sown in gardens near to the homesteads; sorghum and maize, some distance away in separate fields which were rotated after a few years. (Maize was known to grow well in soil previously planted with sorghum.)[98] Sorghum, in particular, had been densely sown by broadcasting seed in small fields, perhaps in order to facilitate guarding and reduce labour in the hoeing season. In the early decades of the century, this pattern of cultivation began to change. Maize, planted at more widely spaced intervals, was more readily adapted to mixed cropping. It was sown, in larger fields, together with pumpkins, sweet cane, beans and even sweet potatoes. The maize sprouted first, and after it had been hoed a couple of times, pumpkin runners began to fill the spaces in between the stalks, drowning out the weeds. The beans would twine themselves around the maize stalks. This pattern of cultivation enabled day-to-day labour in the fields to be cut down; it was more suited to intensive inputs of labour at widely spaced intervals, where possible aided by ox draught. Larger fields could be ploughed after the rains. Communal work parties could be arranged for a couple of hoeing sessions and for harvesting. Hoeing throughout the growing season became less necessary, and the fields did not have to be guarded while the crops were ripening. The timing and extent of adaptions made differed from homestead to homestead. However, it is clear that the concentration on maize opened the way to more extensive mixed cropping in a single field, a system which enabled smaller productive units to maintain their output.

Such changes were also integrally linked to labour migrancy. As the individual productive units were even more dependent on draught to maintain output, a period of wage labour to establish a working herd was essential. As there was, in general, less male labour available to each homestead, the absence of men for long periods threatened to inhibit agricultural production. However, male labour was only essential in the ploughing season and perhaps at harvest. From the late 1930s, if not earlier, monthly figures of migration to the gold mines indicate that the pattern of migration was assuming marked seasonal characteristics (Table 3). Where possible, men would leave home in December, January and February. They were usually limited to six- or nine-month contracts and could return by October for ploughing.[99] August was also a peak recruiting month, for men leaving at this time could return for the harvest in June. The number of migrants leaving during the winter months of May, June and July was far smaller. While the pattern of seasonality should not be exaggerated – only about 40 per cent of men left in the four peak months – and other factors affected the decision about when to leave home, it reflected the changes in family structure and cropping.

Not only could those families with adequate draught plant maize more extensively without having to increase the input of labour in cultivation, they could also sow more subsidiary vegetable crops. This evidence suggests that total and perhaps even per capita output may have continued to increase during the decades when mass migrancy became institutionalised. Such an argument should be advanced with caution. Although the lack of labour in each productive unit did not necessarily inhibit production, there is little doubt that some families found that their labour became too thinly stretched. Women had to spend proportionately more time looking after children, gathering firewood – which in any case was becoming more scarce – and drawing water. Total output probably varied even more from year to year, for maize was less resistant to drought than sorghum. As cash could be earned and grain purchased in an emergency, families were probably prepared to take greater risks so that they could capitalise on a good season. Further, in the longer run, the new system of cropping had its costs. More extensive and deeper ploughing brought with it the danger of topsoil loss, and even erosion in steep fields. Maize tended to exhaust the soil more rapidly, a process hastened by the dropping of field rotation and the shortage of new plots, which was becoming evident in some areas by the 1930s.[100] Yet all in all, the adaptions in cropping did lead at least to further extension of cultivation, if not to higher yields.

There are estimates of grain production in each district of the Transkeian Territories. In 1904 and 1911, total grain production in Pondoland was estimated at between 350,000 and 450,000 bags (Table 7). By the 1920s, returns of the crops produced in Pondoland had risen to around 500,000 bags in average seasons and 700,000 in good seasons. On the basis of population figures, it can be calculated that per capita output in average years increased from something under 2 bags a year in the first decade of the century to between 2.3 and 2.5 bags in 1921. Only by 1936 had it decreased to below 2 bags again. These figures were, however, arrived at by estimating the number of homesteads in a district, the average landholdings of each homestead and the average yield per morgen in any particular year.[101] (Officials calculated that average landholdings varied between two and a half and four morgen, and yields between 4 and 8 bags per morgen. Consumption was thought to be about 2 bags per person every year.) Any of these estimates was subject to error, for no records were kept of the relevant figures. As the system of taxation was not based on output, or even the quantity of land held, there was no reason for the administration to bear the cost of more detailed census work. One official felt that the returns were 'utterly useless'.[102] The agricultural census supervisor in the Territories was a little less pessimistic.

> Outside the surveyed districts [he wrote] no one knows the extent of land allotted for arable purposes, and it is impossible to state with any degree of accuracy how much of the land usually under cultivation is under cultivation at any particular time. It is all guess work based on impressions made upon the minds of untrained men. The returns are not useless and as they cost little or nothing and give us a fair, even if vague notion of the general position, they are worth having.[103]

101

The statistical returns cannot therefore be used to prove or disprove the arguments advanced in this section.

The analysis above is based on a generalised view of the productive capacity of the homesteads. There were some families which were, even in the 1920s and 1930s, producing considerably more than they needed for subsistence and others which produced much less.[104] The uneven levels of production within Pondoland in itself guaranteed a market for the larger producers. It does seem, however, that the adaptions made in cropping, coupled with the increase in stock numbers, enabled many families to remain self-sufficient in their basic foodstuffs in good and average years, at least till the 1920s. Considerable imports were necessary in bad years, particularly in 1919–20 and in 1926–7, but in good and average years the surplus produced in some homesteads was probably nearly sufficient to offset the shortfall in others.[105] Producers still sold considerable quantities to the traders; one leading trader in Libode district remembered purchasing as much as 6,000 bags a year in the mid-1930s, a figure which suggests that the quantity sold had not diminished very markedly, and had perhaps even increased when compared with turn-of-the-century figures. But although some grain found its way to other stations in the Territories, very little was exported. Grain was rather redistributed through the traders within Pondoland, on a commercial basis, or sold and bought back. The evidence suggests that the rural economy of Pondoland was able to recover after the major natural disasters of 1912–13 and 1919–20. It is worth noting that consumption of foodstuffs not produced in Pondoland, even of such basics as sugar, which was later bought in large quantities, remained very low until the 1930s, when per capita output almost certainly began to decline. In general, the position of the homesteads in Pondoland by the 1930s was considerably better than in other parts of the Territories.

This relative success in maintaining production has, however, to be set against the intensification of direct levies on the population of Pondoland after 1925.[106] The Native Taxation and Development Act of that year introduced a flat-rate poll tax of £1 on all African males over eighteen throughout South Africa. While poll taxes had been in force elsewhere, the effects of this Act immediately at least doubled the burden in the Cape. In Eastern Pondoland, married men had to find 10s. per wife for the hut tax, 2s. for the education tax, and 6s. 6d. for dipping levies, as well as the poll tax. After 1927, when the Council system was imposed in the area, the burden increased to parity with Western Pondoland, as a 10s. Council tax replaced the former separate levies. When, a few years later, stock rates were imposed, in addition to the Council tax, to cover dipping, the tax burden again increased. The 1925 measure maintained the principle, in a segregationist era, that expenditure in the African reserves should largely be financed by direct taxation of their populations. Despite objections in both Pondoland and Zululand, it overrode the old Cape principle that taxation in the Territories be the responsibility of married men, and it thus contributed further to separate the liabilities of father and son and to undermine the control of homestead heads. It was also more directly a levy on wages rather than on production; indeed, it was increasingly collected at the labour centres. Over and above the new system of direct taxation, indirect taxation on such important articles as blankets also rose steeply as the Pact government raised tariffs on imports in order to protect South Africa's infant industries. Reliance on wages not only for the process of household reproduction, for accumulating resources to produce, but also for taxation and expenditure on commodities was increased. However, the general pattern suggested in this chapter is that access to land, stock and household labour remained critical for the great majority of homesteads. Indeed, the tendency for homesteads to fragment, at the same time as population increased, resulted in increased demand for these resources. This sustained the general demand for communal grazing lands and automatic grants of arable plots to married men. The patterns of production and the nature of demands in connection with land will become clearer in the ensuing discussion of local political authority and the position of the chiefs.

4
Chiefs and headmen in Pondoland, 1905–1930

1 The dipping crisis and the new paramountcy

Rather than destroy the chiefs in the Transkeian Territories, except for those who had openly rebelled against the Colony, the administration sought to deprive them of many of their independent powers, make them dependent on the state, and use their remaining authority to ease the implementation of colonial rule.[1] Bokleni in Western Pondoland, and especially Dalindyebo in Thembuland, were held up, in contrast to Sigcau, as models of the Colonial chief. After Sigcau's death in 1905, however, the administration attempted to mould his successors to accept their role in the Colonial state.[2] Sigcau's heir, Marelane, was about fifteen years of age when his father died. As he was considered too young to succeed, Mhlanga, son of Mqikela's first wife, was appointed regent by the chiefs and people with the approval of the administration. Sigcau had intended to send Marelane to the United States to further his education; at the turn of the century the paramount had developed some links with Ethiopian churches in the Territories which were organising such educational trips for Transkeian youths.[3] But Colonial officials, intent on making not only an educated and progressive, but also a co-operative, chief out of Marelane, were wary of 'American' ideas which they felt were espoused by the separatist church movement. They advised Mhlanga to keep him in South Africa, and in 1907 Marelane went to Lovedale, the leading Eastern Cape mission school. The principal attempted to instil Christian and colonial ideas into him and even hesitated to allow him home for holidays lest he slip back into Mpondo politics and Mpondo values.

> The lad shows promise of so much force of character [the principal wrote to the Chief Magistrate in 1908] that if he could be secured a respite of another year, he might be able to resist successfully the evil that will be presented him and develop into a useful man, able to exercise wisely and profitably the large measure of power which still clings to the Pondo chieftainship.[4]

104

The administration encouraged Marelane to stay until, at the end of 1909, he was needed to resolve the crisis in which Mhlanga's regency ended.

Mhlanga's accession coincided with administrative attempts to enforce preventive measures against East Coast fever. As the Mpondo would not accept Councils, which financed tank-building in the rest of the Territories, they had to agree, in 1906, to a one-off dipping levy of 2s. 6d. on every hut-tax payer.[5] In 1909, when the disease reached southern Natal, the administration informed Mhlanga that the levy would be introduced on an annual basis in preparation for compulsory dipping.[6] The first collection had only raised enough to build sixteen tanks in the whole of Eastern Pondoland. At the same time, restrictions on cattle movements began to be enforced more strictly. A fence was built dividing Pondoland from Natal and a *cordon sanitaire* cleared on either side. Bizana district, which bordered on Natal, was cut off from the rest of Pondoland and itself divided into twelve zones among which cattle could not be moved. According to the administration, Mhlanga agreed to these proposals. But when the news became general, it occasioned widespread resentment in Pondoland; large deputations were organised to express popular views on the issue.

Officials attributed the opposition to a combination of Mpondo ignorance and conservatism on the one hand and to political agitation on the other. 'Surely when you agreed to the erection of these tanks', the Chief Magistrate told a deputation in 1909, 'you knew that they would be used; you did not think that the putting up of the tanks would frighten the disease away as a scarecrow frightens the birds in the lands.'[7] The anti-dipping campaign, they suspected, was orchestrated by a group of councillors, backed by Masarili, Mqikela's great wife, who had adopted Sigcau, seeking to discredit Mhlanga and take control of the regency. 'They were endeavouring by opposition to Government measures supported by him to secure his downfall'; Mhlanga, on the other hand, 'had stood loyally by the government and should be supported'.[8] Indeed, competition between sections of the royal family did provide a focus for popular opposition. During the crisis it emerged that there was great concern about the readiness with which the regent had accepted the administration's demands; he was felt to be unresponsive to the views of the councillors and chiefs. Considered in this perspective, the complaints that Mhlanga had not consulted his people before agreeing to the proposals must be regarded as more than a smokescreen to cloud other issues. The regent was being manipulated into a passive and collaborationist position; the precedent for unilateral state intervention was being set. Their right to consultation was one of the few means that the Mpondo subchiefs and people had to modify and influence state policy. Masarili took on the role of defending

105

the interests of the minor chiefs and people as she had done in the 1880s when Mhlangaso was ousted.

Underlying the general concern about the form of state intervention were more specific grievances. Any new taxation was undesirable; all the more so a regular tax, over which the people would have no influence in the future, to implement an unpopular measure. Many believed that dipping would do as much harm as good. They had agreed to the dipping of small stock in 1903 after Sigcau carefully consulted his people, but some argued that when dipping first started, many of the small stock had died. 'Now we are told that our cattle will be dipped with the same dip that killed our sheep and goats.'[9] The Chief Magistrate felt that they wrongly attributed death from wireworm to the dip. But there may have been other dangers for stock which had not been dipped before, especially if they were not handled carefully at the tanks, or if the solutions used were too strong. During rinderpest, rumours were rife that the disease and combative measures had been brought by the administration to undermine African society. Such rumours began to circulate again; the treatments for rinderpest, over and above the precautions taken by the Mpondo themselves, had not after all met with much success. Further, some believed that the regular gathering of large numbers of cattle at the tanks would facilitate rather than retard the spread of East Coast fever and other diseases.[10] And especially in later years, spokesmen frequently argued that the long (often weekly) trips to the dipping tanks weakened cattle for draught and affected milk supplies.

Though their ideas about disease were often expressed in relation to the ideology of witchcraft, the Mpondo were well aware that some cattle diseases were spread by contact between infected animals; this was one of the reasons for opposition to dipping, and they had, as has been pointed out, isolated their herds at various times in the nineteenth century in order to stop the spread of disease. Some cattle movements were also stopped as a sign of mourning on the death of a paramount chief.[11] Indeed, such restrictions were being enforced in Western Pondoland after the death of the chief Bokleni in 1912, at the time that East Coast fever made its appearance, and in 1915 the regent Mangala was still fining people for moving brideweath cattle. Restrictions on cattle movements were thus not a completely new form of intervention into the way in which homesteads managed their herds. Part of the chiefly concern about the regulations probably stemmed from the usurpation by the state of chiefly authority in this respect; magistrates actually intervened to stop enforcement of mourning regulations. Popular opposition was stimulated not only by the fact that the new restrictions were in some ways harsher, but that the people had no control over the authorities which enacted and enforced them. The

Colonial response to East Coast fever came at a time when mistrust of the administration, which was beginning to regulate homestead life more closely, was increasing. Restrictions were used as a pretext to abolish advances; they coincided with the introduction of dipping. At the same time, government fences, which were becoming anathema to the Mpondo chiefs and people, were being built; people in Pondoland were aware of events in Zululand, where the sugar farmers were moving into some of the best coastal lands.

Langasiki, the Ngutyana chief in Bizana, who was one of the most reluctant to buckle down and bear the burden of Colonial rule, summed up popular feelings at a large meeting in December, 1909.

> When Government first imposed the 2/6 tax they said that dipping is not compulsory. Now the disease is in Natal and a fence as high as this building [the magistrate's office at Lusikisiki] has been built to prevent the cattle coming to this side. We want all the Government Vets to go to Natal and stamp out the disease there. Government must not kill the children where the disease is not. When government came to the country they said they had come to maintain us, that we might grow, not to destroy us and not to take away our land. We must come under Government with our own blankets and the ground would remain with us always. What have we done today that he should kill our cattle. Our cattle are our own food. We do everything for Government, dig his roads and his mines. We thought we were good subjects to Government. We were praising Government. We do not understand Government that now tramples on our heads and treats us like dogs. We are his children, we fill his house with money in one day, when we have none we work for it. What wrong have we done? I ask Government to tell us what wrong we have done.[12]

His impassioned speech perhaps revealed his ignorance of the way in which East Coast fever could be carried by ticks alone rather than by infected cattle. Yet it made clear the depth of suspicion with which the administration was regarded. East Coast fever restrictions and dipping were associated with other forms of intervention and regarded as punitive measures.

The administration did not sit by idly while the forces of opposition gathered. The magistrate of Kingwilliamstown district, senior official in the Eastern Cape, was sent to Lovedale to obtain Marelane's assurance that he had no part in the disturbance and to inform him about the situation.[13] Marelane was rapidly subjected to a crash course on East Coast fever and the measures that could be taken to prevent it. When Mhlanga died at the end of November 1909, the new chief was whisked back to Pondoland, fully prepared. His presence had little immediate effect. A number of chiefs and councillors had determined to contest the dipping regulations in court.[14] A collection of one shilling from each hut-tax payer was initiated and payment in itself came to signify commitment to resisting the government. Magistrates detected further intrigues by one of Mqikela's sons, who disputed the legitimate right of Sigcau and his successors to occupy the paramountcy. At one stage, in February 1910, officials felt they had lost the new paramount to the forces of opposition. However, after Marelane's formal installation in that month, the Chief Magistrate placed a great deal of pressure on him, threatening to withdraw the subsidies of all the chiefs in Pondoland and arrest them as well. Ultimately, there was little the Mpondo could do short of violent resistance, and the implications of revolt were too well known. The collection broke down, and by early March Marelane was in a position to censure his councillors publicly for misleading him and announce that the government proposals would be accepted, though everyone realised that the 'Pondos generally dislike[d] the idea of dipping their cattle'.

Marelane's accession was seen by the administration to herald a new era in relations between the paramountcy and the administration. Officials' image of the paramountcy began to change. Whereas Sigcau had been seen as backward-looking and the major factor in retarding the advancement of a people hungry for the benefits of civilised rule, Marelane was cast in the role of a collaborative and modernising chief, dragging his people out of the darkness by their all too often absent bootlaces. Whereas a decade before, Sigcau's attempts to resist had seemed to be constrained by the passivity of the people, now the paramountcy was being used to neutralise opposition by the lesser chiefs, who had popular support. The transition was not as stark as these images suggest, but the dipping crisis certainly did highlight changes in the political balance within Pondoland.

The administration's hopes for Marelane were, to some degree, realised. In 1911, when East Coast fever first broke out in the Territories, the paramount organised his own guards on the borders of Pondoland to prevent cattle movements and helped to enforce other regulations.[15] Between 1913 and 1915, he weathered another crisis over dipping which, if anything, was more serious than the first.[16] In 1913, when the disease had already killed the cattle, the administration decided to levy a further tax of five shillings annually, not only on hut-tax payers, but on all adult males. There were still too few tanks in Pondoland to permit compulsory dipping of all the cattle. The threat of increased taxation, coming on top of an unprecedented series of natural disasters between 1911 and 1913, stimulated a new wave of resistance. In parts of East Griqualand, dipping tanks were blown up and some men took to arms. The Mpondo were, at one stage, thought to be implicated in this rebellion, which lasted, in various phases, for three years between 1914 and 1917.[17] Marelane himself was associated with rumours of resistance to the tax and to the war effort. The people of Eastern Pondoland did not in fact volunteer for the Native Labour Contingent in any numbers, and the paramount apparently advised neutrality. There does not, however, seem to have been any open violence in Pondoland, and Marelane was personally given the credit for keeping the Mpondo out of the disturbances. (It is difficult to assess his role fully, as one file dealing with this episode is missing from the archives.) The paramount was able to secure acceptance of the additional tax and compulsory dipping, although he did succeed in persuading the administration to limit the tax to hut-tax payers. Though the benefits of dipping were to some extent recognised, the underlying resentment of state measures surfaced on a variety of occasions in the next decade.[18]

Not only did the new paramount co-operate with officials at times of crisis, when he was under great pressure from the administration, he also took 'progressive' initiatives himself, particularly in the educational sphere. In these he was greatly aided, or more likely led, by Tshongwana, 'one of the best educated and most capable of the Lovedale Native teachers of this time', who became the paramount's secretary, and was 'strictly speaking . . . from accession the brains of the chief'.[19] It was later recalled, when the *Christian Express* unhappily had to publish an obituary for Marelane in 1921, that the young chief had applied to take Tshongwana with him when he was rushed back to Pondoland at the end of 1909. It is possible, however, that Tshongwana's appointment was actually organised by the administration.

Since Mhlangaso's rise to power in the nineteenth century, in which his mission education played some part, the Mpondo chiefs were well aware of the advantages of literacy in a colonial world, though many had an ambiguous attitude to the effects of education. Sigcau had not been entirely remiss in this sphere. He had given £100 to Emfundisweni mission school in the 1890s, had authorised and arranged labour for the erection of schools, and had educated his own children, including one daughter, beyond primary level. However, at his death there were still only twenty-eight schools in Pondoland, all primary, and the number of pupils was only 1,434, or about 2 per cent of children between five and fifteen.[20] Marelane instituted, with administrative approval, an annual two-shilling education levy, which brought in between £2,000 and £3,000 a year to fund primary schools. By 1921, the number of schools in Eastern Pondoland had increased to ninety-four and the number of pupils to between five and six thousand. The paramount's energies were particularly devoted to funding a Teachers Training College at the Methodist centre of Emfundisweni in Flagstaff district. A sum of £1,200 was initially raised, and in 1921 there were 142 student teachers at the institution. (At this time, education in the Territories was funded partly by the missions and partly by the Councils, the state providing some support for teachers' salaries and school inspectors.) The man appointed as principal of Emfundisweni Training School, W. D. Cingo, was himself a descendant of one of Faku's brothers, the leading Mpondo educationist of his time, advisor to and occasional spokesman for Marelane, and later author of traditional histories. He was an advocate of progressive Christian values and co-operation with the state; his college became a symbol for the new developments in Pondoland.

Marelane was appointed to the Cape Province Native Education Commission in 1919, as a representative of the Native Affairs Department, in recognition of his services to education.[21] Whatever his influence with the Commission, it was an unusual step on the part of the Department and signified the importance attached to the attitude of the paramountcy not only at a local, but at a national level. Tshongwana, who attended the Commission's sittings, seems to have played a more important role than Marelane himself. When the secretary died in 1919, while the Commission was still in session, Cingo felt that Marelane gave up his struggle and went to pieces. There are certainly a number of reports, from that time onwards, which reinforce this view.[22] Marelane started to drink heavily, and his behaviour excited comment from both the administration and his advisors. Even his new secretary, Gordon Dana, who had been educated at university in the United States, and was not as sympathetic to the administration as Tshongwana, expressed his concern about the chief to officials.[23] Yet despite Marelane's decline in the last two years of his rule – he died, prematurely, of pneumonia in 1921 – he had, with the aid of men like Tshongwana and Cingo, stamped a new character on the paramountcy as an institution.

The new paramount was not, however, merely a tool in the administration's hands. From his accession, Marelane and his advisors attempted to use their position of favour in such a way as to restore some of the powers of the paramountcy which had been so impaired after annexation. During the dipping crisis, Marelane had direct access to the upper, decision-making echelons of the administration, access which had been denied to Sigcau and even to the paramounts before annexation. It had long been Colonial policy to insist on an official intermediary between the Mpondo chiefs and the Chief Magistrate: a British resident before annexation, and an Assistant Chief Magistrate in Lusikisiki afterwards. The latter official had been withdrawn from Pondoland after Sigcau's death and, despite Marelane's requests, was not again appointed. All communication was supposed to take place through the agency of the Resident Magistrates in Pondoland. Nevertheless, the years of the dipping crisis, drought and East Coast fever (1909–15) were punctuated by frequent meetings between the Chief Magistrate himself and Marelane, who was thus in a position to express his views directly to the top Transkeian official on a large range of important issues.

Any concessions made to the paramount depended on administrative adjustments, which could be reversed, rather than major legislative or policy changes at the national level. 'Native policy' was in flux during the first decade of Union as a programme for South Africa as a whole was being formulated; the propagandists of segregationist ideologies were beginning to regard 'traditional' political authority in the African areas in a more favourable light.[24] But while there was no longer any desire, at the national level, to destroy the chiefs – they had, in the main, been subject to adequate controls – neither was any major concession made in proclamations governing the Native Territories. A departmental circular of 1914, which tried to define the role of chiefs more clearly, merely reiterated existing policy, at least in regard to chiefs in the Transkeian area.[25] Some were recognised and subsidised at the government's pleasure, yet could excercise no 'autocratic powers'. They were not employees of the state, nor public servants – unless they also acted as headmen – but should represent the people to the administration on the one hand and 'by example and precept and the proper use of . . . influence ensure the due carrying out and administration of the law' on the other. Official favour and close access to the senior administrators in the Territories were therefore particularly important to the Mpondo paramount at this time. Shifts in official thinking, and in the position of the paramount, were sometimes made in the heat of a dispute; in certain cases more general administrative principles were subsequently formulated.[26] Such changes are often difficult to identify, as they could be specific to a particular dispute or disguised by constant articulation by officials of earlier administrative principles. However, it is clear that in the course of the dipping dispute, officials began to recognise that a strong paramount in Pondoland, if co-operative, would be an invaluable asset in implementing state measures and entrenching Colonial rule in the area. The concessions made to Marelane reflected both the remaining power of the Mpondo paramountcy and the changing attitudes of officials about the way in which rural communities could be controlled.

Although the chiefly struggle in Pondoland was shaped by relationships peculiar to the area, Marelane was not alone in his fight. In the Transkeian Territories as a whole, chiefs were on the offensive. In Zululand, Solomon began a determined campaign to win formal recognition – for which the

Mpondo chiefs did not have to fight – during the decade after Union.[27] The degree to which the chiefly struggle was co-ordinated in the Union as a whole is unclear – by no means all chiefs were in a similar position – but strategy coincided on at least some points. When Solomon tried to organise a large hunt as a symbol of his authority in 1916, for example, Marelane requested permission for a similar event in Pondoland. Marelane's demands were certainly echoed by and probably influenced by the Western Pondoland chiefs after Bokleni's death in 1912. The latter had generally co-operated with the administration; he eased his people into magisterial rule, taxation, dipping and even the Council system in 1911. But Bokleni's heir, Madukula 'Victor' Poto, was a minor at the time of his father's death, living with and being educated by a Methodist missionary.[28] In 1913, Poto's mother, Mangangalizwe, was appointed joint regent with Mangala, brother to Bokleni. Mangangalizwe was sister to the Thembu paramount and shared his conviction that the most suitable role for a colonial chief was to co-operate with the administration; she was also an enthusiastic lay preacher for the Methodist church. Mangala, on the other hand, was anxious to rebuild the authority and extend the powers of the chieftaincy. By 1915, he had succeeded in warding off a claim to the regency by one of Poto's brothers and in isolating Mangangalizwe from the Councils of Western Pondoland. He came to dominate the paramountcy for the next seven or eight years, and his struggle was perhaps more bitter than Marelane's, his demands more far-reaching. (A considerable number of people from Western Pondoland, including some of Bokleni's sons, did, however, volunteer for the Native Labour Contingent.) Partly because of this, partly because he was less useful to the administration, he evoked a far less favourable response from officials than Marelane. But Mangala did go out of his way to establish a closer relationship with the Eastern Mpondo paramount and seems, on occasion, to have given the lead in defence of chieftaincy.

2 The struggle of the paramountcy

There were clear limits to the kind of concessions that the administration was prepared to make to the chiefs: claims for control over natural resources, concessions, traders and tariffs were not seriously entertained. However, on issues such as death duties and settlement fees, the administration showed some flexibility. It became essential for the chiefs to define and isolate such customary rights as a basis for their demands. Marelane and his councillors often couched their arguments in the language of custom, recalled the powers of the paramount before annexation, and exhumed the agreement between the Cape and Sigcau in 1894. His paramountcy, while clearly progressive in some respects, therefore took on a 'traditionalist' character in others. The political skills of the paramounts were geared to maintaining control through the headmen and reasserting their rights to those customary dues which could still provide a substantial income. The Chief Magistrate, however, may have exaggerated the latter element in their strategy when, in 1920, he summed up the state of play in Western Pondoland.

> As the chiefs can no longer exact presents from the people by force, the latter are not as ready to contribute to the chiefs exchequer as they used to be, when there was no escape from so doing . . . The chiefs of Western Pondoland, guided by Mangala since the death of Bokleni, have observed that the people are slipping away from them. This touches them in pocket, as well as in other ways, but it is the financial side that weighs most with Mangala.[29]

The payment of dues must be seen in the wider context of chiefly attempts to maintain power.

Marelane raised the issue of immigration into Pondoland soon after his accession.[30] In 1910, he disputed the right of Sigidi, chief of the large Nci subchieftaincy in Tabankulu, to admit immigrants without the permission of the paramount. Sigidi had claimed his own settlement fees prior to and after annexation. But Marelane argued that Sigcau had been promised the right to vet all immigrants in 1894 and that this promise should now be kept. The Chief Magistrate, in a remarkable reversal of administrative policy, immediately overruled a previous decision in favour of Sigidi. The promise apparently made to Sigcau was subsequently enforced throughout the whole of Eastern Pondoland. In 1915, after a dispute between Mangala and the Konjwayo chief in Ngqeleni district, similar rights were extended to the western Mpondo paramountcy.

The Chief Magistrate's decision was clearly predicated on a more sympathetic relationship between Marelane and the administration. In addition it seems that officials were now becoming concerned about the movement of settlers into the Transkeian Territories, as some districts were becoming overcrowded. Population movements often involved the movement of stock, which could result in breaches of the East Coast fever regulations. African tenants in the European farming districts around the Territories were under pressure as farmers began to bring land under production rather than rent it out; the Cape's Location Act of 1908 made it more advantageous to remove them, and magistrates had been giving passes without consulting Transkeian officials.[31] The Chief Magistrate ensured that the system of passes was tightened up, but also used the paramountcy to keep a watch on immigration. If local headmen omitted

113

to report new immigrants, Marelane's indunas were likely to hear of their presence and relay the information to the administration. Conversely, when immigrants came with their passes to the magistrates' offices, they would be sent to the Great Place to obtain consent. 'I . . . took the pass to Chief Marelane', related an aspirant settler in 1913, 'and he said I should pay him £5 before he would consider my application.'[32] The paramount's approval was conditional on a fee, usually a beast or its cash equivalent. The right to vet all immigrants implied access to settlement fees and other dues throughout the Pondoland districts.

Marelane's actions, especially during a dispute over his rights to death duties from Mhlangaso's old followers, indicates that this issue was also close to his heart.[33] After he had made a number of abortive attempts to end his period of exile, Mhlangaso was allowed to return to Pondoland in 1905 on condition that he settled in Bizana rather than Nthlenzi, lived as a commoner rather than a chief, and had limits placed on his freedom of movement. However, Mhlangaso's following was not to be denied, and after Sigcau's death they gave him a platform on which to re-enter chiefly politics. In 1909, Mhlangaso emerged as one of the major spokesmen at a meeting about dipping.[34] For reasons that are not entirely clear, Mhlangaso's views on dipping seem to have changed by the end of that year. What is more clear is that the administration lifted the restrictions which barred him from attending the Great Place so that he would have more freedom to work against his old rival, Masarili, who was prominent in the anti-dipping movement. Although there are no records of any promises being made to Mhlangaso for his co-operation during the dipping crisis, he certainly felt that the administration had given him the go-ahead to reassert his rights to chieftaincy.

One of Mhlangaso's first steps in rebuilding his position was to start a collection of death duties from his ex-rebel followers in Nthlenzi location, an act which in itself testifies to the importance of such payments in the eyes of Mpondo chiefs. He could hardly have chosen a more sensitive spot, for Nthlenzi was the location over which Sigcau had fought and was the site of one of Marelane's homesteads.[35] The paramount himself claimed all rebel dues and had tried to collect them soon after his accession. Marelane was, in fact, suspected of assaulting a rebel who rebuffed him in 1911, although the administration never brought him to court as they had Sigcau. When Mhlangaso started his collection, with some success, Marelane immediately called on the administration to protect his rights over the death duties in Nthlenzi. Of his two new-found allies, the Chief Magistrate chose to support the paramount on whom he had pinned so much hope for the future: Mhlangaso's status as a commoner was confirmed. He was not, however, so easily deterred; he continued to collect dues from his sympathetic followers and even tried to establish the homestead of his son in Nthlenzi. Only at the end of 1912, when the location was on the brink of violence, was he finally brought under control after many demands for administrative intervention by the paramount. The issue of death duties symbolised broader conflicts between the chiefs. Marelane had, with the aid of the state, won another important victory over a subchief and, if he could levy them, a new source of dues.

The administration still stuck by its principle that death duties could not be collected by force. Indirect evidence suggests, however, that the chiefs continued to try and enforce their rights. In 1924, after violent conflict over the paramountcy's rights to claim the dues from one group of Nci people in Flagstaff, an official found it necessary to warn chiefs again that 'compulsory exaction of death duties will not be countenanced'.[36] When enquiries were made about the causes of the fight, magistrates in Eastern Pondoland were of the opinion that death duties were still regularly collected; they did not seem particularly concerned about such chiefly activity. As late as 1935 conflict broke out on a similar issue in Lusikisiki. The general freedom allowed to Marelane's indunas probably made it easier for him to levy his dues, including the education tax, which was collected by the chiefs rather than by the magistrates. Monica Hunter gained the impression, during her fieldwork in the early 1930s, that death duties were no longer paid by most commoners; her comments may refer largely to Western Pondoland.[37] The oral evidence collected in Eastern Pondoland is contradictory.[38] While death duties probably continued to be of importance both as a symbol of chiefly authority and as a source of revenue for the chiefs during Marelane's time and perhaps during the next decade, it seems that many families stopped paying these dues in later years.

Although officials accepted some chiefly nominees for headmanships immediately after annexation, and sometimes consulted either with the paramount or other leading chiefs when the original nominees had to be replaced, they gradually developed a procedure of appointment which allowed the people of a location to show their preference by a show of hands. The popular vote was not final, but it certainly undermined further the power of chiefs to secure posts for their own men. Marelane had some freedom to send indunas around the country, but he could not coerce people to meet his demands, especially if they were supported by local headmen who could appeal to the magistrates. He realised, as had Sigcau, that sympathetic headmen were essential to the maintenance of chiefly power. The paramountcy had also to extend its control over headmanships if positions were to be found for all the sons and brothers of the royal family. While Sigcau had arranged with the magistrates for the placement

115

of his sons before his death, and most were accepted by the people of the locations to which they were assigned, his eldest son, Toli, remained at the Great Place.[39] The location in Tabankulu in which Toli was supposed to 'form a tribe' was under a headman who, with the support of the people, refused to stand down. Nci and Cwera chiefs in the district also felt threatened by the proposed presence of a senior member of the royal family so close to their centres of power. Marelane, stung by the rejection, and concerned that his inability to place Toli was considered an indication of weakness, suggested that a new principle be laid down for the appointment of headmen in Eastern Pondoland.

> We have two classes of headmen [he wrote to the Chief Magistrate in 1911] viz. Chiefs and Commoners. According to our custom the position of headman is hereditary only in respect of Chiefs and their heirs . . . Briefly my proposal is to the effect that commoners should be informed that they are merely acting for my children, who will replace them when they attain manhood. And that whenever a headman dies I should be given an opportunity of recommending a successor.

Officials again refused to make any concessions in principle. They reminded Marelane, as they had Sigcau, that the days when every son of a chief could become a chief were past. However, the Chief Magistrate indicated that he was generally in favour of royal nominees, when they were acceptable to the people, because they could usually command greater respect and because this tightened the hold of the administration over the royal family. Moreover, after yet further difficulties were experienced in finding a location for Toli, the administration created one for him in 1915 by excising contiguous portions from a number of other locations in Lusikisiki without regard to protests from local headmen who were losing both land and people.

The administration also protected Marelane from attempts by minor royal lineages to place out their sons and widen the area under their authority, a reversal of the policy adopted during the first ten years after annexation. Mhla?ga, the regent between 1905 and 1909, claimed chieftainship and the right to place his sons in a number of locations between the Msikaba and Mtentu rivers in Lusikisiki district.[40] He legitimated his claim on the basis of a grant allegedly made by his father, Mqikela, but hoped that it would be recognised as a reward for his co-operation during the regency. Sigcau, on the other hand, had regarded the area as a potential chiefdom for his eldest son, Mswakeli. He was keen to have a regent headman appointed to one location in the area in preparation for the time when Mswakeli completed his education and reached manhood. During his regency, Mhlanga tried to push Mswakeli into the Flagstaff district, and the regent's heir pressed Mhlanga's claim after Marelane's succession. But the new paramount was able to call on the administration to install his brother Mswakeli in 1911.

Official decisions were not always so clear-cut, partly because the basis for appointment had now become confused.[41] A variety of factors came into play in any dispute over headmanship. Where the post was in the control of a chiefly family, the heir was usually appointed, although the administration reserved the right to depose a candidate whom they considered incompetent or unsuitable. Officials reiterated the principle that the people should be consulted in any dispute, and they continued the practice of organising a show of hands at public meetings within the location concerned. But the popular vote could be embarrassingly fickle, swinging from one candidate to another if more than one meeting was held.[42] Officials did not try to dissuade either paramount or minor chiefs from trying to put pressure on the people during disputes, and they never felt that they were bound to follow the result of the vote. Further, from Marelane's accession, they took the paramount's claim to any location seriously, thus opening the way to complex disputes between paramount and local chiefs about the history of control over the area. The chiefs, in turn, tried to use the administration in furthering their claims even if these had little historical basis. The administration felt that it had to take all these, often conflicting, criteria into account in order to secure a headman who was sufficiently popular to secure the support of the people, sufficiently pliable to cooperate with the state's demands, and sufficiently acceptable to the paramount or other powerful chiefs who had the power to make his position difficult if they did not approve of the appointment.

The cost of such ill-defined criteria of selection was protracted and often bitter disputes over headmanships. Although there are by no means adequate records of all disputes, it seems that Marelane did indeed succeed in placing his nominees in some locations over which the paramountcy did not previously have control.[43] After Marelane died in 1921, and his brother Mswakeli became regent, the paramountcy maintained the pressure on the administration. Two of Marelane's senior sons, Botha and Nelson, were placed in important locations in Flagstaff which had not previously been under paramount control.[44] Mswakeli was even able to slip one candidate into a contested post in the face of popular disapproval, which eventually became so heated that the paramount's nominee had to be withdrawn. The issue of headmanship remained central to chiefly politics throughout the 1920s. Mswakeli's demands were, if anything, more extreme than Marelane's. He tried to have the procedure for nomination altered by reintroducing what he called the 'custom of bringing'.[45] Instead

117

of the vote being organised by the magistrate, it would be organised in the presence of the paramount's councillors, and the successful nominee would then be 'brought' to the magistrate for approval. Even this request was a compromise. In a moment of anger, Mswakeli revealed his true feelings. 'All the locations in Eastern Pondoland "belong" to the Great Place ... when I make a nomination I do not want it put to the vote.'[46] Both he and Poto in Western Pondoland, who succeeded as paramount in 1918, argued that by accepting popular nominees the administration was allowing backward-looking rather than progressive headmen to succeed.[47] The increased stridency of the demands for control of appointments in the 1920s probably reflects both increasing concern on the part of the paramountcy about its local political control and a resurgence of chiefly aggression. At no point, however, did the magistrates make any major concession in principle, though they continued to encourage the paramounts to nominate candidates and involve themselves in the procedure for selection.

An essential part of the paramountcy's strategy in maintaining local political control was to monopolise the role of intermediary between the administration and the people. The chiefs were well aware that headmen had direct access to the magistrates and could bypass the paramountcy in presenting popular grievances. They were also concerned that their role would be further diluted if Councils, along the Glen Grey model, were imposed in Pondoland; these could even threaten the institution of chieftaincy itself. Bokleni, who had accepted a changed role as a colonial chief, was not averse to the Council system in the first decade of the century, but was reluctant to take the plunge without the agreement of the eastern Mpondo paramount and bided his time in order to obtain better terms. When he was eventually won over in 1911, his councillors insisted that Western Pondoland should have its own separate General Council, that the paramount should nominate all Council members, and that the customs and system of land tenure which were central to chiefly power should not be subject to alteration by the Councils.[48] These concessions were, in the main, granted, although he was allowed to nominate only four out of six councillors in each District Council and two out of the three General Council members from each district. The powers delegated to him were far greater than those to other Transkeian chiefs, and the Pondoland General Council tended to operate as a permanent, slightly restructured, consultative committee between the paramount's nominees and the magistrates.

Marelane was initially in favour of a similar arrangement for Eastern Pondoland, and the administration was prepared to offer similar concessions to him during the dipping crisis.[49] Officials felt that acceptance of the Council system in the area would reduce conflict over the financing of dipping and placed considerable pressure on the paramount to accept. But Marelane held back. He was, after all, able to secure access to the administration on his own terms for a number of years during the crisis, and this enabled him to make significant gains; the Pondoland General Council and the Transkeian Territories General Council were not seen to be effective in persuading the administration to act on their motions. He had also to take into account popular opposition to the tax and the popular association of the Councils with the dipping programme which resulted in revived anti-Council agitation throughout the Territories.

So ineffectual did Mangala regard the Western Pondoland General Council which he had inherited from Bokleni that he tried to withdraw from the system.[50] He was particularly annoyed by the tight controls which officials maintained over Council finances and by the fact that the administration could and did refuse to accept paramount nominees. Officials had also been suggesting that, for ease of administration, the Pondoland General Council be amalgamated with the Transkeian Territories General Council, a move which was considered a threat by the chiefs. They feared that they would be swamped by representatives from the rest of the Territories. Not only would the Council in Pondoland cease to play a protective role for the paramountcy, but the Mpondo could be forced to accept majority resolutions inspired by southern Transkeian councillors, who could articulate demands inimical to Mpondo chiefs.[51] In fact, Mangala had, in 1918, attempted to counter this development by launching a proposal for a new General Council composed of the whole of Pondoland and large parts of East Griqualand, which the Mpondo paramounts would be able to dominate. This unsuccessful scheme – which had met with a favourable response at a large meeting held in Eastern Pondoland in 1918 – seems to have been seen as an alternative to complete dissociation.

The administration had not made further attempts to extend the Council system to Eastern Pondoland during the decade after Union, for the structure of 'Native administration' in the country had not yet been re-defined. After the 1920 Native Administration Act, however, which provided for the extension of the Council system to areas outside the Territories, pressure was renewed. Mswakeli still preferred to remain outside the system, but eventually accepted, in 1926, on condition that he was given an elected Council constituted under Act 23 of 1920, rather than one on the Transkeian model, and that it remain separate from the other Transkeian Councils.[52] Officials could not understand why the 'most backward and ignorant' people in the Territories should demand an elected Council designed for the urban areas; 'in asking for such a system', the

Chief Magistrate suggested, 'they are actuated by a feeling of pride or sentiment and wish to have something different from either the TTGC or the existing PGC'. But the aim of Mswakeli and his advisors, although it was not revealed to the government in a series of negotiations which eventually led to a meeting with the Minister of Native Affairs, was rather different. They wished to circumvent the official control over nominees and funds that characterised the Transkeian system. This, they felt, was best guaranteed by a fully elected Council. According to Dana, they felt that they would be able to control the procedure for electing the councillors.[53] In 1927, however, the administration closed negotiations and unilaterally imposed the Transkeian Council system in Eastern Pondoland, at the same time creating a new General Council of all the District Councils in Eastern and Western Pondoland. In the late 1920s, officials felt that there was no longer any justification for the expense of maintaining two separate Council systems in the Territories and suggested that the Pondoland General Council be amalgamated with the TTGC. Despite their reservations, the Mpondo chiefs, under the leadership of Poto, who had thrown in his lot with the Council system, accepted.[54] They were guaranteed that the Mpondo paramounts would still be recognised, that their powers of nomination would remain and that chiefly rights and privileges would not be impaired. The first session of the United Transkeian Territories General Council met in Umtata in 1931.

The battle for local political control also spread into the sphere of education.[55] Money raised through the education levy was administered as a Trust Fund by the administration; the schools themselves, in accordance with the policies concerning African education, fell under the ultimate control of the Cape Province Education Department. Marelane and his councillors, however, were insistent that, as the fund had been raised by a voluntary levy from the people rather than by a government tax, they should have some say over how it was disbursed. After the initial proclamation governing the Trust Fund was promulgated in 1917, Marelane was allowed, along with the magistracy and the Education Department, to vet all expenditure. The issue was further discussed by the Native Education Commission in 1919, where it was agreed that an Advisory Committee be established as a new level of local authority under the Education Department. This committee, which to some extent served the function of the General Councils in the rest of the Territories, was unique to Eastern Pondoland, and recognised the critical role played by the chieftaincy in the area. Marelane accepted the idea in 1921, after consulting mass meetings, but disagreements arose over the weighting of Mpondo representatives, magistrates and missionaries. The paramount wanted to ensure that magistrates would not dominate and to include enough popular representatives to allay suspicions about how the Fund was spent. He proposed that the Mpondo nominees, appointed by himself, be in the majority and that magistrates have no right to vote. He was forced to back down when the Chief Magistrate insisted that officials vote and that the Mpondo representatives be equal in number to others. However, he secured a compromise which gave very real representation to Mpondo chiefs and people; again, the decisions about education reflected the political balance that had been reached between paramount and the administration in Pondoland.

The most striking feature of the period after Marelane's accession in Eastern Pondoland was the success of the paramountcy in maintaining a measure of local political control and the ability to levy certain dues, despite a system of administration which was essentially designed to minimise chiefly influence and power. The paramounts were highly sensitive to any infringement of their powers and resorted to complex political manoeuvres in order to maintain them. Where possible, they tried not only to prevent administrative infringement of their powers, but also to employ the administration in bolstering up their position and regaining certain rights from local chiefs and headmen. In doing so, they projected a mix of the ideologies of progress and tradition. Marelane and Poto, in particular, showed that they were not merely hidebound chiefs clinging to the past, yet they were always highly sensitive to the use that they could make of appeals to tradition. In fact Poto, with the aid of Mangala and his Mfengu secretary, Makiwane, in 1927 published a full-length book on Mpondo history and customs, emphasising the role and powers of the paramounts; Cingo wrote a similar book in the 1920s.[56]

The changing attitude of the administration to the chiefs stemmed, initially, from the problems faced by officials in maintaining order in Pondoland and in increasing the effectiveness of government intervention. State attempts to radically restructure local political relationships had been abandoned. Given the nature of local political power and the continued strength of the paramounts, officials had little alternative but to bargain. The administration was certainly not prepared to make many major concessions to the paramounts; indeed, they refused more chiefly demands than they granted. But, having accepted that chiefs would not be displaced, officials were concerned to remould the institution of chieftaincy and to incorporate chiefs into the bureaucratic structure. This was achieved in Pondoland partly by allowing royal and chiefly families to dominate many of the headmanships, and partly by giving certain powers, such as those over immigration and the local Council system, to the paramounts. The recognition of chiefs and of their more bureaucratic role was enshrined in the 1927 Native Administration Act, a cornerstone of segregationist policy, which largely confirmed the position in the Trans-keian Territories.[57] The state had ultimate control over the appointment and recognition of chiefs, who served at its pleasure; the administrative duties of headmen were more closely defined. The Act also provided for a more segregated system of justice. Chiefly courts could be recognised, and 'native law and custom' was to be more extensively applied in civil disputes. It is interesting to record that Victor Poto's court was, in 1929, one of the first recognised in the country. Mswakeli's court was similarly elevated in 1931. The survival of the chieftaincy, and the use made of chiefs and headmen in administering Pondoland, had important implications for patterns of production, stratification and political conflict in the area.

3 Chiefs, headmen and the land

Throughout the early decades of the twentieth century, the chiefs and headmen in Pondoland displayed great sensitivity to any threats on the part of the state either to dispossess the Mpondo of their land or to change the system of communal tenure. Though the paramounts, at least, had not been averse to granting concessions prior to annexation, they did not construe the terms of these grants as providing traders or concessionaires with permanent title to the land. When their political power had been reduced, the chiefs began to reflect a deep-seated fear that the administration would bow to pressure from such interests. As Union 'Native policy' swung towards the entrenchment of the system of reserves after the first decade of the century, the dispute over land did not assume a central position in the relationship between chiefs and the state. There were, nevertheless, some areas of disagreement over land policy, and chiefly insistence on the preservation of communal tenure had important implications for the nature of rural production.

The paramounts opposed, on a number of occasions, the alienation of even small areas of land for state purposes. They had had to accept the reservation of commonages around the magisterial centres, but in future years councillors maintained that these had been 'gifts' to the administration and therefore could not be cut up into farms or urban plots as had been done with the land around Umtata magistracy.[58] Sigcau contested all claims by the traders to rights over the sometimes extensive grants that he and his predecessors had made; he even tried to prevent the erection of a lighthouse on the coast of Lusikisiki, partly so that no precedent might be set by which the administration could claim land for such purposes, partly because he felt it would disturb access to coastal winter grazing. Some Europeans in the Territories felt that land would be more

122

productive if it were opened to colonists.[59] Such opinions stimulated chiefly
fears that successful cash cropping might lead to confiscation of land.
When granting plots in the fertile Mngazi valley near Port St Johns town,
Bokleni, according to Mangala, specifically 'instructed Gawe [one of the
grantees] and other men not to plant fruit trees or make other improvements lest they should attract Europeans'.[60] Similar fears led to unease
about cotton-planting and Council extension schemes. In a period when
winter grazing was increasingly dependent on stubble, fencing of cash
crops threatened communal access to grazing lands. Government schemes
to assist in fence-building met with a poor response.

It was this concern about the implications of any commoditisation of
land that led the eastern Mpondo paramount to support at least some sections of the Natives Land Act of 1913. The position was clearly articulated
by Cingo, one of Marelane's chief advisors, during the nation-wide debate
following this piece of legislation. Leaders of the South African Native
National Congress (SANNC) were firmly opposed to the sections of the
Act which fixed African reserves, prevented purchase of land by Africans
outside of these and small 'scheduled' areas, and weakened the position
of tenants on European-owned farms.[61] During the SANNC campaign to
mobilise support and funds for a deputation to England, H. Selby Msimang,
Congress Secretary, held a meeting in Kokstad. Cingo used the opportunity to launch an attack on the SANNC policy in a series of letters to
the *Kokstad Advertiser*. His arguments are worth noting in some detail:

> The pivot of this SANNC appeal, as far as we can judge, is 'that
> natives are debarred from purchasing land wherever they choose,
> etc. etc.' But it seems that the same knife is applied to whites as well.
> It is not a fact that more land than what today belongs to natives
> has hitherto been steadily dropping from their hands, with their eyes
> open, into the hands of whites; while much of the proceeds went
> down their throats.
>
> The prospects therefore of the position 50 years hence at this
> course, with multiplied millions of natives, are enough to stagger
> the imagination.
>
> But supposing the whole of South Africa were today cut up into
> farms, and offered for sale to both whites and blacks, what native
> millionaire would secure land for these millions of natives? Not the
> illustrious leaders of the north to be sure. South Africa would at that
> moment become absolutely 'A White Man's Country' and natives
> hurled headlong will-nilly into the mines. The wisdom of these north-
> ern apostles in endeavouring to break the law which debars whites
> from encroaching on native lands and reserves – hitherto the general
> course – is, we confess, beyond our ken.

Our only millionaire, it must be admitted, is 'The Native Land Act' on its main principles (a) the acquisition of further areas for native squatters, (b) the fixtity [sic] of tenure in native areas, etc....

If these enthusiasts of the north own patches of land in the interior (as we believe there are such syndicates) and they fear these might come under European spheres, would it not be calculated downright stupidity on our part should we, solely to secure their claims, jeopardise by foolish agitation, our inherited Cape rights, which are bound to be recognised and honoured by both Commission and Union Parliament.[62]

Few if any inhabitants of Pondoland were tenants; few were in a position to, or had been forced to, purchase land outside Pondoland. It was the very nature of social relations in the area, and the survival of communal tenure, that underlay their support for the Act.

The chiefs also remained on the alert against less direct threats on the land. The administration stuck by Rhodes's principle that no Europeans would be given allotments in communal tenure areas, but they did make an exception for some of the 'Coloured' descendents of early European traders, especially in Lusikisiki district.[63] Marelane was concerned that they, being 'like Europeans' and less concerned to defend communal tenure, might try to use their plots as securities for debts. In this way, European traders and lawyers might obtain some hold on communal land. This same issue underlay a bitter dispute between the administration and the western Mpondo paramountcy. After Gawe, the grantee mentioned above, died in 1915, his plot was eventually given by the magistrate of Port St Johns to another immigrant named Maninjwa.[64] As Gawe had left debts, the magistrate, who dealt with such estates, felt that Maninjwa should pay the costs of improvements made on Gawe's land so that the debts could be cleared. Mangala, the regent, was adamant that no cash value should be placed either on land or improvements in Pondoland. In a stormy meeting with the Chief Magistrate in 1916, he tried to prevent the transaction. He even offered to pay Gawe's debts himself in order that no precedent be set for land being used as a security for debts. He was quite clear about the basis for his argument: 'the reason for the request is to prevent the land going to a European'. In fact magistrates in other districts had been allowing commercial transactions over improvements to land, despite opposition from some headmen.[65] Mangala's argument was not accepted, and in 1918 the Chief Magistrate confirmed that while vacated land reverted to commonage, improvements could 'be removed or sold to the person to whom the site [was] allotted'. But such transactions were not usual in Pondoland.

124

The administration accepted, however, that land held in communal tenure could not be used as security for loans and mortgages. While land-holders elsewhere with title were able to raise capital on the basis of their land, Africans in the reserves had to rely on what they could earn through the sale of produce or through wage labour. The Land Bank, established by the Union government in 1912, restricted its credit to Europeans partly for the reason that its system of loans could not be operated in the African areas. Plots in Pondoland came to be regarded as the exclusive possession of the holder and were often passed from generation to generation, a prac-tice which the administration by and large accepted.[66] But under the land proclamations of 1903 and 1919 regulating communal tenure, land was liable to confiscation for a variety of reasons, and the lack of certainty about long-term rights to plots probably played a part in diverting much of the little income available into stock.

The administration made only one exception to these rules in the Terri-tories.[67] Traders had long argued that they should receive outright titles to their trading stations for the very reason that they also found it dif-ficult to raise mortgages and make improvements when their security of tenure was in doubt. In fact, trading stations were bought and sold as if they were privately owned even before annexation when the traders' tenure was subject to the chieftaincy. Partly because of objections by the chiefs, however, stations remained crown land, subject to confiscation by the state. But by 1919 the government bowed to pressure from traders' associations. It was envisaged then that the whole of the Transkeian Territories would be surveyed, and in a proclamation of 1922 the adminis-tration provided for title to trading stores in surveyed districts. As the survey had hardly begun, Pondoland was not immediately threatened, but both Poto and Mswakeli raised strong objections to this change in principle. Dana argued that in giving titles to the traders, the adminis-tration would be providing them with stronger rights to the land than the people themselves. The paramounts were reluctant to recognise that Pondoland was crown land and therefore ultimately at the disposal of the state. They asserted that the terms of annexation had recognised the land as belonging to the Mpondo nation as a whole, personified in the chief-taincy. Mangala argued that the 'land is mine'; it 'belonged' to the para-mountcy as representative of the people.[68] But the administration insisted on its ultimate right to dispose of land in Pondoland; though the plans for survey in the Territories as a whole were jettisoned in the 1920s, traders in communal tenure areas were able to claim title once their stations had been surveyed.

It would be misleading to suggest that communal tenure in Pondoland was defended by the chiefs alone. A small minority of wealthier, progressive cultivators who wished to fence land, grow winter crops and cash crops, and extend their arable land, found the implications of communal tenure inhibiting.[69] But for the bulk of the population, communal tenure was their ultimate guarantee of access to both arable plots and grazing. Cingo was expressing a general view in his arguments against any commoditisation of land; even if the limited system of individual tenure envisaged under Glen Grey were to be implemented, many families might have found their access to land constrained in the future. It has been argued that the particular process of proletarianisation in Pondoland in the first few decades of the twentieth century was such as to make it essential that most homesteads maintained, and indeed expanded, their arable holdings. As much of the wage income earned was still invested in stock, general access to grazing also remained of critical importance to the majority of homesteads. The form of land-holding in Pondoland was symbolised by the powers of chieftaincy. Further, as will be illustrated below, the allocation of land through chiefs and headmen, rather than by the state, enabled the mass of the people to exercise some control over land through the political processes surrounding local decision-making. The assertion made in another context that 'without chiefs we shall be like squatters' underlay the general unease about any more radical state intervention in the system of land-holding.[70]

This argument should not be taken to imply that there were not changes in the form of land-holding. Indeed, beneath the general support for communal tenure there were different shadings of interest at work; the tensions between chiefs, headmen, administration and the mass of the people over land distribution illuminate the wider ambiguities in the position of chiefs and headmen in the colonial period. In the pre-colonial period, it has been suggested, chiefly control and the ideology surrounding it were expressed in terms of rights over followers, tribute and cattle.[71] Once a homestead had been established, the immediate control over allocation of land and the breaking of new land lay with the senior men of the homestead, though the local political authority was probably consulted. But by the 1920s and 1930s, when homestead sites or plots could not always easily be found in the immediate vicinity of established homesteads, chiefs and headmen took on a far more central role in land allocation. This was an area in which the state permitted the extension of their authority, and in the land proclamations of 1903 and 1919 the responsibility of headmen for allotting plots and homestead sites was formally recognised. Though the state had ultimate authority over land allocation, magistrates could only order a headman to make certain allocations; they could not allot land themselves. The intermediary position of the headmen was thus entrenched, and in practice headmen maintained control over

126

distribution. Magistrates would only intervene in a dispute, but, as in the case of other civil disputes, the majority of cases in Pondoland were settled locally or by referral to the chiefs' courts. (This was not necessarily the case in all Transkeian districts, for some were more overcrowded and in some the authority of particular chiefs and headmen was not widely recognised.) The administration by and large accepted the pattern of distribution of land at annexation. The existing land-holdings were supposed to be registered at the magistrates' offices, but officials admitted as late as 1918 that registration had not been enforced and that they had no clear idea of the extent of land-holding.[72] New allotments were supposed to be inspected by a constable from the magistrates' courts, but this was not always done. The administration did attempt to keep an up-to-date record of hut-tax payers, and until a man had been registered he was not officially entitled to take up a plot through his wife. But the tax register did not record the exact amount of land held by each homestead. The specific form of distribution of land thus depended on the more general political balance within the locations.

Rising pressure for arable plots by the third decade of the twentieth century provided headmen with some scope to use their key position in the distribution of land. The establishment of a homestead had in precolonial times been accompanied by a complex of relationships which involved tribute, services and loans. But the headmen now began to demand payment for the allotment of plots.[73] These were not initially extravagant: in the 1920s magistrates noted that headmen required 'a goat or a sheep'. Some probably demanded more, but the payments were not significantly greater than 'gifts' entailed by any call on a chief or headman. In the next decade, the amount increased to one or two beasts or their cash equivalent. Such claims gave the chiefs and headmen an indirect hold over wage income, as it was often returned migrants who were setting up homesteads or breaking new ground. There was no absolute shortage of land for plots – the bulk of land in each location remained the communal grazing area – but headmen had to be persuaded that they should allow further encroachment on the pastures. The stock population was rising rapidly, grazing land was at a premium, and headmen were often owners of large numbers of animals.

There is also evidence to suggest that some headmen began to accumulate plots, sometimes renting them out, and to exclude those who could not pay or were not their political supporters. As early as 1910, the magistrate of Libode found 200 people without land in Valelo's location. 'This state of affairs', he thought, was 'doubtless traceable to William Valelo who would only allow his friends to plough lands.'[74] The case was unusual, though not entirely exceptional. Valelo, grandson of Faku, and his son

William were fighting a ruthless battle for control in the location in which discriminatory land allocation was only one strategy. Because of his relative independence prior to annexation, and the inaccessibility of the location, neither the magistrates' nor the paramount's attempts to intervene in earlier years had met with great success. But by the 1920s magistrates were speaking of accumulation as a general phenomenon.[75] How far their perception represented a realisation of long-established inequalities of land-holding at a time when the administration was taking a greater interest in ironing these out is unclear. Certainly the types of relationships referred to, especially in districts outside Pondoland, seem to have been a new phenomenon. In Pondoland itself, rentier relationships were insignificant in the general pattern of land-holding at least till the 1930s. But certain chiefs and headmen, either through extending land-holdings through marriage or by reserving very much larger plots for themselves, were clearly expanding their land-holding at a time when pressure on plots was rising. The paramount chiefs were allowed to carve out personal farms.[76] Bokleni, for example, received 3,000 morgen from which 150 homesteads were moved to give him unconstrained access to the land. The eastern Mpondo paramount and Dalindyebo of the Thembu received, similar grants, but this was exceptional.

The administration responded to these developments in an ambiguous way. When W. T. Welsh became Chief Magistrate in 1920, for example, he initially determined to take a hard line against payments for plots, which were not legally permitted in the land proclamations.[77] Yet he soon modified his position. In a comment on agitation by headmen for increased salaries in 1927, he indicated that he was quite aware that headmen did not survive on their government stipend – by this time a minimum of £1 a month – alone.

> He would like to point out that he did not discern the pitiful picture that had been painted by one of the speakers because there were always a great many applicants for headmanships whenever there was a vacancy. He did not know whether the reason for this was because of the perquisites some headmen got, or the extra lands they gave out to themselves or others, or perhaps it was on account of the miserable pittance of £1 they were ashamed to mention.[78]

Unless excesses were reported by people prepared to go to the magistrate behind the back of their chiefs and headmen, magistrates in general condoned, if they did not approve of, such payments. A margin of flexibility helped to keep the chiefs and headmen co-operative; such payments also saved costs that would have been entailed in maintaining closer control. They were not, at this stage, concerned to delimit rigidly the authority of headmen. The land proclamation of 1903, which confirmed that each hut-tax payer was entitled to at least one plot, provided the basis for intervention in cases where tax payers were not granted land. In 1910, for example, Valelo was cautioned and ordered to demarcate plots for all families that had been excluded. The 1919 proclamation, promulgated at a time when land in some districts, though not generally in Pondoland, was becoming shorter, formally introduced the principle of one-man-one-lot into the communal tenure parts of the Territories as a means to ensure access to land for all families.[79] Magistrates began to move towards the goal of limiting each tax payer to one plot, not exceeding five morgen (roughly eleven acres) in only one location. In fact, because plots were often smaller than this size, the implications of the policy were more serious for larger homesteads; for others, it entailed a rationalisation rather than diminution of land-holdings. In any event, magisterial progress was slow. In the late 1920s, they were still discussing with Pondoland General Councillors how best to implement the proclamation and accepted representations that separate lands could be allowed for each wife as long as the total did not exceed five morgen. Some intervention did start at this time, aided by the introduction of surveying chains to measure plots. (Previously they had been measured by pacing.) But oral evidence confirms that in this sphere, as well, a great deal of flexibility was shown by officials until the extensive rehabilitation schemes of later years.

Control over land distribution by chiefs and headmen, for which a maintenance of communal tenure was necessary, did enable them to maintain and perhaps extend their differential access to land. In this respect their interests in the system could differ from those of the mass of the population. However, in general, the system, as it operated in Pondoland at least, continued to guarantee land and grazing to all homesteads; in the last resort appeal could be made to officials to intervene against chiefs and headmen. As will be clear from the argument presented in this chapter, the chiefs and headmen cannot be characterised merely as a 'wealthier peasantry'. Differential access to land and stock did have implications for productive capacity. But at the same time, their income from dues and land grants were probably more important than that from their surplus crops. Indeed, the general constraints on accumulation and marketing were in part the reason for their defence of such rights. As they received a once-off payment from immigrants, it was in their interest to admit as many as possible; similarly there was advantage in meeting popular pressure for allotment of plots. A larger population in their location broadened the base of people from whom they could collect dues. The pre-colonial forms of tributary rights had only been modified and not totally transformed after annexation. There were contradictions in their

129

position, but chiefs and headmen increasingly became the agents of the state in its attempts to squeeze as many people as possible on to the land in the African reserves and thereby limit outright urbanisation and proletarianisation. The entrenchment of chiefs and headmen in the administrative and political structure of Pondoland and the dynamic of local political processes therefore helped to perpetuate migrancy as a specific form of proletarianisation.

5

Rural differentiation, alliance and conflict, 1910–1930

1 Chiefs and headmen, wealthier families and locally employed Christians

The most fundamental change in the rural economy of Pondoland between 1910 and 1930 was the increased dependence of a majority of homesteads on wage labour. Yet, as has been argued, proletarianisation was not in the main predicated on rural differentiation; on the accumulation of resources by a minority of families in Pondoland and the expropriation of land and stock from others. Although the level of dependence on wages differed from homestead to homestead, the great majority of families from which workers came retained their rural homesteads, access to land and, to a considerable extent, access to cattle; the predominant form of proletarianisation was migrancy. This pattern of entry into wage labour had deep implications for the nature of differentiation in Pondoland. It has already been argued that the specific process of incorporation into the larger capitalist economy only modified, but did not transform, pre-colonial forms of political authority. As happened in areas of the Eastern Cape, for example, no significant class of wealthy peasants developed in the colonisation of Pondoland.[1] Pre-colonial forms of rank and authority, which had implications for wealth in terms of income and productive capacity, were to some extent translated into a new context. This is not to suggest that the process of colonisation left social relationships in the countryside intact. The process of differentiation will be explored largely by means of different life histories, which may to some extent be regarded as 'typical', of men who were born and brought up in the early decades of the twentieth century.[2]

Although the general trend in Pondoland was towards increased rates of migrancy, there were certain families whose men were able to escape the general experience of leaving Pondoland to work on the mines, farms and industries of South Africa. And the ability to escape migrancy became an increasingly important element in rural differentiation. Such men tended to have their origins in very different, but increasingly interlinked,

131

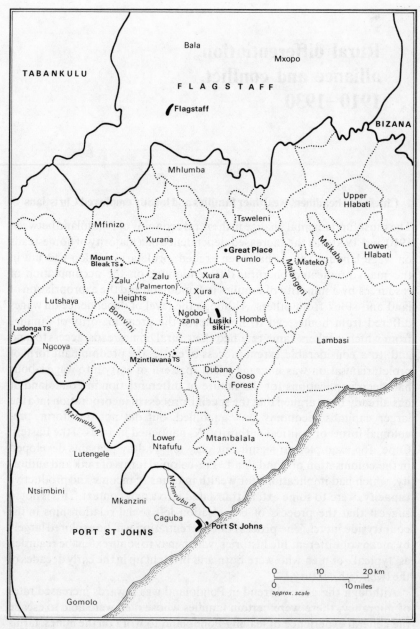

3 Sketch map of locations in Lusikisiki district for identification of place of residence of oral informants (1976/7). TS = Trading Station.

groups. There were those whose birth into families of rank assured them of differential access to rural resources in terms of cattle, labour, land and income from dues. Shading into this group were wealthier families who may have inherited resources but not office and who were able to delay their incorporation into wage labour for a generation longer than most. In contrast, a group of families emerged during these decades who escaped migrancy not so much by defending themselves against dependence on wages and commodities, but by the access they had to better-paid local jobs in church and state. In dealing with the varied experiences of families from such groups, it should be emphasised that within the broader patterns of differentiation, the importance of the 'domestic cycle' should not be neglected. As men became older they would tend to re-establish their rural position. Further, this could have implications for their children, as mobility between these groups and families with migrants was not impossible. However, as will be argued, the patterns of differentiation were to some extent becoming solidified by the 1920s and 1930s.

The paramounts still had the largest herds in Pondoland – probably numbering their cattle in the thousands.[3] Patterns of circulation of stock, which had been so central to their position in the mid-nineteenth century, remained of importance. It was through inheritance, bridewealth, dues, fines and loans that they primarily maintained and increased their herds. The leading chiefs had of course begun to exchange as well as distribute cattle in the nineteenth century. In fact the rituals surrounding sale of stock were drawn, according to traditions, from the early transactions between chiefs and traders: 'When Europeans [buying cattle] were showing their thanks to Mqikela, they took money, put it to their mouths, put sugar in a plate, took Mqikela's hand and kissed it. It became the custom that if a man sells you a beast, you must kiss his hand.'[4] In the twentieth century, the paramounts continued to sell stock when they could – Poto mentioned in 1929 that he tried to dispose of 150 animals in one lot – though the difficulties of sale threw large stockowners back into loaning relationships. They were also amongst the leading innovators in stock-keeping. Nqwiliso kept a flock of 300 'fairly well bred' angora goats; Marelane requested with success in 1914 that the homesteads near his Great Place in Flagstaff, further inland than Quakeni, be removed so that he could 'keep and breed sheep on a larger scale' to compensate for his losses in the East Coast fever.

Although the paramounts were amongst the first to purchase ploughs and wagons, and certainly produced more grain on their fields than any-one else in Pondoland, there is no clear evidence from the turn of the century or before that they were engaged in selling crops.[5] In the next

133

few decades there were still demands on them to distribute grain. They had to provide for the many people attending cases and councils at their homesteads, for the indunas who still served at the Great Place, for the work parties on the fields. Marelane also tried to fulfil the function of providing grain in times of distress, such as in the famine of 1912, when he even purchased a substantial quantity of maize for distribution. But by his own admission, the chiefs could no longer play a significant role during starvations. Poto was probably the first to transform himself into a more explicitly market-oriented crop producer.

> I was amazed to see a person harvest 500 bags [an agricultural demonstrator who worked in his district between 1934 and 1936 recalled]. If you went to see him during the time of ploughing, planting, cultivation, go to his lands, you would find him there together with his wife Matimkulu. Growing mealies, pumpkins, beans. Paramount Chief Poto was a proper farmer, I daresay. He was selling mealies to the traders or to other districts where there was starvation. People took mealies from his place; people from Mount Frere would come with their wagons to cart mealies.[6]

Only the paramount chiefs could gain access to land for crop production on this scale, perhaps fifteen to twenty times the average produced by homesteads in Pondoland; they had large personal farms around their homesteads. Poto in particular was a leading advocate of agricultural improvement. He not only gave his backing to the extension schemes, as did Mswakeli in Eastern Pondoland, but followed and even anticipated the teaching of demonstrators. He purchased a range of implements, used fertiliser, and united his plots into large fields for ease of cultivation.

Work on the paramounts' fields was still predominantly carried out by indunas or work parties from surrounding locations which would be called out at different times in the agricultural cycle; one man remembered seeing fifty teams of oxen on Marelane's fields during the ploughing season. This in itself created pressure on the paramounts and other chiefs with access to labour to redistribute rather than sell, although Poto seems to have been able to translate his remaining control over communal labour on the land into a marketable surplus with more success than the chiefs of Eastern Pondoland. However, even Poto's income from crops, unlikely to have been more than £100 (perhaps £200) at the prices ruling, was relatively insignificant as a proportion of his total income. Certainly, for the sons of the paramounts, it was their guaranteed place as headmen rather than their fathers' success in marketing that assured their position in rural society. Most of the paramount chiefs from the time of Sigcau and Bokleni were educated. Marelane, Mswakeli and Poto all went beyond primary school, as did their sons, and this made them amongst those with the highest formal school qualifications in Pondoland. But the paramounts' children did not in general have to work in professional employment.

The lesser chiefs and headmen were a highly differentiated group. Though none would rival the paramounts, they were in a broadly similar position both as regards their income and the constraints surrounding its disposal. Amongst them were some of the largest stockowners and market-oriented crop producers.[7] One headman in Tabankulu, the sheep district *par excellence* of Eastern Pondoland, kept a flock of around 1,000; one in the same district as Poto grew, with the aid of an agricultural demonstrator, 300 bags of grain on his fields. Commoner headmen, a minority in Pondoland, although they usually received smaller subsidies, were not necessarily disadvantaged and could be freer from the constraints surrounding those who had a hereditary chiefly position. Further, the position of the headmen in the interstices of the Colonial state allowed them to develop powers which were not necessarily rooted in chiefly authority. Chiefly headmen, on the other hand, were more likely to find posts for their heirs, and possibly some of their other sons. Some headmanships did come to rest with branches of chiefly families which had no direct claim to genealogical primacy – the patterns of succession in Pondoland had indeed always allowed for competition between branches of the family –and even some commoner headmanships became hereditary despite Marelane's claim to control them. What all headmen had in common was their political authority and its implications for differential access to income and resources.

In general, at least some of the sons of headmen could escape migrancy. They might go once or twice to the mines under pressure from their peer group, for, once migrancy had become institutionalised and social interaction between youths gradually became more oriented around a migrant culture, even those for whom there was no necessity to migrate were drawn in. The experience of a son of a Kwetshube headman, born around the time of East Coast fever in Lusikisiki, illustrates both this phenomenon and the broader position of a headman's family in the early decades of the century.

I went to the mines once, my father stopped me from going again. I went surreptitiously with other youths – thirteen of us together on the day we left. I was still young, herding cattle; I was not married. When I went, my father had eighty-seven head of cattle. He asked: 'Why did I leave these cattle? What was I working for?' There were blankets bought for me and brass leg bangles. He said, 'What was my complaint?' He wanted to beat me for going that time.

135

I just said that I was keen to go to the mines; I only went once. The reason that I stayed was that I was going to take over the headmanship. He had three lands from his three wives. He did not work himself on the lands; only his indunas. There was only one plough – indunas were driving the oxen and ploughing. If one of them wanted to marry, he paid the bridewealth. It was young men who came and stayed; he was buying them blankets and giving them *amasi* [soured milk]. He would brew beer and people would come to hoe. He never went to hoe; he would slaughter a beast for them. He was not selling mealies to the traders – he gave them to those who did not have. No money was paid. Not all headmen did so in his day, but I saw him doing this. He did not keep sheep though he was given sheep and goats by his people for slaughtering.[8]

His father was perhaps unusual in continuing to distribute grain alone rather than selling, but this part of the account may be romanticised, projecting the 'traditional' conception of subchieftaincy. But there is evidence to suggest that other headmen found their scope for accumulation constrained by popular demands.

Not all of his father's eleven sons were able to escape migrancy. Indeed, in families of headmen, as in those of wealthier commoners, there was clearly a differential rate of migrancy. An heir in the great house in particular, as in this case, would be less dependent on a wage to marry and accumulate a herd; he would inherit his father's homestead and position. A man who migrated many times to the mines recalled:

I went away in about 1918 to Durban to work. I went there only once and to the gold mines after that. My father died while I was away and my eldest brother became head of the homestead. He never went away to work; he worked only in Lusikisiki with Merbe [the butcher] buying cattle from the people for the butchery. My older brother did not pay my *lobola*.[9]

Men who stayed at home were more likely to become involved in managerial activities in surrounding homesteads with migrant heads. Even if not headmen, they would spend more time at the homesteads of the local chiefs, acting as councillors or in court proceedings. These were all activities which could provide scope for entrenching a rural position. It should not be surmised, however, that a position of local authority depended entirely on escape from migrancy. Some migrants were able to establish a similar position once they had ceased to migrate.

Those families which were able to maintain a relative independence from wage income without the benefit of headmanships or without radically altering the organisation of production in their homesteads were characterised by their size. Hunter counted three or four homesteads with over fifteen people out of twenty-two on a hillside in Ngqeleni in the early 1930s; the average homestead housed about **eight people**.[10] Family labour and differential access to communal work parties rather than indunas were one key to their independence, though children from poorer homesteads would live with them and work, especially as herds. They would be in a position to capitalise on good seasons and struggle through bad, perhaps sending sons to work in emergencies. They would not usually sell much grain, but rely on wool and tobacco, hides and cattle for cash income. When their grain could not sustain them through bad seasons, they could fall back on their herds. Their position was defined, above all, by the wealth in cattle; these were the homesteads with herds numbering something approaching one hundred head. Hereditary wealth no doubt remained a critical element in their position. The indiscriminate ravages of East Coast fever necessitated that they be in a position to re-accumulate. This would of course be easier for men who had large families (and more daughters), who were important commoner councillors or who belonged to minor houses of the chiefly lineages. However, the constraints or accumulation, by no means absolute in the pre-colonial period, were far looser by the early twentieth century, and there was scope for men without rank or political influence to build a substantial rural base. But as these families broke up, usually only one branch, based around the eldest son of the great house, would be able to survive in a similar way. The attitude of such men, including many of the headmen, to education was ambiguous. Aside from the expenses involved, the need for family labour and the desire to entrench more general control over children militated against schooling. At the same time, their wealth in itself made education less urgent. 'Wealthy natives did not care for education', remarked a councillor in 1916. 'The question often put to a Native boy who went to school was "Why do you try to learn. Your father is wealthy"'.[11] Yet, as this statement suggests, the heads of such families might perceive the need to educate at least one of their children; factors such as the position of the local headmen in relation to schooling could play an important part in such a decision.

The nature of the administrative system that was established in Pondoland and the pattern of state intervention in the area not only enabled many chiefs and headmen to maintain a relatively privileged position, it also created an increasing number of local salaried jobs in the administrative hierarchy. The Native Affairs Department and the other state departments which had some responsibility for administration in the Territories absorbed Africans as clerks, interpreters, policemen and prison orderlies. More particularly, the state initiatives taken under the auspices of the Councils or the Eastern Pondoland Trust Fund tended to depend on African rather than European officials.[12] Dipping assistants, even some supervisors, agricultural demonstrators and teachers in the expanding educational institutions were predominantly African. The established mission churches also began to make more extensive use of African evangelists and even ministers. Whereas a mere handful of such jobs were open immediately after annexation, there were probably over 500, perhaps substantially more, available in Pondoland by the 1930s. The salaries earned varied from about £60 to over £120 a year, at least two to four times the amount earned by migrants on one contract.[13] But all these jobs demanded education up to standard four, and some salaried posts, such as teaching and demonstration work, required secondary education, additional specialist training and some command of English.

Education at this level was only available at the mission institutions, which still played a leading role in organising, though no longer in funding, schools, and it was usually accompanied by the teaching of Christian doctrine. The origin of the group of men who came to fill local salaried positions must be sought in the small Christian community in Pondoland. Mission activity dated back to the 1830s, but despite the key political position of men like Jenkins, the early missionaries were unable to attract a significant number of Mpondo people to their message.[14] Many of those settled on the three major Methodist stations, Buntingville, Palmerton and Emfundisweni, in the nineteenth century were early immigrants from the Cape or Natal. In the decades immediately before annexation, as has been suggested, the missionaries came to be identified with the colonial powers, and the advances made by the early missionaries were, if anything, reversed. There could have been no more than a few hundred Christian families in Pondoland at the time of annexation, and the great majority of them were mission station residents. The mission effort in Pondoland was intensified after annexation. Though the Methodists remained by far the most important church, the Anglicans put new life into St Andrews and started stations and small hospitals at St Barnabas, Ntlaza in Western Pondoland and Holy Cross in Eastern Pondoland; other denominations, including the South African General Mission and the Presbyterians, also worked in Pondoland.[15] They met with limited success. As late as the early 1930s, by which time a few chiefs, notably Victor Poto, had become Christians, less than 5 per cent of the population in Pondoland were adherents of the mission churches. The proportion was probably less in Eastern Pondoland and Port St Johns. Nor is there evidence to suggest that separatist Ethiopian and Zionist churches attracted a significant following.

Even this relatively small growth in the Christian community was to a considerable extent accounted for by turn-of-the-century immigrants. For, as has been suggested in previous chapters, there was continuous migration into the Pondoland districts from the Eastern Cape and southern Transkei, and to a lesser extent from Natal, during the later decades of the nineteenth century and in the early decades of the twentieth century. The primary cause of migration was shortage of land in the overcrowded locations of the Eastern Cape. As Bundy has shown, parts of this area, and the southern Transkei, were affected by declining resources far earlier than Pondoland. Mfengu families, in particular, thousands of whom moved from the Eastern Cape into Fingoland in the 1860s, began from the 1870s to seek land further afield. Some moved more than once, first to areas such as East Griqualand, and then, when the latter began to suffer the same problems as their home districts, to the relatively underpopulated parts of Pondoland.[16] Amongst those from districts which had been more thoroughly colonised, where the mission effort had been more aggressive and more successful, were men who were Christians and had a smattering of literacy. Especially after annexation, the new waves of immigrants settled in the locations rather than on the mission stations. The Christians were often, but not always, monogamous, and their families were probably smaller than Mpondo families. Aside from their identity as Christians, their willingness to invest more in implements, their experimentation with new crops and new techniques of cultivation distinguished them from the bulk of the Mpondo families around them. Their herds were sometimes unremarkable, but the men were prepared to expend more labour in the fields and to use the better resources available in Pondoland to survive and sometimes prosper from the produce they sold, even if they had been forced to migrate to work at an earlier phase of their lives. Although the mission residents and the new Christian immigrants were not mainly responsible for the increase in crop exports at the turn of the century, Christian families were amongst the largest producers.

At the turn of the century, when little state employment was available, some augmented their income from transport riding, petty trading or 'running' for recruiters. But while the first generation of immigrant Christian families may have been able to survive by such activities and by marketing produce, the oral evidence collected suggests that they saw little future for their sons as independent peasants. The difficulties facing producers in the early decades of the century, the shock of rinderpest and East Coast fever, coupled with the importance accorded to formal education in Christian cultural attitudes, led almost all of these families to send their children to school in preparation for employment. Education, which opened the door to local salaried employment, increasingly became the route by which migrancy could be escaped.

This transition from wealthy Christian immigrant father to locally employed son was apparent in a number of interviews. Mhatu, a Christian from Gcalekaland who came to Lusikisiki early in the twentieth century, was remembered by his sons and others as one of the most innovative farmers in his and surrounding locations. He was one of the few to irrigate his fields – by diverting a stream through furrows – in order to grow winter crops. He sold oat hay as well as the staple crops in Lusikisiki and was remembered particularly for his successful stands of wheat, a rare crop in the coastal districts. In the 1910s and 1920s, he sent his sons to school; one became a teacher; another, after reaching standard six at Palmerton, apprenticed as a printer. Mpateni, the agricultural demonstrator from whom the information on Poto's agricultural activities was drawn, came from a Hlubi family which moved from Whittlesea (Hewu) in the Ciskei to Cala, thence to Tabankulu and eventually to Lusikisiki before East Coast fever. His grandfather was 'an ordinary man'. His father, a Christian, after acting as a labour runner and migrating himself for some years, fenced his land, grew wheat and peas, constructed a harrow from an upturned sledge and mixed grass and manure for fertilizer. He produced fifty or sixty bags a year, selling all but twenty. He and Mhatu arranged their own marketing, thus avoiding the difficulties inherent in dealing with the traders. (Such families were among the few wagon-owners in Pondoland). He too sent his son to Palmerton and put him through the new agricultural school in Flagstaff, paying fees out of the proceeds of his crop.

It was not only in the already Christian families that such generational transitions took place. There were comparable changes, sometimes over one generation, sometimes over two, in Mpondo families.[17] In most cases, conversion to Christianity, usually orthodox Methodism, featured in the family history. Those who landed up in local employment often, though not always, came from wealthier Mpondo families. W. D. Cingo, Principal of Emfundisweni, was descended from an important chiefly lineage in Lusikisiki.[18] Xinwa was son of one of the wealthier commoners in Gomolo location, Port St Johns. Under pressure from the local headmen, he attended school and reached standard five during the First World War. After a period at home, helping his family on the lands – they did particularly well out of wool and tobacco – he went on one trip to the mines in 1920 to earn bridewealth. He then 'came home and farmed'. In 1925, his education enabled him to gain local employment as a dipping foreman. He had, meanwhile, become a Methodist. Mathandabuzo, from Mfinizo location, where the Cingo family held sway, was also born at the turn of the century into a generation of which many had to migrate.

His family was able to keep him at home, yet they saw no need for education. Inspired by the first agricultural demonstrator, Nkonya, who arrived in 1923, he adapted his methods of cultivation after founding his own homestead and was soon producing well over one hundred bags of grain, much of which he sold in surrounding locations. He became a part-time peripatetic evangelist for the Methodist church, living for the next couple of decades largely off his income from the land. In turn he sent his children to school; they became teachers and nurses.

The other major element in the locally employed group in Pondoland in the 1920s and 1930s was first-generation-educated immigrants who had come specifically to take up employment.[19] Most came from families which had experienced a similar transition in other parts of the Transkei and Ciskei in the nineteenth century. Tennyson Makiwane, Poto's secretary in the 1920s, was descended from a famous Mfengu Christian family. Gordon Dana, secretary at the eastern Mpondo Great Place, had been sent by his father, a leading member of the Ethiopian movement in Qumbu and a substantial crop producer, to school and university in the United States. On his return in 1913 with a B.A. degree from Lincoln College, Dana had entered the Native Affairs Department as a clerk and interpreter before being employed by Marelane. Nkonya, the first agricultural demonstrator in Lusikisiki, was brought up by his mother, a teacher, and an uncle, a priest, in the Tsomo district of Fingoland. A number of the other early teachers, demonstrators and junior civil servants in Pondoland came from the large, well-educated Christian communities in the Eastern Cape.

The advantage of local employment was not only that it provided a salary, it also enabled such salary-earners to maintain production. They had land, implements and stock from their fathers, access to capital from their salaries and some knowledge of new techniques. Though the process of incorporation into the capitalist economy worked against the development of opportunities for marketing of surplus produce outside Pondoland, the unevenness of production in the Territories guaranteed limited yet sufficient scope for marketing within the area. State policy and the role of headmen within it militated against extensive land accumulation, yet those families with sufficient resources and local political influence, including some of the leading Christian immigrants, could acquire enough land to produce very much more than they needed for home consumption. Those salaried Christians who came from Mpondo families or from immigrant fathers were clearly at an advantage, but first-generation-salaried immigrants usually established homesteads in the Pondoland locations and could build up their herds and agricultural resources.

Xinwa, for example, continued to produce wool and tobacco for sale

after he became a dipping foreman. Mpateni's productive efforts super-
seded even those of his father.

> In 1937, I did the ploughing myself. I was a demonstrator here in
> Flagstaff. I harvested 120 bags. Following year, 150 bags. And that
> caused me to buy a wagon for carting those mealies to Tabankulu
> where there was starvation or to Tonti, other side of Emfundisweni.
> I was selling mealies there, by my wagon, to Coloureds who were
> sawing planks. I took thirty bags to Tonti and then sold one bag for
> two planks; each plank was twelve feet. I took those planks to Holy
> Cross Mission where there were carpenters. Each plank at Tonti was
> five shillings. I sold them at Holy Cross for ten shillings.[20]

A wagon facilitated independent marketing and small-scale entrepre-
neurship; Mvunela, an immigrant teacher in the coastal location of
Mtambalala, augmented his salary by carting wood from the nearby
forests for sale in the magisterial towns during his school holidays. But
even those larger producers without wagons were able to dodge the trading stores. Once it was known that a man regularly had grain for sale,
people from surrounding locations would come to his homestead to
purchase. The entrepreneurial activities of this group of men usually
depended on their own labour, but some were in a position to employ
additional workers on their fields; as in the case of surrounding homesteads, they also used communal work parties, although they did not
usually participate in parties organised by other homesteads.

The larger producers and independent petty entrepreneurs of the turn
of the century had engaged in similar activities. The new generation,
sometimes their sons, were not only able to rival their fathers' output
but at the same time earned salaries. The wealthier Christians of the
1920s and 1930s were not usually simply peasants; their ability to maintain production was integrally linked to their position and income from
salaries. In fact, it is likely that their salaries became an increasingly
important element of their income and that their profession took pre-
eminence in deciding how their labour time was spent. None of those
interviewed forsook their salaries to try their hand at surviving off the
land alone. If they told stories of men who had taken this step, they stressed
that it was unusual. They, in turn, educated their children to the highest
level possible.

These educated Christian families lived in a manner which reflected
their above-average income. They had square houses built of mudbrick
rather than wattle-and-daub huts. They wore clothes and shoes rather
than blankets. They bought furniture, a far wider range of household goods and imported foodstuffs. They socialised in tea parties and

mission gatherings rather than at beer drinks. But their expenditure was governed by a philosophy of thrift, reinforced by the fact that they were far more deeply affected by the rise in the price of commodities, especially after the First World War. Yet the wealthier families of the 'school' community in Pondoland, although small in number in comparison to some other parts of the Territories, were clearly able to maintain a lifestyle of a different character from all but the wealthier chiefs and headmen. (Very few were able to become headmen in Pondoland.)

2 Migrants and the rural poor

By the end of the first decade of the century, the vast majority of migrants from Pondoland, well over 80 per cent, worked underground in the gold mines on the Rand. The major change in patterns of migrancy over the next couple of decades was the shift by substantial numbers of workers especially from the coastal districts of Eastern Pondoland and Port St Johns to the sugar fields of Natal. In the late 1920s, and especially after the depression in the mid-1930s, there was limited diversification in patterns of migrancy as demand in secondary industry and the coastal cities grew. In the absence of annual figures for the number and destination of migrants from each district after 1910, it is impossible to specify the precise fluctuations between each sector. But by 1936, out of a total of about 30,000 migrants from Pondoland districts, some 18,000 to 19,000 (60 to 65 per cent) still worked in the Rand mines, and perhaps 5,000 to 7,000 (around 20 per cent) on the Natal sugar estates; the remainder gravitated to a wide variety of jobs in the coastal cities, in smaller towns in Natal and the Cape, and on farms.[21] Migrants from Pondoland remained predominantly mine and sugar-estate workers, and this shaped the particular relationship between wage labour and rural production that characterised the area.

Though the educated element in the population of Pondoland was small, even in the 1930s, by no means all were able to find local jobs. Not all Christian families could afford post-primary education, and local men had in any case to compete against the much larger pool of educated Africans from other parts of the Cape. If local employment could not be found, there was little alternative but to migrate. Such a fate befell one of the sons of Mhatu, who had completed standard six and been employed as an apprentice printer at Palmerton mission press.[22] In 1922, his apprenticeship was terminated and he was forced to go to Durban to work in a soap factory. He returned in the mid-1920s, was married and allotted a land next to his father's, but soon had to return to work, this time in the mines, for two years. Just before his father's death in 1930, he went to Port

143

Elizabeth, where he found employment as a cook on a fishing trawler. His younger brother was in the meantime completing his teacher training course, and the responsibility for supporting the family fell on the eldest son. He worked on the trawlers for over a decade, returning only for short holidays. His experience, shaped by the barriers facing African skilled workers and the problems of finding work during the depression, was probably typical of that of the better-educated Christian migrants. Even if they had, for a short time, to work on the Rand, they soon extricated themselves and gravitated towards the more open and varied job market in the coastal cities. A member of the Palmerton Christian community who reached standard four moved to the Kynoch explosive factory near Durban after four spells in the mines in the 1920s.[23] Such men left home without contracts, thus increasing their options on the labour market. If possible, they found jobs which gave them the chance of some upward mobility. Their literacy, often coupled with a smattering of English, gave them an advantage in town. They stayed in employment more continuously, coming home only for a couple of months a year at the most. Sharing a wider cultural identity than most migrants from Pondoland, they avoided the restrictive environment of compounds and home groups. They were likely to spend more of their wages in town and remit less home; smaller urban employers seldom organised the remittance schemes which were an integral part of the system of payment of the Rand. While they were working, agricultural activities at home would take second place. Yet, as their wages tended to be higher than those of underground workers, they were not necessarily poorer and could afford to maintain, at least in part, the lifestyle of Christians.

The feature of migration to the mines, by contrast, was that it provided a more controlled environment. In the first decade of the century, the persons and property of mine workers were in constant danger both during their travels to and from Johannesburg and in the mines. Young men 'went forward in a group' for protection, and advances gave some protection to their families.[24] But the mining industry, in its efforts to secure a regular and controlled labour force and prevent desertion, progressively diminished the hazards attending mine migrancy during the next couple of decades. The Native Recruiting Corporation (NRC) gradually achieved, by the 1930s, a monopsonistic position over the labour supply, ousting smaller recruiters and contractors whose operations included advances, varied contracts and what the mining industry considered other irregularities. NRC recruiters offered standard contracts of six and, more usually, nine months. In the 1920s, an Assisted Voluntary Scheme was launched to cater for those who preferred 'voluntary' rather than contract labour. In effect the NRC was taking control over the 'voluntary' labour force. (Workers from Pondoland preferred the standard contracts, in contrast to the trend away from these in the mine labour force as a whole.) By the 1920s, workers no longer walked for days to the nearest railhead. Their passes were organised for them at the major recruiting centres in the magisterial towns, they were loaded on to special motorised busses ('Mbombelas') for Kokstad and Umtata, and then they travelled by special trains to the clearing centre of the Government Native Labour Department at Germiston. Once on the Rand, workers lived in compounds, though these were not closed. Workers from Pondoland tended to gravitate to particular mines, in which they were often housed as a group, and tended to be absorbed into drilling jobs. Underground teams were mixed, but the predominant experience of mine labour was increasingly one of the compound, the home group and organised travel. While such institutions, as van Onselen has pointed out, served as means of ideological and physical control over the labour force, they were also conducive to the maintenance of close links with home districts and of 'ethnic' identities at work.[25]

The strength of rural identity, coupled with the availability of well-established schemes for remittances and deferred pay, contributed to a high rate of repatriation of wages by migrants to the mines. Not only were mine workers likely to remit more than those working in other sectors, but, observers noted in the 1930s, Mpondo mine workers deferred more of their pay than those from other Transkeian districts.[26] Even as late as the 1940s, when some incomplete figures are available, it seems that about 45 per cent of mine workers from Lusikisiki were deferring their pay in full and that perhaps 60 to 70 per cent of the total earned was repatriated. Such high rates of reinvestment in the rural economy were possible because migrants could establish rural homesteads and accumulate herds from wages; conversely, they made it possible for families to continue to supplement mine wages with rural productive activities.

Illiterate, unilingual migrants had little choice but to remain as underground workers for much of their working life. Though many would work over a long period, they tended to contract irregularly, with gaps of a year or more between spells. One interviewee made twelve trips in about twenty-two years; another contracted fourteen times in twenty-seven years.[27] (In view of the health hazards in underground work, the average number of contracts undertaken by mine workers from Pondoland was probably considerably less than these examples suggest.) They were not target workers as conceived by the mines. For a certain period of their lives they depended on their earnings to establish their homesteads and herds, and sometimes to purchase food. But neither were they

145

dependent, as were Christian workers in town, on wages for their day-to-day subsistence. Rural productive and social activities played a far more important role in determining their pattern of migrancy. Although there was little scope for upward mobility in the mines, those who acquired drilling skills and could exceed the minimum demanded on each shift could earn more than the basic wage.

Wages on the Natal sugar estates were lower than in the mines.[28] In the early 1930s, unskilled cutters and weeders – most Mpondo migrants worked at these jobs – received around £2, considerably less than the basic mine wage of about £3, for thirty shifts. Aside from the possibility of advances, Mpondo workers did find some advantages in employment on the sugar estates. Work was above ground, though by all accounts the dangers of work in the sugar fields were not significantly less than in the mines; contracts were usually for six months, and workers could spend longer periods at home even if they migrated yearly; the estates were also more accessible. Most of the workers on the sugar estates came from the coastal districts of Lusikisiki, Bizana, Port St Johns and Flagstaff, which were nearer to Natal; it seems that some of the traders in these areas, who specialised in sugar recruiting, were in a position to influence the choice of migrants as migration became more closely linked to indebtedness.

But the supply of labour to the sugar fields was also guaranteed by the less restrictive controls on recruiting for agricultural industries. The estates were allowed to, and prepared to, employ men who had been rejected by the NRC on the grounds of health. They were also allowed to recruit youths of between sixteen and eighteen years, while the mining industry was supposed to employ only over-eighteens. Regulations providing that parental permission be obtained before youths under eighteen could be employed were never successfully implemented. Evidence suggests that youths of under sixteen also found their way to the estates in some numbers. The sugar recruiters were prepared to use far more coercive means in acquiring labour; they would round up groups of youths in trucks and carry them back to Natal without passes or contracts. Throughout the 1920s, there were many complaints about conditions on the sugar fields and about the fact that children were returning with no money; some were not returning at all.[29] Migration to the estates, in particular, illustrates the extent to which families were losing control over their children.

However, many older men did go to the sugar fields on contract. The division between mine workers and sugar-estate workers was predominantly geographical. But there are suggestions in the evidence that it was particularly men from poorer families, more heavily indebted to traders, with more regular need for male labour at home, with fewer options on the labour market, who migrated to Natal. These points, as well as further evidence of differentiation between branches of the same family, emerge in the experience of a worker from Lusikisiki, born shortly after the turn of the century.

When Marelane died [1921] I was already working on the sugar plantations. My father's eldest brother was a wealthy man at that time. He received many cattle from his father; he had sheep too. He never went to the mines. His father asked him to look after the homestead when he died. This was the custom – the eldest son took over the homestead. He had a plough and two or three lands, but he could have had more if he had wished to. My father had no oxen and no plough. Three he had were increase from one animal he had loaned from his mother's family but these were paid as bride-wealth. We had to ask assistance from the son of his eldest brother [who in turn had succeeded to take over the original homestead]. We used to grind maize and take it to his eldest brother to get milk. I heard that my father went to work in Natal, but he came back with no money. He did not loan from the headman. There were people who did so but my father told me I should not form such a relation-ship with headmen and chiefs because if anything of theirs dies, you still have to pay for it. My mother was the second wife. The first wife gave birth to many children but they all died. Eight chil-dren died during the influenza [1918]. One daughter survived from the first wife; myself and my sister survived from the second. I was a herd before I went away to work. I was herding cattle belonging to my father's brother's sons. They did not pay me a tickey. In those days you used to get a goat for herding but here were no goats there so I got nothing. They had come to ask me to help them during the East Coast fever. I never put my foot in a school; I never saw a school there in Msikaba in those days. The church was not here. Many people were going to the mines of the time I went to *Mobeni* [the sugar estates]. They were going on cattle advances at the time. These are the cattle we got after East Coast fever. I learnt there were cattle at Carter's place and that I could join and get a beast. I had to work six months for the beast, a young heifer, which I received on my first contract. When Marelane died I was at the sugar estates for the second time; I was recruited by Mr Carter and received money this time. I went three times on my own afterwards. If you contract and fall ill, you are not allowed to come home. I did not like that. When I went on my own I stayed eight or nine months. I used to go up in April after ploughing and hoeing and stayed eight months or so. The pay was one shilling a day. The people who went to the gold mines used to get more, but I did not want to go there. I was working the land with my father and could not leave him to do it alone. I went to the sugar fields because I wanted a beast. I went with family and friends from here – we all went up together on foot and caught the train from Izingolweni. We were hoeing sugar cane. An Indian foreman was in charge of us and he beat us. That was how it was. My intention was to get that beast; I was not concerned what happened to me.[30]

The characteristics of poverty spring out from the narrative: a father from a minor house with no cattle; a family devastated by influenza so that labour was short; a youthful experience working as a herd for other homesteads; a pattern of migrancy dictated by the agricultural cycle; a desperate need to earn cattle to sustain the homestead. In fact, Mgeyana was later able to find local employment as a herd at Lambasi, accumulate a considerable number of cattle, and escape his early circumstances of poverty, but some of the migrants to the sugar fields were less likely to escape the downward spiral into indebtedness.

Migrants from the bulk of families in Pondoland, probably over 80 per cent of the total, experienced some variation in the patterns of migration to the mines and sugar fields. By the 1920s and 1930s, some were also moving out of mine and estate labour into unskilled jobs in town, but even the latter were sometimes able to maintain close-knit home group networks and links with the rural homesteads. It is to such families – the average producers of perhaps ten to twenty bags of grain a year, the average stockowners with herds of less than twenty head and a few goats and sheep – that the generalised analysis of household production, presented above, most clearly applies.[31] Though they were able to maintain rural production, they were too short of labour and capital to innovate further or engage in petty entrepreneurial activities. Though they may have received help from neighbours in the shape of work parties at various phases of the agricultural cycle, they could not employ people to work in their fields nor attract clients. The women of such families, who already had to spend more of their time on child care and the gathering of water and wood, probably gave more labour to the wealthier homesteads in their locations than they received back in the work parties they organised.

Patterns of consumption in such families did not change dramatically in the first few decades of the century. They still lived largely in wattle-and-daub huts, constructed out of local materials with local labour and arranged as of old in a semicircle around the cattle kraal. The men purchased clothing for their trips to the labour centres, but at home they usually wore blankets and went barefoot. Though rural fashions changed continuously, the women also used blankets as their basic item of clothing, to which were added German prints in the 1930s. Even the price of the limited number of commodities purchased in such households rose significantly in relation to wages in the decade after the First World War; this in itself inhibited expenditure on consumer goods. The expense of adopting a Christian lifestyle was one factor in limiting the rate of conversion and the social changes that usually accompanied it. Hunter noted that 'some pagans maintained that they do not wish any member of the family to become a church adherent and wear European clothes, "because dressed Natives are always poor"'.[32] Only a minority of Christian families could be assured of finding employment which brought sufficient cash to maintain a Christian lifestyle.

Families with migrants were not necessarily the poorest in Pondoland; a significant number of homesteads could not even be assured of any wage income. The size of such homesteads was usually smaller than the average. In itself, a small homestead did not indicate poverty. Some of the salaried professionals were, for a time, single or lived in a nuclear family unit. Women involved in craft activities such as potters and doctors often lived alone with a few children and could earn enough to stave off poverty. But to have neither education nor a craft nor family labour made it difficult either to produce or to earn. Poverty was closely linked to the process of homestead disintegration. Old couples could find their children marrying and leaving them with no means of support; those who were already poor were probably more vulnerable to isolation. Widows could be left with children and no paternal home to return to. Such families sometimes had no stock at all – surveys suggest that as many as 30 per cent of families in other Transkeian districts were without stock in the 1940s, though the proportion in Pondoland in the 1930s was almost certainly smaller – and could cultivate little more than a garden and a small field.[33] Young men from minor houses who had recently established a homestead might find themselves in a similar position and could even, by the 1930s, be denied immediate access to a plot; breaking away from a larger family unit also had its costs. Yet as long as they could migrate, they had some prospect of building up their rural resources.

Those men who were too old to migrate and those of all ages who were too weak or ill for the heavy manual work in the mines and sugar fields could still find casual daily labour, or sometimes more regular work, on council road gangs. Their wages, between one and two shillings in the 1920s, were not markedly less than those earned by migrants, but they did not receive free food and housing while at work. Domestic servants in the magisterial villages and on the trading stations were probably drawn from such poorer families whose women also had to find some cash income. They would receive around one pound a month. (The demand was limited by the small size of the European population.) Wealthier kin or larger homesteads in the neighbourhood sometimes absorbed the poor, providing them with keep to do odd jobs around the homestead, or took on boys to herd cattle. Those who were dependent on poorly paid local employment or on wealthier homesteads and those who were coming to the end of their lives, had little chance of breaking out of the trap of poverty.

Patterns of wage employment, in part determined by rural cultural and economic differentiation, in turn tended to reinforce the divisions within rural society. The wealthier chiefly and Christian families in Pondoland were, to some extent, able to entrench their position through their political power, their cash income, their access to education and rural resources. The work experience of educated Christian migrants served to maintain their cultural identity and economic position in the rural areas. Migrants from the bulk of families worked in industries in which the labour force was highly controlled and which became increasingly aware of the importance of cementing the rural links of their workers. At the same time, the wages they earned were insufficient to allow them to break out of the chains which bound them into the system of migrancy. Those families without migrants had little chance of raising themselves out of poverty.

Though the process of proletarianisation in Pondoland was largely reflected in increasing rates of migrancy, in the break-up of large homesteads, in a more seasonal pattern of migration, and in the emergence of the rural poor, some people did go to the towns permanently. It would be simplistic to relate urbanisation to rural poverty alone. Educated Christians who could find no local employment and who had fewer rural ties might gravitate towards jobs in town. Youths who had been dragooned into labour in the sugar fields and who deserted could be absorbed into the locations of Natal's cities. Some mine workers formed liaisons on the Rand, and women who had absconded from their parents' homes might escape to domestic service or brewing activities outside Pondoland. In view of the nature of the material used in this study, it has been difficult to assess the importance of permanent urbanisation. Hunter's book does include a chapter on urban African communities in East London, but she does not specifically follow up Mpondo communities in town.[34] It is also difficult to periodise urbanisation. Individuals had no doubt been leaving Pondoland in small numbers since the turn of the century, but it seems that the most marked movement took place after the 1930s. Judging from population figures, which may not be accurate, the rate of increase in the rural population of some Pondoland districts was beginning to fall off markedly between 1936 and 1946 (Table 1). It was also in this period that arable land in some locations became more scarce and that employment opportunities in the rapidly growing manufacturing sector became more widely available.

To specify the degree of differentiation within Pondoland at a particular moment requires a static analysis of a community which was in flux. The settlement units, which must be the basis for such an analysis, were rapidly dissolving and being reconstituted; the trajectory of each homestead's fortunes depended on a complex of factors. A homestead might move from a position of having no cattle to having at least an adequate herd in a relatively short space of time. At the same time, wealthier homesteads might splinter and find the resources of each constituent element depleted. There are in any case no adequate figures which could be used in such an analysis. But underlying the processes of flux, mobility and the domestic cycle, patterns of differentiation described were becoming more clearly visible. Considered in terms of rural resources alone, the ownership of stock and the capacity to produce crops, the degree of differentiation was perhaps not markedly different from that at the turn of the century. The inability of wealthier families to invest in land on the other hand, and the ease with which migrants could purchase stock in the 1920s on the other, offset the tendencies towards a polarisation between rich and poor. But cash income from employment was becoming increasingly important in differentiating rural families. Moreover, the implications of relative wealth and poverty were changing in a society which had been incorporated into the larger capitalist economy and the South African state.

3 Patterns of alliance and conflict

Although the new patterns of social differentiation received expression in shifts in associational activity, the political process surrounding the chieftaincy remained deeply embedded in the early twentieth century. The issues confronted by the people in Pondoland and the forms of their response have to be considered in the context of the complex and changing relationships between chiefs, headmen and people. Internal conflict and reactions to the successive acts of state intervention were often translated into battles for local authority in disputes over headmenships or competition between different branches of chiefly families, or were articulated in mass meetings at the Great Place which guided and constrained incumbent chiefs. At the same time, however, the dynamic of dispute in Pondoland was infused, in a colonial world, with broader ideologies and influenced by broader movements. It has not been a major aim of this study to examine changing ideology closely, although this issue has been dealt with implicitly in the foregoing analysis. What follows is a brief attempt to identify the social expressions of differentiation, and to relate them to the chiefly politics on the one hand and more widespread movements in the rural areas of South Africa on the other.

A dominant theme in the anthropological writing on the African areas taken over by the Cape Colony has been the cleavage between 'school' and 'red'; between those who broadly accepted missionaries and the cultural and economic implications of conversion and who expended far more on consumer items, and traditionalists who sought to defend, as far as possible, their own culture and material life.[35] The implication in such analyses has been that major political divisions stemmed from this cultural cleavage. It is clear that in parts of the Eastern Cape and Transkei where Mfengu and Christian Xhosa communities absorbed elements of colonial culture, became progressive farmers, and supported the Colony in its wars of conquest, the legacy of hostility ran deep. In areas such as Qumbu district, East Griqualand, where immigrants identified as Mfengu were given substantial tracts of land after the Mpondomise revolt of 1880, the divisions between the two communities remained one of the major foci of local politics through the early decades of the twentieth century.[36] However, by elevating cultural criteria as the primary instruments of analysis, the anthropological literature has not come to terms with the specific situations in which such cleavages assumed central political importance. Further, the process of colonisation in the Cape threw up a variety of local conjunctures in which political divisions were by no means always focussed around 'school' and 'red' communities.

In Pondoland, indeed, such cleavages were not of central importance. It was not only because immigrant and Christian communities were small and, aside from the mission locations around Palmerton, Emfundisweni and Buntingville, generally scattered, but also because of the way in which they had been absorbed into the chiefdom. Although missionaries were identified as agents of colonialism, especially by Mhlangaso, in the struggles before annexation, they had for much of the nineteenth century played a role which the chiefs valued; their activities did not deeply threaten the political power of the chiefs. By the twentieth century, there was no deep legacy of hostility over the role of mission communities. New immigrants, who settled out of the mission locations, were often initially dependent on the chiefs and headmen for land and cattle. At the same time, the resources available in Pondoland gave them greater opportunities to extend production than they had had in their home districts. At least in the first decade of the century, when arable land was plentiful and the cattle population relatively small, cash cropping and fencing stimulated little opposition. In the time of Bokleni and Poto in Western Pondoland and Marelane and Mswakeli in Eastern Pondoland, educated immigrants were welcomed by the paramounts for the skills they could offer. These chiefs had thrown their support, admittedly sometimes under pressure from the state, behind schools, dipping and new agricultural methods. It was the immigrant Christians, as much as officials, who were the agents for the implementation of these schemes. Early in his rule, Marelane assured officials that he would favour immigrants 'whose presence may be beneficial to the Pondos, religiously or educationally'.[37] Though his declaration may in part have been designed to pacify those in the administration who were concerned that his new powers over immigration might be misused, it is clear from the character of his paramountcy that he encouraged a limited process of subcolonisation, so long as he could retain some control over it. Mangala, in Western Pondoland, was on occasion more hostile to such immigrants.[38] But his concern was more to protect jobs in Pondoland for local educated men than to dispute the necessity for such jobs to be filled. 'They wanted Pondo money to go into the pockets of Pondo people', his councillor demanded when discussing dipping appointments. 'They did not wish to own cattle which would eventually be the inheritance of other tribes.'

The spread of Ethiopian church movements in the Cape was in certain cases not unrelated to the struggle by chiefs to maintain their position.[39] Mhlangaso, when at the height of his power in the early 1880s, had attempted to take over the Methodist missions in Pondoland, install his own African ministers, and establish a church under his control; his initiatives predated the better-known episode of Tile and Thembu church by a couple of years. Sigcau initially supported the Methodists, in opposition to Mhlangaso. However, at the turn of the century, when he was looking for allies against the Colonial government, he had welcomed Ethiopian ministers from the African Methodist Episcopal Church. Ethiopians, largely from Eastern Cape Mfengu communities under severe pressure by the turn of the century, were by this time causing considerable anxiety to the officials in the Territories; their political message was self-help, educational achievement and eventual political freedom for Africans. Officials discerned, probably correctly, in Sigcau's strategy an alliance between those opposed to Colonial rule. The Ethiopians encouraged him in his claims for the rights of chiefs, in his desire to present his case in England, and in his ambitions to educate his children

153

in the United States. When it became clear, however, that these churches could do little to improve his position and when the administration placed pressure on him to drop his involvement with his new allies, the movement ceased to gain ground. A few ministers did become established, notably Samson Mtintso, who remained associated with the paramountcy in Marelane's time and became involved in the latter's attempts to extend his influence in locations in Tabankulu district. But the response from most headmen was hostile.

It was the very fact that the wealthier peasants and petty entrepreneurs had, by the 1920s and 1930s, become dependent on education and salaried jobs that defused conflict between them and the chiefs. As in the case of the chiefs, they had become a group more dependent on the state. The accommodation increasingly received institutional expression. Aside from men such as Tshongwana and Dana in Eastern Pondoland, Makiwane and later Bam in the west, who were directly employed by the paramounts as secretaries, others such as Cingo became close advisors. Poto, in particular, attempted to balance his councils and courts between the traditionalists and the educated minority. During the conflict over Gawe's land in Port St Johns, Mangala had asked disdainfully of the new immigrant occupant, 'Who is Maninjwa? I do not know him.'[40] He was a Methodist who married into an important local Methodist family and became an advisor in Poto in the 1920s. Leading Christians also served on the state-constituted Councils, sometimes as nominees of the magistrates but often as the nominees of the paramounts, who controlled the majority of appointments. Hunter noted that in 1931 seven out of thirteen councillors from Eastern Pondoland in the Pondoland General Council were educated immigrants, the rest being of chiefly families. Some of the local District Councils were of similar composition.

The social and religious networks surrounding the Methodist church, the common experience of mission schools, underpinned the alliance between educated groups and some of the chiefly families. Poto was, like his mother, a lay preacher. Although Marelane and Mswakeli were not practising Christians, they were involved in a number of local mission institutions. Common interests and background also provided the basis for participation in new associational activities. In the wake of agricultural extension work from the early 1920s, farmers' associations, credit societies, and co-operatives were formed in Pondoland.[41] The response was slower than in other parts of the Territories, but in most districts associations, dominated by wealthier progressive agriculturalists and a few chiefs, were started. They served mainly to arrange bulk purchase of seed and implements and provide loans; as in the case of the agricultural extension programme as a whole, farmers' associations benefited, and were used by, a relatively small group of larger producers.

The concerns of the paramounts in the early decades of the century were essentially local; they were bound up with defending their own position and acting as intermediaries between the administration and the people in Pondoland. Their strategy may have been influenced by that of other Transkeian chiefs and that of the Zulu paramount – they certainly remained in touch through messengers in this period – but there is no evidence of a national organisation to forward their interests. The SANNC attempted to provide a broad enough front to represent chiefly interests, and Marelane was included in the Council of Chiefs established as part of the movement.[42] The initial Congress position on the Land Act was not, as has been suggested, supported by the paramount. Though Congress demands later changed to provide for protection of the reserves, as well as freedom for Africans to purchase land, the radicalisation of elements of the Congress, especially in the Transvaal, in the period after the First World War again opened the gap between them and the Mpondo chiefs. Marelane maintained contact with the movement through his secretaries but did not become involved in mobilising his people in its support. Mangala turned to the more conservative Cape breakaway from the Congress, the Bantu Union. He attended the Union's convention in 1919, but largely sought help from them in pursuit of his claims for an increased salary and for control over headmen and land; no permanent alliance seems to have developed. Similarly, although a number of men, including the paramounts, were able to vote for candidates in the Union parliament – Marelane supported the South African party under Smuts – the legislation drafted by Hertzog's Pact government which threatened the vote did not become a major issue in Pondoland as it had in other Cape districts.

There were a number of issues on which the paramounts, by virtue of their unselfconsciously 'progressive' stance, their association with educated immigrants, or their apparent willingness – they were usually in fact highly ambivalent – to further the implementation of state measures, were at odds with popular opinion. The lines of conflict were most clearly revealed during the dipping crisis, which left a deep legacy of unease about state intervention.[43] They again became apparent when the agricultural extension scheme was launched in Eastern Pondoland. Mswakeli himself was in favour. Yet as Nkonya, the first demonstrator, related, the regent's position came under attack.

> I remember the first meeting I had, arranged by Chief Mswakeli some time in 1923, when I got here. Matwassa [headman of the location around Palmerton mission] and a few people from this

155

location had accompanied us. A few older chiefs like Bodweni were in favour. All the Pondos? No, they don't want it. They said: 'It's going to kill this land. Wait until the young chief grows up and takes his place. You cannot accept an undertaking like this. You have no right.' He [Mswakeli] was told in the face. They were angry. It was not just talk. In 1925, Professor Jabavu, who was a lecturer at Fort Hare, took a tour during the December holidays and held one of his meetings at Qaukeni. He talked mainly about agriculture. When he finished his talk, Chief Mswakeli asked the Pondos if they had any questions. The only educated chief there was Lamayi Langa of Flagstaff district. He stood up and supported what had been said by Dr Jabavu. But all the meeting murmured against. Mswakeli got angry. He said all must be stopped. He said what Jabavu has said is going to be done in due time. The noise was too high to say anything. It was better to keep quiet.[44]

The tensions that emerged during the meetings again reflected the feeling of lesser chiefs and popular opinion that the paramountcy, as in the case of the dipping crisis in the hands of a regent, had been too receptive to decisions taken by the administration. Again the role of the chieftaincy came under question, providing a focus for discontent about the broader implications of agricultural improvement; the fencing of land, the disturbance of winter grazing patterns and the threat of stock limitation, which had already become an issue. Many lesser chiefs and headmen eventually accepted demonstrators, but their position in successive phases of state intervention was always split. On the one hand, as salaried headmen, they were under great pressure from the administration to co-operate; on the other, they reflected popular opposition and suspicion.

As illustrated in the discussion of dues and land, the chiefs and headmen clearly had sectional interests. The chiefs, headmen and wealthier immigrant families drew the greatest benefit from educational and agricultural expenditure. Agitation for increases in the salaries of headmen and Council employees was a constant theme in Council deliberations. As the largest stockowners, they had their dipping costs subsidised. For although stock ownership was unequal, dipping was funded out of the general revenue raised by a flat rate levy on all hut-tax payers. It was only in the late 1920s that the more differential stock rates related to the number of animals dipped by each owner, in force in most other Transkeian districts, were introduced. It was also in the interests of chiefs and headmen that migrants' wages continued to come back to rural society.[45] Though evidence is lacking, it seems that some headmen attempted to take a direct levy on migrant wages. Their continued ability to levy dues,

their charges for plots of land usually from men who were engaged in setting up homesteads, now depended increasingly on income from wages
rather than on production on the land alone. Throughout the 1910s and
1920s, chiefs and headmen advocated tighter controls over migrants and
their wages; they suggested unsuccessfully that it should be made compulsory for every migrant to inform the headmen when leaving and returning and that deferred pay be made compulsory. In general, they recognised
the importance of pass laws as a means of control over the labour
force. Their complaints about migration of youths to the sugar fields
reflected a similar concern about the loss of control over migrants and
wages. And some even proposed that pass laws be extended to women in
order to prevent uncontrolled movement to town, for the loss of daughters implied not only a reduction of family labour but of a source of bridewealth.

Yet on many of these issues they were also articulating demands broadly
favoured by the people. Their defence of communal tenure, while
underwriting their own position, protected commoner land-holdings.
Demands that taxation be limited to married men underwrote the authority of homestead heads. Controls over migration would work towards the
same end, although as migrants themselves became homestead heads,
popular opinion seems to have become more ambiguous. Arguments in
favour of the use of Council funds to provide grain at subsidised rates
during times of shortage and for increases in the wages of road labourers
also reflected popular demands. Indeed, the continual mass meetings held
on most major issues provided a forum for such demands to be aired;
the councils of the chiefs especially in Eastern Pondoland were still dominated by lesser chiefs and headmen and sometimes included commoners. As the meeting about extension schemes indicates, consensus by no
means always prevailed. But the political process surrounding the chieftaincy, and the chiefly role as intermediary between state and people,
could to some extent contain conflict and provide a vehicle for the articulation of popular demands. In this context, popular movements led
from outside the ranks of the chieftaincy, such as surfaced in East Griqualand – where chiefly authority was far weaker – during the dipping crisis,
made little impact in Pondoland in the period under discussion.[46]

It was only in the late 1920s, when the successive impact of the new
poll tax and the droughts of 1926–7 weakened the position of many families, that an independent popular movement took hold in Pondoland.
One of its major forms of expression was widespread pig-killing.[47] Episodes
of pig-killing had occurred on a number of occasions in Pondoland and
surrounding regions in the late nineteenth and early twentieth centuries:
in 1886 at a time of political and economic crisis; in 1906 during the

Bambatha rebellion in Zululand; and again in the mid-1910s after the dipping crisis and rumours of a census. An analysis of this response must ultimately rest on an understanding of the way in which people explained disturbance in their society; the episodes certainly recall the cattle-killing in the Xhosa chiefdoms in 1857. What is of importance in the 1920s is that pig-killing became absorbed into a broader popular movement which clearly articulated popular discontent with dipping, taxes, government-controlled education and mission churches.[48] The movement, harnessed and spread by Wellington Buthelezi and others, did not originate in Pondoland. Indeed, Buthelezi's support was based largely in East Griqualand, Fingoland and the western Transkei, where rural communities had been more thoroughly transformed and where the rural crisis of the late 1920s bit more deeply. Yet Buthelezi's message about the necessity to kill pigs, about the coming of American blacks – an image which harked back to the early Ethiopian movements – in aeroplanes to free Transkeian people from oppression did spread through Pondoland districts. In Western Pondoland, the movement was directly linked to Buthelezi's organisation. In the coastal districts of Eastern Pondoland, however, as in some other parts of the Territories, local leaders absorbed and retranslated his ideas. Pigs were killed in some numbers in 1927 and perhaps again in the next couple of years. People refused to pay taxes, and those in coastal locations in Lusikisiki cleared a piece of flat land at which they assembled to await the arrival of the aeroplanes.

Despite their disappointment, the so-called Wellington movement was sustained for a couple of years. It became locally known as the 'ICU' after Clements Kadalie's Industrial and Commercial Workers' Union, the major African trade union of the 1920s. Kadalie, having split from the centre of the movement which he had built, moved to East London to head the Independent ICU in 1928. In the next couple of years, he specifically attempted to build his organisation in the rural areas. Though he was banned from the Territories, some of his committee did succeed in establishing links in the southern Transkei and had correspondents in Pondoland districts. But for the mass of rural people in Pondoland, the ICU name and the spirit of the movement were absorbed and welded into an ideology dominated by Buthelezi's millennial thinking. Although a few headmen were caught up in the surge of popular feeling, the paramounts, councillors and at least the more prominent members of the Christian community felt threatened by, and were strongly opposed to, the movement. They co-operated with the state in bringing it under control. Poto, though interested in the ICU in its more orthodox form, made his position clear – and underlined his value to the administration – in a request for a rise in chiefly salaries in 1928: 'If the chiefs were loyal, it was

158

easy for the people to be loyal, but if they were not loyal, the people would not be loyal. Dr Wellington and his followers were trying to cause trouble in various parts of the Territories but because of the good rule of the chiefs, they could not succeed.'[49] The Wellington movement and the ICU version of it in Eastern Pondoland do not seem to have obtained such a strong hold as in East Griqualand and the western Transkei. In these areas, the movement was accompanied by the establishment of independent schools and churches – a rejection of the state's apparatus of ideological control in the Territories. These were movements generated in areas with a different experience of colonisation and proletarianisation which spread to Pondoland because elements of their ideology resonated with local popular consciousness.

Such widespread and organised political movements were constrained by chiefly power and administrative action. The changing position of the rural population was as much reflected in adaptions of social organisation at the local level. One of the most important developments were new forms of association derived from the migrant experience. It is not within the scope of this study to analyse the response of Mpondo migrants at the work place. On a number of occasions, such as in 1906, when problems over the advance system reached their peak, and in 1920 during the black miners' strike on the Witwatersrand, some Mpondo workers did take organised action.[50] Yet in 1913 Mpondo workers were persuaded not to join a strike, and in 1920 at least one group remained at work during the general withdrawal of labour. Without a far closer analysis of changing forms of control at the work place and of conflicts between various levels of the differentiated African labour force, often expressed in 'factional' disputes, it is difficult to assesss exactly how the particular pattern of migrancy from Pondoland shaped the development of worker organisation and consciousness. What is clear is that Mpondo migrants and those who stayed on the Rand were absorbed into urban gangs, described by van Onselen, and by 1930, at least, had formed their own major gangs.[51] After a major fight between Mpondo and Shangane workers at Crown Mines in that year, in which the Mpondo 'General' Jackson of the Shozi society was killed, a newspaper commented that 'the Pondo gang has been growing in force for some time. It is similar to the notorious Ninevite gang and has been responsible for innumerable knifing cases.'[52] A few years later the magistrate in Lusikisiki linked the decreasing control over migrants from his district on the Rand and in Durban to the 'evils of "laita" and other gangs in the bigger labour centres'. Councillors were concerned about 'immoral practices' of homosexuality in the compounds which were associated with these gangs. What is of particular interest is that such forms of organisation appear to have been transposed

159

back into the rural setting in subsequent years. Beer-drinking groups in Pondoland borrowed the hierarchical form of organisation of urban gangs, taking the names of their offices from the rural administrative hierarchy. Parties at which beer was sold were held in rotation and appear to have played the role of redistributing migrant earnings in the rural areas. New forms of youth groups, which may be called gangs, seem to have been linked particularly to those youthful migrants returning or deserting from the sugar fields. Such groups were viewed as a threat by both the administration and chiefs; whether they became of political significance must at present remain an open question.

It was around organisations such as farmers' associations, church and educational institutions and the Councils on the one hand, and beer-drinking groups, new youth groups and gangs on the other, that patterns of rural differentiation began to solidify. Yet the issues surrounding the chieftaincy remained of critical importance. In the late 1930s, the question of succession to the paramountcy in Eastern Pondoland gave rise to a major conflict. Marelane's accepted heir, Mandlonke, was installed on Mswakeli's death in 1934.[53] Three years later he committed suicide, leaving no sons. Successors were sought amongst Marelane's surviving sons. Botha, Marelane's eldest son by his first wife and a known government supporter, received the backing of the administration and also some of the leading chiefs and councillors, such as Poto. But Botha's opponents argued that according to Mpondo custom, the eldest son of the first wife of the paramount could never succeed. The large mass of the people threw their support behind Nelson, who claimed to be son of one of the *qadi* (support) houses of Marelane's great wife. He was put forward as a candidate who would be far more sensitive to popular opinion and less co-operative with the administration. After holding a commission of enquiry, the administration installed Botha under an armed guard. Nelson's supporters responded by boycotting the installation. When it became clear that violence would produce no result, they took Nelson's claim to the Supreme Court in 1942. (The case was lost.) The political process surrounding the chieftaincy again came to the fore when a mass revolt against the state's rehabilitation and Bantu Authorities programmes was organised in Eastern Pondoland in 1960. Botha, like Mhlangaso in the 1880s, like Sigcau when he tried to help labour recruiters, was accused of 'selling' the country for his own benefit. One demand of the popular movement was a revival of Nelson's claims, although by this stage new forms of popular expression and organisation were to some extent by-passing the chieftaincy.

Postscript

By the 1930s, the economic position in Pondoland could still be favourably compared with that in many other parts of South Africa's reserves.[1] To take but a few indicators: rates of migrancy were lower; the number of cattle per capita was slightly higher; soil erosion was limited and landlessness rare. The people of the area were not necessarily 'wealthier' than those in other African communities; indeed, wealth and poverty are elusive concepts at a time when the penetration of commodity relationships was uneven. Mpondo homesteads were probably more self-sufficient, in general, in basic foodstuffs. But they also probably had a lower cash income: on average, the income of Mpondo migrants may have been lower, for education was less general, and, being amongst the last into the labour market, they tended to work in lower wage sectors such as the sugar fields. The feature of the area was that the homesteads were relatively less dependent on wage income, that access to rural resources had not been severely constrained, and that wages could still be invested in rural production. Yet in the regional political economy of South Africa as a whole, the people of Pondoland shared the relative poverty of African rural communities and were subject to the pressures operating on all the reserves. Available statistics are not entirely reliable but, together with other evidence, strongly suggest that in the next few decades there was a decline in the total number of stock held and the total amount of crops produced in Pondoland. Though the decline was not dramatic in absolute terms, it was much more significant per capita as the population continued to increase. The local variations within South Africa's reserves almost certainly became less marked.

But the aim of this study has not merely been to illustrate that the people of Pondoland became locked into the colonial economy later than those in some other parts of South Africa, that they remained more independent from wage labour in the early decades of the twentieth century, that in the longer run Pondoland became a labour reservoir. Rather it has

161

been argued that the character, as well as the timing, of change differed significantly. (The analysis presented might apply more closely to parts of Zululand and the northern Transvaal, as well as to the British protectorates in southern Africa. Indeed, the possibility of Britain assuming control over at least parts of the Transkeian Territories was mooted in the 1880s.) Moreover, although there was a generalised process of proletarianisation throughout the region in the early twentieth century, manifested in increasing rates of migrancy, in changing terms of labour tenancy and in outright urbanisation, the trajectory of rural struggle was varied. Perhaps the example which illustrates this point best is the response to the Land Act of 1913, a central issue in South African society at the time.[2] The debate between Cingo, Msimang and others over the Act's implications was a brief encounter, not regarded as of great importance by the SANNC secretary. Yet it pinpointed crucial spheres of divergence between rural communities. For the people in Pondoland, the Act promised to entrench their right to land. For tenants and 'squatters', and for those who depended on the right to purchase for their access to land, the constraints envisaged, coming on top of previous legislation by the separate colonies, were a major threat. Such differences had important implications for the possibility of broad-based responses to the demands of capital and the state in the country as a whole.

In addition to emphasising the particularity of social relationships in Pondoland, this study has attempted to examine the complexity of social change in more detail than has been possible in general studies of the peasantry. Contemporary observers certainly commented on the distinctive character of Mpondo society in the 1930s. The magistrate of Lusikisiki, it will be recalled, prefaced his comments on cattle sales in the 1930s by asserting 'the fact that the Pondos are probably the most conservative tribe in these Territories'; he welcomed, however, what he considered a new response, and it persuaded him that such an opinion might have to be modified.[3] General Smuts concurred with the first sentiment, though as a man dealing with conflicts arising from rapid African urbanisation, and following segregationist policy as one of the solutions, he was less keen to welcome change: he wrote in his preface to Monica Hunter's *Reaction to Conquest* that the 'Pondo is unusually conservative and tenacious of his old culture, and in Pondoland the disintegration of native life is by no means so alarming as in other parts of South Africa'. For him it was the fact that the Mpondo had 'not been so intensely subjected to European influences as the neighbouring Bantu tribes' that explained their condition. Monica Hunter allowed the subjects of her analysis more scope to shape their world in her theory of 'selective conservatism', but her general conclusion was similar. What these observers, informed by ideas of westernisation and 'culture contact', failed to appreciate – and here Monica Hunter must to some extent be excepted – was the degree and complexity of change in Pondoland. A society which had depended on communal production in hunting, raiding and cultivation to recover from the Mfecane had become predominantly pastoral in the mid-nineteenth century and had developed extensive trading relationships with the colonies. In the late nineteenth century, the organisation of production and patterns of trade were deeply affected by the introduction of new technology, particularly the plough. In the early twentieth century, mass labour migrancy had been entrenched. These changes had been echoed by shifts in the locus of control over production and rural resources, by changes in the nature of chieftaincy and the composition of rural homesteads. It is true that many features of pre-colonial society persisted into the twentieth century. But neither lack of 'contact' nor 'selective conservatism' can alone explain why they did. The concept of conservatism is also inadequate to describe the changing form and role of social institutions and practices in a new situation.

It has been argued, on the contrary, that the particular and sometimes ambiguous pattern of state intervention, and the nature of capitalist penetration into Pondoland, rather than lack of state intervention and 'contact', moulded the shape of rural society. It is worth summing up a few of the points made: communal tenure was able to survive as a result of the reversal of Cape policies on the land once labour migrancy had been entrenched; the nature of cattle-keeping and attitudes towards cattle in the 1920s and 1930s cannot be divorced from the effects of state intervention to control East Coast fever; the enforcement of customary law, especially family law, in Colonial courts played some part in maintaining the strength of the homestead heads and the continued payment of bridewealth; the institution of chieftaincy, initially anathema to Colonial officials, became more acceptable to a state confronted with the problems of maintaining rural order. There *were* features of Colonial policy in the field of education, agriculture and the control of rural resources which encouraged the modification of old practices. Migrant labour in particular contributed to the dissolution of large homesteads. But the central direction of policy provided the framework for the persistence of certain social relationships.

However, it has also been stressed that state policy and an analysis of capitalist penetration can only contextualise patterns of change in Pondoland. At various historical moments the possibility of more radical transformation did emerge. Only through an analysis of the political balance in the area, the complex relationship between paramount, subchiefs and people, and the conflicts over authority within the homesteads can the

163

response of people in Pondoland be understood. Because of the specific nature of proletarianisation, the fear that land might be alienated, and the increasing importance of control over land to the chiefs and headmen, protection of communal tenure became a central demand. The fragmentation of homesteads, coupled with the necessity of maintaining rural production, drove most rural men to accumulate herds. Continued demands for bridewealth emphasised this tendency and were another means of ensuring that migrant wages were invested in productive resources rather than in consumer goods. And the rising cost of commodities, compared with the price of cattle, made rural households wary of extending their range of purchases – one of the implications of conversion to Christianity. These tendencies militated against the emergence of clearly distinct classes within Pondoland; and it is in this context that the political processes surrounding the chieftaincy remained important. Peasants in southern Africa have been seen as actors during the rise of peasant production but more acted upon in decline. This study has tried to cast its subjects as actors even when their independence as producers was being undermined.

Rural communities contributed to shape not only their own world but the larger society of which they were becoming part. Although the analysis of the origins of migrancy from Pondoland cannot necessarily be generalised, it indicates that migrancy, as one specific form of wage labour on which much of the early industrialisation in South Africa was based, was not simply determined by needs of capital. The mines and farms of South Africa transformed the rural societies from which labour was drawn and increasingly dominated the South African state; at the same time the nature of accumulation in South Africa was deeply affected by the dynamic of relationships in African societies. Similarly, the way in which the people of Pondoland struggled to defend their resources, and the specific nature of their demands, eased the implementation of some elements of segregationist policy in South Africa in the early twentieth century. This is not to argue that segregation emerged merely as a result of the defensive position of African people in Pondoland, or indeed South Africa's reserves as a whole. It was a complex response by dominant groups to conflicts in the industrial, urban and rural settings that cannot be addressed on the basis of the material set out here. But at a certain moment in South Africa's history, the trajectory of struggle in areas such as Pondoland allowed the state to deflect conflict from the towns and entrench some of the forms of pre-colonial society in the reserves. As demands for labour were intensified in later decades, new points of conflict arose in the rural areas. But segregation has provided the basis for central features of present-day South African society, and in this sense the

African communities which were less deeply transformed, and absorbed later, into the capitalist economy came to play an increasingly important role in the shaping of state policy.

Much groundwork is still necessary before an overall view of rural communities in South Africa can be constructed. Linkages between town and country, between work place and homestead, between plantation worker, tenant and reserve dweller have to be investigated before a fuller picture of the diverse experiences of dominated groups in South African society can emerge. But only when the view from below has been integrated into analyses of the political economy of the country as a whole can the peculiar path of capitalist development in the region be fully grasped.

Tables

While some of the figures used in the construction of these tables are based on careful enumeration by officials and others, some are merely estimates and therefore of doubtful value. Even where figures were carefully recorded, they may not, for a variety of reasons, represent the situation accurately. The tables have nevertheless been presented because they give some rough indication of, for example, the size of population, quantity of stock kept and extent of crop production in Pondoland. Where necessary, comments have been appended to the tables indicating the way in which figures were collected and possible errors. Such figures have been widely used in secondary works on the Transkeian Territories, though they are seldom subjected to critical analysis. The comments attached to these tables may serve to warn those who are confronted by Transkeian statistics of possible inaccuracies.

Table 1A *Returns of population for Pondoland districts*

District	1896 (estimate)	1904	1911	1921	1936	1946
Bizana		32,909	42,366	45,204	57,651	55,835
Flagstaff		25,713	27,780	31,861	43,134	43,505
Libode		24,728	25,421	28,990	38,249	41,707
Lusikisiki		41,691	44,015	53,670	69,795	83,114
Ngqeleni		37,655	36,648	40,352	46,853	53,679
Port St Johns		8,519	17,888	21,147	24,376	25,868
Tabankulu		29,294	37,509	40,243	46,280	49,961
Total	185,000	200,509	231,627	261,467	326,338	353,669

Table 1B *Average annual percentage increase over previous census year*

District	1911	1921	1936	1946
Bizana	4.1	0.7	1.8	− 0.3
Flagstaff	1.1	1.5	2.4	0.1
Libode	0.4	1.4	2.1	0.9
Lusikisiki	0.8	2.2	2.0	1.9
Ngqeleni	− 0.4	1.0	1.1	1.5
Port St Johns	15.7	1.8	1.0	0.6
Tabankulu	4.0	0.7	1.0	0.8
Total	2.2	1.3	1.7	0.8

Table 1C *Density of population per square mile*

District	1911	1921	1936	1946	Average size (sq mi, 1921)
Bizana	60	64	82	79	709
Flagstaff ´	65	75	102	102	428
Libode	48	54	72	78	535
Lusikisiki	48	58	76	90	931
Ngqeleni	83	91	106	121	446
Port St Johns	54	63	73	77	340
Tabankulu	73	78	90	97	517
Total	60	68	84	91	3,906

Note: All the census figures from 1904 onwards were based on very detailed enumeration in each location. In general, officials reported that they received co-operation from the headmen and people in Pondoland during census counts. The archives of the Department of Statistics are not available, thus making any critique of the returns highly speculative. Most of the figures are likely to be underenumerations, but the extent of error in any one year cannot, on the material available, be specified. Some of the more glaring anomalies, such as the decline in population in Ngqeleni between 1904 and 1911 and the vast increase in Port St Johns over the same period, can be explained by changes in district boundaries. The slower overall rate of increase revealed by the 1921 figures as compared with the 1936 figures is probably the result of the impact of influenza in 1918. An analysis of annual percentage increases by district between census years shows that these varied very considerably. The variation is unlikely to be the result of markedly different patterns of natural increase in these districts, where social conditions were broadly similar. They are probably best explained by inaccuracy in enumeration on the one hand, and patterns of migration on the other. Some districts received more immigrants from outside Pondoland, and there were movements between districts as well. The levelling off of population

167

between 1936 and 1946 in Bizana, Flagstaff and Port St Johns, while it may be due to inaccuracies, may also be the result of permanent out-migration of families to the cities, or possibly to other districts such as Lusikisiki.

These tables are based on the actual population as enumerated in the districts on census day. They do not include absentees. For this reason, the rural population figures display an increasing predominance of women. If figures for absent men were added to the total population figures, the annual average percentage increase over the previous census year would be slightly higher: 1.5 rather than 1.3 for 1921 and 1.8 rather than 1.7 for 1936. The figures given for absentees in 1921 and 1936 (see Table 2) are based on returns collected in the rural districts, not on an enumeration of people from Pondoland at the place of their work. (The latter has been the practice in finding '*de jure*' population figures since 1960.) The absentee figures themselves are therefore suspect.

Table 2 *Labour passes given in Pondoland districts, 1896–1912, and number of absentees, 1921 and 1936*

Year	Bizana	Flag-staff	Lusiki-siki	Taban-kulu	Libode	Ngqeleni	Port St Johns	Total
1896	1,195	94	53	324	113	189	15	1,983
1897	891		273	315	57	182	4	1,722
1898	1,767	472	343	949	353	235	8	4,127
1899	1,290	200	166	314	38	72	1	2,081
1900	1,946	271	233	596	185	198	44	3,473
1901	3,269	714	274	771	166	173	21	5,388
1902	3,790	1,431	423	611	662	867	48	7,832
1903[a]	5,488	1,323	725	943	285	577	201	9,542
1904	4,766	1,660	1,154	1,029	458	699	294	10,060
1905	3,632	1,800	775	1,426	947	1,249	403	10,232
1906	3,748	1,739	1,842	1,578	507	750	125	10,289
1907	3,588	2,088	1,318	1,418	599	1,095	180	10,286
1908	3,231	2,383	1,525	1,254	746	1,026	183	10,348
1909	2,879	2,645	1,400	1,228	1,336	774	252	10,514
1910	3,783	3,893	1,819	1,773	3,313	1,661	672	16,914
1911	4,203	2,615	1,671	1,271	1,731	432	511	11,434
1912	5,592	3,780	2,432	2,193	1,753	782	402	16,934
1921	3,117	2,181	4,078	3,044	2,138	3,062	1,122	18,742
1936	5,342	3,795	5,183	4,827	3,701	4,583	1,830	29,261

[a] For the period July 1903 to June 1904.

Note: Figures for 1896 to 1909 are taken from the published Cape *Blue Books*. Figures for 1910 to 1912 are from the published Union *Blue Books* and *Reports of the Native Affairs Department*. Monthly figures of the passes issued in each Transkeian district were issued in the Cape *Government Gazette* from 1901 to 1909 (see Table 3). These figures do not agree exactly with the annual figures in the sources above, although the discrepancy is not great. After 1913 the Native Affairs Department ceased to publish an annual report, and in the irregular reports which were issued there are no figures of labour migrancy by district. It proved impossible to find such figures in any of the archival collections consulted. The 1921 and 1936 figures are drawn from a return of absentees from each district in the census reports. They reflect only the number of absentees recorded on the day of the census, not the number of passes issued, and therefore are not strictly comparable with the earlier figures.

As the 1896–1912 returns indicate only the number of passes issued, and not the actual number of migrants who left the Pondoland districts, they may be underestimates. However, administrative files in the archives suggest that few workers left without passes at this period. They had, after all, to contract and take passes if they were to obtain advances. A far more serious objection to these figures arises from the fact that workers from the Transkeian Territories did not have to obtain passes in their home districts, although they were encouraged to do so. The figures of labour passes issued were supposed to be regularised by officials so as to reflect the actual district of origin of each worker, but no archival information could be found which indicated that this was in fact done efficiently. The table shows that substantially more passes were issued in Bizana than in other Pondoland districts throughout the period 1896–1912. (Flagstaff figures are also high.) Although there is information which suggests that rates of migrancy from Bizana were higher than those from other districts in Pondoland, they are unlikely to have been as much higher as this table indicates. Bizana and Flagstaff villages were, however, the major recruiting centres in Eastern Pondoland, as they were situated on transport routes out of the area. It is likely that some workers from other districts obtained their passes in these villages. A comparison of the 1912 and 1921 figures tends to confirm this point. The latter, which reflect the actual number of absentees, show a reduction in Flagstaff and Bizana and an increase in the other Pondoland districts.

A further problem arises. Did many Mpondo workers contract outside Pondoland? If so, the figures used in the text may be seriously misleading. It is probably true that a number of migrants from the Western Pondoland districts obtained passes in Umtata between 1896 and 1912. On the other hand, considerable numbers of migrants from the East Griqualand districts of Mount Ayliff and Mount Frere contracted for work in the Pondoland recruiting centres, partly because of the availability of advances in Pondoland, and partly because they could leave as Mpondo workers, who were apparently in great demand on the mines. It is impossible to say whether or not these two anomalies cancel each other out. The great increase in 1910, which was apparently not caused by any natural disaster, is probably made up largely of workers from outside the Pondoland districts. Cattle advances, abolished in other districts in 1909, were still available in Pondoland in 1910.

Table 3 *Seasonality of labour migration, 1901–9 and 1937–45*

	1901–9		1937–45	
	Average number of migrants	Per cent of total	Average number of migrants	Per cent of total
Jan.	838	8.6	1,406	13.6
Feb.	859	8.8	1,092	9.9
March	864	8.9	929	9.0
April	795	8.2	837	8.1
May	832	8.5	822	7.9
June	746	7.7	706	6.8
July	858	8.8	739	7.1
Aug.	757	7.8	889	8.6
Sept.	705	7.2	868	8.4
Oct.	768	7.9	743	7.2
Nov.	774	8.0	692	6.7
Dec.	936	9.6	712	6.9
Total	9,732	100.0	10,372	100.2

Note: Figures for 1901 to 1909, for all Pondoland districts, are calculated from returns in the Cape *Government Gazette*. No other monthly returns of labour passes issued could be found, either in published or unpublished sources. Publication of these figures in the *Government Gazette* ceased in April 1910 at the time of Union. Figures for 1937 to 1945 were found in the Mine Labour Organisation back files in Johannesburg and reflect only workers recruited for the gold mines by the Native Recruiting Corporation from Eastern Pondoland. The two sets of figures are not strictly comparable. The note appended to Table 2 applies to the 1901–9 series. There are also missing figures and occasionally what appear to be gross overestimates. These have been filled in or ironed out. The result is thus not highly reliable. When the labour supply for the industry was, as a whole, adequate, it enforced a quota system on recruiters in the Territories. Only a certain number of workers were accepted from each district in particular months, and some effort was made to spread recruiting more evenly through the year. Quota systems were vigorously applied in the 1930s. In fact some figures for 1934–6 which were found in the Mine Labour Organisation files suggest that the pattern of migration for the Territories as a whole did not have a marked seasonal characteristic in these three years. During the late 1930s and early 1940s, quota systems were relaxed, though not abolished, and, as the table illustrates, a more marked seasonal pattern emerged. It is possible that if workers had been completely free to choose the date of their departure, the pattern of migration in 1937–45 would have been even more seasonal. No quota systems were applied in the first decade of the century.

Table 4 *Percentage of men absent*

	Pondoland	East Griqualand	Thembuland	Transkei	Transkeian Territories (total)
1896	2.5	11.4	16.5	21.9	13.4
1904	10.1	13.8	14.7	20.1	14.5
1911	9.6	14.7	16.1	23.4	16.5
1921	13.5	18.7	17.3	18.9	17.0
1936	17.1	24.7	24.4	25.7	22.8

Note: The percentages tabulated are calculated from labour migrancy and population statistics (see Tables 1 and 2). Total male population figures used in the calculation for this table were arrived at by adding absentees to the actual enumerated population. In view of the reservations made about both sets of figures, this table should be regarded with a great deal of caution. The percentages given in each year are not always calculated on strictly comparable data. To calculate, very roughly, the percentage of 'economically active' men (those between fifteen and forty-five years of age) absent, figures given should be multiplied two and a half times.

Table 5 *Cattle holdings, Pondoland districts*

Year	Total	31 December	Percentage increase or decrease over previous year	31 August	Loss or gain between 1 January and 31 August
1895	130,000				
1896	175,000				
1898	76,981				
1899	83,300				
1904	134,967				
1911	279,591				
1914	75,848				
1915	54,238				
1918		102,028			
1919		123,290	20.8		
1920		146,011	18.4		
1921		186,333	27.6		
1922		221,451	18.8		
1923		262,881	18.7	238,957	+ 17,506
1924		295,204	12.3	279,126	+ 16,245
1925		330,416	11.9	303,022	+ 7,818
1926		338,178	11.4	343,951	+ 13,535
1927		414,210	12.5	382,868	+ 14,690
1928		447,124	7.9	No figure	
1929		476,918	6.7	448,666	+ 1,542
1930		511,407	7.2	479,182	+ 2,264
1931		509,347	− 0.4	No figure	
1932		521,467	2.4	No figure	
1933		502,555	− 3.6	No figure	
1934		475,663	− 5.3	472,400	− 30,155
1935		501,466	5.4	472,086	− 3,577
1936		504,329	0.6	488,896	− 12,570
1937		489,301	− 3.0	488,548	− 15,781
1938		484,537	− 1.0	472,741	− 16,560
1939		501,310	3.5	477,923	− 6,614

Note: Figures for 1895 to 1899 are taken from Cape *Statistical Registers*. They are estimates made by magistrates. The returns for the pre-rinderpest years (1895 and 1896) are almost certainly gross underestimates. Figures for 1904 and 1911 are culled from the census returns. It is not clear whether they are estimates or whether they were the result of homestead-by-homestead enumeration, as in the case of the population figures. The 1914 figure is an estimate. The 1915 figure is based on a head count of cattle taken in the districts by veterinary officials and may be fairly close to the mark. Figures from 1918 onwards are based on dipping returns. As compulsory dipping was rigorously enforced only from the early 1920s, they may initially reflect increases in cattle dipped rather than cattle numbers, but these figures are probably the most accurate of any of the series available on the Transkeian Territories.

Figures for the total number of stock as on 31 December of each year were appended to the *TTGC Proceedings*. From 1923, additional figures giving the number of stock on 31 August of each year were included. (These are also in the *Agricultural Census* reports.) The December figures were collected after the spring calving and thus at a time when the cattle population was near its annual height. The August figures, taken at the height of the winter dry season, were collected when the cattle population was reaching its lowest level.

Table 6 *Sheep and goat holdings:*
Pondoland districts

Year	Sheep	Goats
1895	34,500	62,500
1896	37,750	67,800
1898	48,550	112,140
1899	62,000	120,250
1903	183,404	250,104
1904	168,223	276,621
1907	193,048	241,974
1908	218,757	243,016
1909	228,179	209,091
1911	193,046	154,065
1922	287,197	—
1923	313,456	297,135
1924	370,354	323,450
1925	386,449	321,700
1926	456,476	346,929
1927	505,202	378,635
1929	504,225	372,682
1930	570,979	347,697
1934	405,337	236,624
1935	420,778	245,643
1936	485,202	287,714
1937	485,422	274,367
1938	446,847	234,804
1939	475,612	231,610

Note: Figures for 1895 to 1899 are from the Cape *Statistical Registers*. They are estimates, possibly underestimates. Those for 1903 and for 1907–9 are from *Reports of the Chief Inspector of Sheep* in the Cape. In this decade the state attempted to enforce compulsory dipping of sheep, and these figures may be reasonably accurate. Figures for 1904 and 1911 are taken from census returns. (See note on Table 5.) Figures from 1922 onwards are included both in appendices to the *TTGC Proceedings* and the *Agricultural Census* reports. Compulsory dipping of all sheep had been abolished by this time; only those herds with scab had to be dipped. However, the sheep inspectors of the Department of Agriculture made regular inspections of the flocks in their districts and must have been in a reasonable position to estimate the number of animals. The returns are probably not as accurate as the cattle returns.

Table 7 *Grain output: Pondoland districts*

| Year | Bags or muids (200 lb) | |
	Maize	Sorghum
1895	121,500	78,000
1896	128,000	79,000
1898	148,000	105,500
1901	227,545	—
1904	274,230	101,625
1911	351,285	81,715
1920	307,730	16,872
1923	588,668	25,700
1924	506,000	17,250
1925	498,549	16,828
1926	517,564	18,961
1927	564,809	27,652
1929	741,107	71,502
1930	590,732	70,165
1933	724,041	35,729
1934	320,425	16,549
1935	139,532	8,023
1936	631,395	22,189
1937	592,000	26,484
1938	810,000	26,950

Note (see ch. 3, sect. 4): Figures are drawn from the Cape *Statistical Registers,* census returns, *Agricultural Census* returns and appendices to the *TTGC Proceedings.* They are all estimates. Producers did not measure their output in bags. Officials knew the number of hut-tax payers and took this as the figure for the number of lands. This correlation is open to many objections. They then estimated the average size of lands and the average yield per acre. They had no accurate means of assessing either. They also introduced a system where yields were compared with a 100 per cent crop in a good year, and estimated the shortfall according to weather and observation. The figures probably do indicate, roughly, the good and bad years. There is no reliable means by which to assess whether the tendency was to overestimate or underestimate the amount of crops produced in any one year or whether the changing method of assessment led to significant variations in these tendencies over the years. The figures on sorghum production are likely to be very wild estimates.

Notes

Preface

1. G. Mbeki, *The Peasants' Revolt* (Harmondsworth, 1964).
2. Further details on the nineteenth century and a lengthy note on sources are included in W. J. Beinart, 'Production, Labour Migrancy and the Chieftaincy: Aspects of the Political Economy of Pondoland, ca. 1860–1930', unpublished Ph.D. thesis, University of London, 1979.
3. D. G. L. Cragg, 'The relations of the Amampondo and the Colonial Authorities (1830–1886) with Special Reference to the Role of the Wesleyan Missionaries', unpublished D. Phil. thesis, University of Oxford, 1959.
4. M. Hunter, *Reaction to Conquest* (London, 1936, 1964).

Introduction

1. For general background see C. W. de Kiewiet, *A History of South Africa, Social and Economic* (London, 1941); M. Wilson and L. Thompson (eds.), *Oxford History of South Africa*, 2 vols. (Oxford, 1969, 1971); S. Marks and A. Atmore (eds.), *Economy and Society in Pre-Industrial South Africa* (London, 1980).
2. The episodes mentioned are dealt with in more detail in succeeding chapters.
3. A. G. Frank, *Capitalism and Underdevelopment in Latin America* (Harmondsworth, 1971), E. Wolf, *Peasants* (Englewood Cliffs, N.J., 1966) and T. Shanin (ed.), *Peasants and Peasant Society* (Harmondsworth, 1971) were amongst the more influential works for Africanists; E. A. Brett, *Colonialism and Underdevelopment in East Africa* (London, 1973), S. Amin, *Neo-Colonialism in West Africa* (Harmondsworth, 1973) and G. Arrighi and J. S. Saul (eds.), *Essays on the Political Economy of Africa* (New York, 1973) extended the analysis to Africa with important variations. C. Bundy, 'The Emergence and Decline of a South African Peasantry', *African Affairs*, 71, 285 (Oct. 1972), and *The Rise and Fall of the South African Peasantry* (London, 1979), M. Legassick, 'Development and Underdevelopment in South Africa', unpublished, 1971, M. Wilson, 'The Growth of Peasant Communities', in Wilson and Thompson, *Oxford History of South Africa*,

176

vol. II, and R. Palmer and N. Parsons (eds.), *The Roots of Rural Poverty in Central and Southern Africa* (London, 1977) applied some of the concepts to southern Africa.

4. A. G. Hopkins, *An Economic History of West Africa* (London, 1973); P. Hill, *Studies in Rural Capitalism in West Africa* (Cambridge, 1970); C. C. Wrigley, *Crops and Wealth in Uganda* (Kampala, 1959).

5. This strand in the literature on peasants is developed in, for example, A. V. Chayanov, *The Theory of Peasant Economy* (Homewood, Ill., 1966); T. Shanin, *The Awkward Class* (Oxford, 1972). Cf. J. Goody (ed.), *The Developmental Cycle in Domestic Groups* (Cambridge, 1958) and Goody, *Production and Reproduction: A Comparative Study of the Domestic Domain* (Cambridge, 1976).

6. Bundy, *South African Peasantry*, chs. 2, 3; R. Moyer, 'The Mfengu, Self-Defence and the Cape Frontier Wars', in C. C. Saunders and R. Derricourt (eds.), *Beyond the Cape Frontier* (London, 1974); S. Trapido, 'White Conflict and Non-White Participation in the Politics of the Cape of Good Hope, 1853–1910', unpublished Ph.D. thesis, University of London, 1970; Trapido, '"The Friends of the Natives": Merchants, Peasants and the Political and Ideological Structure of Liberalism in the Cape, 1854–1910', in Marks and Atmore, *Pre-Industrial South Africa*.

7. S. Trapido, 'Landlord and Tenant in a Colonial Economy: The Transvaal 1880–1910', *Journal of Southern African Studies*, 5, 1 (1978); P. Delius, 'The Pedi Polity Under Sekwati and Sekhukhune, 1828–1880', unpublished Ph.D. thesis, University of London, 1980; T. Keegan, 'The Restructuring of Agrarian Class Relations in a Colonial Economy: The Orange River Colony, 1902–1910', *Journal of Southern African Studies*, 5, 2 (1979); H. Slater, 'The Changing Pattern of Economic Relationships in Rural Natal, 1838–1914', in Marks and Atmore, *Pre-Industrial South Africa;* M. Morris, 'The Development of Capitalism in South African Agriculture: Class Struggle in the Countryside', *Economy and Society*, 5 (1976).

8. J. Goody, *Technology, Tradition and the State* (Oxford, 1971); Barrington Moore, *Social Origins of Dictatorship and Democracy: Lord and Peasant in the Making of the Modern World* (London, 1967); E. Laclau, 'Feudalism and Capitalism in Latin America', *New Left Review*, 67 (1971); R. Brenner, 'The Origins of Capitalist Development: A Critique of Neo-Smithian Marxism', *New Left Review*, 104 (1976); T. Ranger, 'Growing from the Roots: Reflections on Peasant Research in Central and Southern Africa', *Journal of Southern African Studies* 5, 1 (1978); G. Kay, *Development and Underdevelopment: A Marxist Analysis* (London, 1975): E. Terray, 'Long-Distance Exchange and the Formation of the State: The Case of the Abron Kingdom of Gyama', *Economy and Society*, 3, 3 (1974).

9. For recent attempts to reconceptualise peasants, to dispense with the category and to typify simple commodity producers and commoditisation, see J. Ennew, D. Hirst and K. Tribe, '"Peasantry" as an Economic Category', *Journal of Peasant Studies*, 4, 4 (1977); H. Bernstein, 'Notes on Capital and Peasantry', *Review of African Political Economy*, 10 (1977);

J. Banaji, 'Modes of Production in a Materialist Conception of History', *Capital and Class*, 3 (1977); H. Friedmann, 'Household Production and the National Economy: Concepts for the Analysis of Agrarian Formations', *Journal of Peasant Studies*, 7, 2 (1980).

10. See M. Legassick, 'Gold, Agriculture and Secondary Industry in South Africa: From Periphery to Sub-Metropole in a Forced Labour System', in Palmer and Parsons, *Roots of Rural Poverty*; 'South Africa: Capital Accumulation and Violence', *Economy and Society*, 3, 3 (1974); and 'The Making of South African "Native Policy", 1903–1923: The Origins of Segregation', unpublished paper, ICS, London, 1972; H. Wolpe, 'Capitalism and Cheap Labour-power in South Africa: From Segregation to Apartheid', *Economy and Society*, 1, (1972); Morris, 'South African Agriculture'.

11. See esp. S. Marks, 'Natal, the Zulu Royal Family and the Ideology of Segregation', *Journal of Southern African Studies*, 4, 2 (1978).

12. For general literature on 'articulation' and 'modes of production', see for example E. Terray, *Marxism and 'Primitive' Societies* (New York, 1972); H. Wolpe (ed.), *The Articulation of Modes of Production* (London, 1980); M. Klein (ed.), *Peasants in Africa* (Beverly Hills, Calif., 1980) and D. Seddon (ed.), *Relations of Production: Marxist Approaches to Economic Anthropology* (London, 1978).

13. Cf. P. Delius, 'Migrant Labour and the Pedi, 1840–1880', in Marks and Atmore, *Pre-Industrial South Africa*; P. Harries, 'Kinship, Ideology and the Origins of Migrant Labour', unpublished, 1980.

1. The political economy of Pondoland in the nineteenth century

1. Victor Poto Ndamase, *Ama-Mpondo: Ibali ne-Ntlalo* (Lovedale, 1927); M. Wilson, 'The Nguni People' and 'The Sotho, Venda, and Tsonga', in Wilson and Thompson, *Oxford History of South Africa*, vol. I; W. D. Hammond-Tooke (ed.), *The Bantu Speaking Peoples of Southern Africa* (London, 1974), esp. articles by B. Sansom; R. Derricourt, 'Settlement in the Transkei and Ciskei before the Mfecane', in Saunders and Derricourt, *Beyond the Cape Frontier*; J. H. Soga, *The South Eastern Bantu* (Johannesburg, 1930); A. T. Bryant, *Olden Times in Zululand and Natal* (London, 1929); J. B. Peires, 'A History of the Xhosa c. 1700–1835', unpublished M.A. thesis, Rhodes University, 1976; E. M. Shaw and N. J. van Warmelo, 'The Material Culture of the Cape Nguni', *Annals of the South African Museum*, 58, 1 and 2 (1972, 1974).

2. For a more detailed account of the Mpondo chiefdom in this period and for sources, see Beinart, 'Political Economy of Pondoland'; 'Production and the Material Basis of Chieftainship, Pondoland c. 1828–1880', in Marks and Atmore, *Pre-Industrial South Africa*; and 'Economic Change in Nineteenth Century Pondoland', *ICS, SA Seminar*, 7 (1977). For Zulu, see M. Gluckman, 'The Kingdom of the Zulu of South Africa', in M. Fortes and E. Evans-Pritchard (eds.), *African Political Systems* (London, 1940); J. Omer-Cooper, *Zulu Aftermath* (London, 1966); J. J. Guy, 'Ecological

Factors in the Rise of Shaka and the Zulu Kingdom', in Marks and Atmore, *Pre-Industrial South Africa*; D. Hedges, 'Trade and Politics in Southern Mocambique and Zululand in the Eighteenth and Early Nineteenth Centuries', unpublished Ph.D. thesis, University of London, 1978.

3. M. H. Lister, *Journals of Andrew Geddes Bain* (Cape Town, 1949), 111 n. 59.

4. P. Bonner, 'The Rise, Consolidation and Disintegration of Dhlamini Power in Swaziland between 1820 and 1899', unpublished Ph.D. thesis, University of London, 1977; J. R. D. Cobbing, 'The Ndebele under the Khumalos, 1820–1896', unpublished Ph.D. thesis, University of Lancaster, 1976; L. Thompson, *Survival in Two Worlds: Moshoeshoe of Lesotho 1786–1870* (Oxford, 1975).

5. WMMS, SA Box 7, J. Cameron to Secs., 24.5.1836.

6. The documentation of Pondoland in the mid-nineteenth century is not sufficiently dense to allow a detailed reconstruction of the chiefdom, nor do the documents often expand on social relationships within the society. Traditions collected and relationships observed at a later period have to some extent to be projected back into the mid-nineteenth century. An attempt has, however, been made to locate these relationships in the specific context of the period. Poto, *Ama-Mpondo* and Hunter, *Reaction to Conquest* provide information on many of the issues addressed. Interviews in Pondoland and a wide variety of twentieth-century sources which illuminate and refer back to earlier periods have also been important.

7. Interviews, Nelson Sigcau, Xinwa, Fono, Nonkonyana, Laqwela. The following construction of the polity differs considerably from the argument in W. D. Hammond-Tooke, 'Segmentation and Fission in Cape Nguni Political Units', *Africa*, 35, 2 (1965); it has more in common with the approach in Peires, 'History of the Xhosa' and 'The Rise of the "Right Hand House" in the History and Historiography of the Xhosa', *History in Africa*, 2 (1975).

8. Poto, *Ama-Mpondo*, 17–21; Hunter, *Reaction to Conquest*, 379, 382–4; District Record Book, Lusikisiki, tradition related by Maninha (*sic*) *c.* 1927; Hammond-Tooke papers, Correspondence on *Sigcau* v. *Sigcau*; interview, Mgoduka.

9. See Hammond-Tooke files, RM Bizana to CMT, 11.11.1924, Privileges of Heads of Clans Granted by Paramount Chiefs, for a later account of the status of immigrant chiefs.

10. See Beinart, 'Political Economy of Pondoland', ch. 2, sect. 1.

11. I. Schapera, *The Tswana* (London, 1976). For comparative information on this and following paragraphs, see Delius, 'Pedi Polity'; Bonner, 'Dhlamini Power'; Guy, 'Ecological Factors'; Sansom, 'Traditional Economic Systems', in Hammond-Tooke, *Bantu Speaking Peoples.*

12. This practice was mentioned in many interviews; see CA CMT 3/50, Asst CMT to CMT, 21.7.1898.

13. Poto, *Ama-Mpondo*, 56; Hunter, *Reaction to Conquest*, 136–9; interviews, Heathcote, Fono, Mgeyana.

179

14. See this ch. sect. 2; WMMS, Mason to Secs., 29.9.1860, 29.1.1861 and *passim* for an impression of stock-holding at the time.

15. Hunter, *Reaction to Conquest*, 190; the following points have been elaborated particularly by Jeff Guy. Poto, *Ama-Mpondo*, has lists of the paramounts' wives.

16. J. Wright and C. de B. Webb (eds. and trans.), *The James Stuart Archive of Recorded Oral Evidence Relating to the History of the Zulu and Neighbouring Peoples*, vol. II (Pietermaritzburg, 1979), 74.

17. Paragraphs on marriage owe much to Monica Wilson's writings and comments and to discussions with Peter Delius; see Delius, 'Pedi Polity', ch. 2 and 3, esp. 71–4; P. Bonner, 'Classes, the Mode of Production and the State in Pre-Colonial Swaziland', in Marks and Atmore, *Pre-Industrial South Africa*, 93.

18. See Poto, *Ama-Mpondo*, 55 and Hunter, *Reaction in Conquest*, 384–5 for a general list of payments. There is extensive discussion of tributary rights, some of it referring to the past, in the archival collections on Pondoland from annexation. See this ch., sect. 4 and ch. 4, sect. 2.

19. I. Schapera, *Tribal Legislation among the Tswana of Bechuanaland Protectorate* (London, 1943) and *Tribal Innovators: Tswana Chiefs and Social Change 1795–1940* (London, 1970).

20. J. J. Guy, *The Destruction of the Zulu Kingdom* (London, 1979); J. B. McI. Daniel, 'A Geographical Study of Pre-Shakan Zululand', *South African Geographical Journal*, 55, 1 (1973).

21. Following based on, for example, Hunter, *Reaction to Conquest*, 'The Effects of Contact with Europeans on the Status of Pondo Women', *Africa*, 6 (1933) and 'Results of Culture Contact on the Pondo and Xhosa Family', *South African Journal of Science*, 29 (1932); A. Steedman, *Wanderings and Adventures in the Interior of Southern Africa*, vol. II (London, 1835; repr. Cape Town, 1966); WMMS; interviews, esp. Vulizibhaya, Kohlabantu.

22. J. van Tromp, *Xhosa Law of Persons*, 124; Hunter, *Reaction to Conquest*, 212; CA CMT 3/640/72; interview, Mathandabuzo.

23. Interviews, esp. Nonkonyana.

24. Steedman, *Wanderings*, vol. I, 261–2.

25. See ch. 2, sect. 1 and ch. 3, sect. 4.

26. Lister, *Journals of Andrew Geddes Bain*; J. Stuart and D. McK. Malcolm, *The Diary of Henry Francis Fynn* (Pietermaritzburg, 1969); WMMS, Jenkins papers; PRO CO 48/408, Curries Report, March 1861; B. A. le Cordeur, 'The Relations between the Cape and Natal, 1846–1879', *Archives Yearbook for South African History*, 1965, pt I.

27. PRO CO 48/485, Rutherford to Frere, 4.1.1878 in Frere to Hicks Beach, 22.5.1878 includes shipping figures.

28. WMMS, Box 24, F. Mason to Secs., 30.3.1860; W. Taylor, *Christian Adventures in South Africa* (London, 1867), 466; B. J. T. Leverton, 'Government Finance and Political Development in Natal, 1843 to 1893', unpublished Ph.D. thesis, University of South Africa, 1968; F. Algar, *Handbook to*

the Colony of Natal: 1865 (London, 1865), 23, 24; Witwatersrand University, Church of the Province Library, A55, Reminiscences of R. T. A. James; PRO CO 179/68, Table enclosed in Scott to Newcastle, 21.11.1863.

29. *Kaffrarian Watchman*, 15.4.1876; CA CMT 3/51; Cragg, 'Amampondo', ch. IV; WMMS, Jenkins papers, Jenkins to W. Shaw, 21.8.1854; Cape of Good Hope, *Return of Papers on Pondo Affairs*, A. 105 – 1880, 38, 72; PRO CO 48/485, Blyth to Littleton, 10.12.1877 in Frere to Hicks Beach, 22.5.1878; BPP, *Correspondence Respecting the Affairs of Pondoland*, C. 5022, 1887, 68; *BBNA*, G. 13 – 1880, 164.

30. WMMS, SA Box 24, Impey to Secs., 7.6.1858; SA Box 19, Mason to Secs., 30.3.1860, 30.3.1863; SA Box 20, Allsopp to Secs., 23.8.1865; Box 21, Kirkby to Secs., 12.3.1873; Jenkins papers, T. Shepstone to Jenkins, 18.7.1855; Diary of H. C. Shepstone, 5.12.1871, 5.3.1872; Cape of Good Hope, *Report of the Commission of Enquiry into the Disease among Cattle, Known as Redwater*, G. 85 – 1883, 214–18.

31. WMMS, SA Box 19, F. Mason to Secs., 29.9.1860.

32. Taylor, *Christian Adventures*, 446.

33. PRO CO 48/407, Currie to Grey, 18.3.1861 in Grey to Newcastle, 13.4.1861; WMMS, SA Box 21, Allsopp to Secs., 9.2 1869; Diary of H. C. Shepstone, 26.3.1872; WMMS, Jenkins papers, item 169, Frere's memorandum, 1878; *BBNA*, G. 33 – 1882, 69; *Kokstad Advertiser*, 1882–3, *passim*; *Journal of African History*, 13 (1972), issue on firearms in Africa.

34. Taylor, *Christian Adventures*, 466; *BBNA*, G. 21 – 1875, 87; G. 16 – 1876, 29; G. 13 – 1880, 167; interview, Xinwa.

35. Rainfall figures in the District Record Books survive only for the twentieth century. These indicate that rainfall on the coast in Port St Johns and Lusikisiki was around 50–5 inches a year, near the Great Place around 40 inches, diminishing progressively to less than 30 inches in Tabankulu in rough proportion to the distance from the coast. WMMS, SA Box 19, Mason to Secs., 1861–3; SA Box 23, Cameron to Secs., 13.4.1877; *Kaffrarian Watchman*, 10.10.1877, 7.11.1877.

36. *Kaffrarian Watchman*, 15.4.1876.

37. R. Ross, *Adam Kok's Griquas: A Study in the Development of Stratification in South Africa* (Cambridge, 1976); le Cordeur, 'Relations between the Cape and Natal'; Cragg, 'Amampondo'; *BBNA*, G. 21 – 1875; Cape of Good Hope, *Memorandum on the Pondo Settlement of 1886*, G. 10 – 1887.

38. APS, C. 149 – 103, Umquikela (*sic*) to Sec., APS, 1.8.1883.

39. *BBNA*, G. 21 – 1875, 29; G. 8 – 1883, 167; G. 3 – 1884, 149; Bundy, *South African Peasantry*, 49, 55, 71–5.

40. CA O'D, Accession 1403, esp. vol. 27, Letters Dispatched, 1881–3, vol. 29, Letters Dispatched, 1887–92 and Diaries 1–10; *BBNA*, G. 13 – 1880, 160; G. 3 – 1884, 149; Natal, *Report of the Trade Commission, 1885–1886* (Pietermaritzburg, 1886), 74. For a more detailed account of trade in these years, see Beinart, 'Political Economy of Pondoland', ch. 1, sect. 3.

41. For further details, see Beinart, 'Political Economy of Pondoland', ch. 2, sect. 1 and 'European Traders and the Mpondo Paramountcy, 1878–1886',

Journal of African History, 20 (1979); CA NA 162, Oxland to SNA, 30.12.1881; CA NA 164, Scott to Under SNA, 12.3.1889.

42. Cf. Goody, *Technology, Tradition*.
43. See esp. *Kokstad Advertiser*, 1892–3.
44. Le Cordeur, 'Relations between the Cape and Natal'; Craggs 'Amampondo'; C. C. Saunders, 'The Annexation of the Transkeian Territories (1872–1895) with Special Reference to British and Cape Policy', unpublished D.Phil. thesis, University of Oxford, 1972; C. W. de Kiewiet, *The Imperial Factor in South Africa: A Study in Politics and Economics* (Cambridge, 1937); A. Atmore and S. Marks, 'The Imperial Factor in South Africa in the Nineteenth Century: Towards a Reassessment', *Journal of Imperial and Commonwealth History*, 3, 1 (1974); N. Etherington, 'Labour Supply and the Genesis of South African Confederation in the 1870s', *Journal of African History*, 20, 2 (1979).
45. Cape, *Return of Papers on Pondo Affairs*, A. 105 – 1880 documents this period.
46. F. Brownlee, *The Transkeian Native Territories: Historical Records* (Lovedale, 1923); Cape of Good Hope, *Report of the Commission of Enquiry on the East Griqualand Rebellion*, G. 58 – 1879; Beinart, 'European Traders'; Cragg, 'Amampondo'; *Kokstad Advertiser*, 1883–6.
47. Cape, *Memorandum on the Pondo Settlement*.
48. For a more detailed treatment, see Beinart, 'Political Economy of Pondoland', ch. 2, sect. 3; J. W. MacQuarrie, *The Reminiscences of Sir Walter Stanford*, vol. II (Cape Town, 1962); *Kokstad Advertiser*, 1891–4.
49. See *Kokstad Advertiser*, 14.2.1894 and CA NA 497 for detailed analyses of the war and Mhlangaso's position; Rhodes University, Cory Library, MS. 15, 799, H. Rock, 'Reminiscences'.
50. C. H. Tredgold and W. P. Buchanan, *Decisions of the Supreme Court, Cape of Good Hope*, vol. XII, 1895, *Cook Bros.* v. *Colonial Government* and records of this case in the Supreme Court Archives.
51. For annexation, see MacQuarrie, *Stanford*, vol. II, 147–67; *Kokstad Advertiser*, Jan. to April 1894; CA CMT 3/952/746; CA NA 440, Commission of Enquiry into Sigcau's Behaviour.
52. CA CMT 3/952/746, Rhodes to Elliot, 18.2.1894 and Elliot to Rhodes, 16.2.1894; CA CMT 3/50, 3/51; CA NA 685/2608, SNA memorandum, 29.5.1908.
53. The best source on the operation of the magisterial system is the *BBNA* series published annually from 1874 to 1910.
54. CA NA 440; CA PMO 144, 146.
55. CA CMT 3/50; Rhodes University, Cory Library, McLoughlin papers, Gladwin to CMT, 21.2.1923.
56. CA NA 686/2610; CA NA 685/2608; CA CMT 3/51.
57. McLoughlin papers, RM Lusikisiki to CMT, 23.7.1925, quoting Asst CMT, 1904.
58. CA NA 685/2608, SNA to Asst CMK, 26.11.1904; see CA CMT 3/952/752 and CA CMT 3/953/45 (1).

182

59. CA NA 510/268, RM Bizana to Asst CMT, 23.12.1901 and enclosures and 30.12.1901; CA NA 685/2608, RM Flagstaff to CMT, 10.12.1903 and enclosures.
60. CA NA 561/1017, SNA to Asst CMT, 5.7.1902 and following correspondence; CA NA 550/879, CMT to SNA, 25.8.1902 and following correspondence; CA CMT 3/52, Asst CMT to CMT, 27.4.1901; CA CMT 3/593/45 (1), *passim.*
61. *BBNA*, G. 25 – 1902, 57; G. 46 – 1906, 52; G. 12 – 1904, 69 and *BBNA, passim*; cf. CA CMT 3/50, RM Bizana to Asst CMT, 11.9.1896; CA CMT 3/52, Asst CMT to CMT, 29.9.1901.

2. Crops, cattle and the origins of labour migrancy, 1894–1911

1. Bundy, *South African Peasantry*, 110ff; Trapido, 'Liberalism', in Marks and Atmore, *Pre-Industrial South Africa.*
2. *Kokstad Advertiser*, 18.4.1894.
3. Vindex, *Cecil Rhodes: His Political Life and Speeches, 1881–1900* (London, 1900), 371–89, speech on moving the second reading of the Glen Grey Act.
4. Bundy, *South African Peasantry*, 135; T. R. H. Davenport, *The Afrikaner Bond: The History of a South African Party, 1880–1911* (Cape Town, 1976), 152–5; *South African Native Affairs Commission 1903–1905* (Cape Town, 1905), vol. III, evidence of H. G. Elliot, esp. 191ff.
5. Vindex, *Rhodes*, 381.
6. Trapido, 'Non-White Participation', 317–23; CA NA 526/509; C. Bundy and W. Beinart, 'State Intervention and Rural Resistance: The Transkei, 1900–1965', in Klein, *Peasants in Africa.*
7. MacQuarrie, *Stanford*, vol. II, 239; CA NA, 526/509, esp. Asst CMK to SNA, 22.11.1906 and CMT to SNA, 11.12.1906.
8. CA CMT 3/50, Asst CMT to CMT, 17.2.1897.
9. CA PMO 146, Jenner to Milton, 11.7.1895.
10. Union of South Africa, *First Census of the Population of the Union, 1911*, U.G. 32 – 1912, 34.
11. CA NA 617/1881, SNA to Prime Minister, 5.8.1903; SNA to Asst CMT, 6.10.1904; CA NA 519/410 for details on traders' associations and their demands; CA CMT 3/52, Asst CMT to CMT, 22.5.1901.
12. *BBNA*, G. 46 – 1906, 109.
13. Figures for shipping to Port St Johns are in *BBNA*, 1880–99; Cape of Good Hope, Department of the Treasury, *Report on Trade with the Native Territories*, G. 22 – 1905.
14. Information on crop production from *BBNA*, 1895–8.
15. CA PMO 249, Rinderpest in the Transkeian Territories, Memorandum for the Right Honourable the Premier, signed 'S. Cowper', 6.9.1897 and correspondence; *BBNA*, G. 42 – 1898; *Kokstad Advertiser*, 1897; C. van Onselen, 'Reactions to Rinderpest in Southern Africa, 1896–1897', *Journal of African History*, 13, 3 (1972).
16. CA O'D 11, calculated from figures in diary.

17. CA O'D 44, J. P. Bouverie to J. F. Mackenzie, 18.1.1898.
18. CA PMO 249, Report, RM Port St Johns, 15.12.1897 in CMT to SNA, 13.1.1898.
19. Paragraph based on reports by Pondoland magistrates· in *BBNA*, 1899–1905, and Cape, *Census of the Colony of the Cape of Good Hope, 1904*, G. 19 – 1905.
20. CA O'D 13–15, 44–51; C. C. Henkel, *The Native or Transkeian Territories: The Country between the Cape Colony and Natal* (Hamburg, 1903), 46.
21. *BBNA*, G. 52 – 1901, 54.
22. CA CMT 3/97, RM Flagstaff to CMT, 27.12.1902.
23. *BBNA*, G. 12 – 1904, 55.
24. Cape, *Census, 1904*, G. 19 – 1905, 499, 500.
25. See ch. 3, sect. 3; *BBNA*; interviews, e.g. J. Mhatu; see ch. 5, sect. 1.
26. For sheep, see Stanford papers Ca 3, Hargreaves to Stanford, 30.11.1897; CA O'D 12, 13, 15; Cape of Good Hope, Department of Agriculture, *Reports of the Chief Inspector of Sheep*, esp. G. 35 – 1898, 14, G. 37 –1903, 52 and G. 28 – 1904, 83; Davenport, *Afrikaner Bond*, 155–9; CA NA 686/ 2609, CMT to RM Lusikisiki, 17.2.1903 and enclosures.
27. *BBNA*, G. 52 – 1901, 35.
28. *BBNA*, G. 19 – 1909, 51.
29. Keegan, 'Restructuring of Agrarian Class Relations'; Trapido, 'Landlord and Tenant'; S. Marks and S. Trapido, 'Lord Milner and the South African State', *History Workshop Journal*, 8 (1979); Bundy, *South African Peasantry*.
30. CA CMT 3/847/593 (1), RM Mount Frere to CMT, 24.9.1909.
31. *BBNA*, G. 19 – 1909, 37; Union of South Africa, Department of Native Affairs, *Blue Book on Native Affairs, 1910*, U. 17 – 1911, 117 and reports by Pondoland magistrates.
32. E.g. Union, *Blue Book*, U. 17 – 1911, 115.
33. *Ibid.* 140.
34. CA O'D 7, calculated from figures and notes in diary.
35. Prices from *BBNA*, 1904–9, *passim*; Union, *Blue Book*, U. 17–1911, reports by Transkeian magistrates.
36. Shaw and van Warmelo, 'Material Culture of the Cape Nguni', pt 1, 'Settlement'.
37. E.g. interview, Kohlabantu.
38. Hunter, *Reaction to Conquest*, diagram facing 61.
39. *BBNA*, G. 50 – 1900, 45.
40. E.g. *BBNA*, G. 25 – 1908, 23; Bundy, *South African Peasantry*, 130ff.
41. CA CMT 3/882/670, CMT to SNA, 12.9.1911 and enclosures.
42. WMMS, SA Box 22, J. Cameron to Secs., 19.5.1876; CA NA 162, Oxland to SNA, 13.2.1881; CA CMT 1/57, Whindus to CMT, 14.3.1891. R. F. Sieborger, 'The Recruitment and Organisation of African Labour for the Kimberley Diamond Mines, 1871–1888', unpublished M.A. thesis, Rhodes University, 1975, makes no mention of Mpondo workers in the mines in his detailed tables of the origins of workers in Kimberley.

43. *BBNA*, 1896–1909. The annual tables of labour passes show the destination of workers.
44. P. Delius, 'Migrant Labour and the Pedi, 1840–1880', in Marks and Atmore, *Pre-Industrial South Africa*; P. Harries, 'Labour Migration from the Delagoa Bay Hinterland to South Africa: 1852 – 1895', *ICS, SA Seminar*, 7 (1977), 61–76.
45. *BBNA*, G. 19 – 1909, 77, calculated from figures given; *ibid.* 42.
46. C of M, Witwatersrand Native Labour Association Report No. 93/247 (1906), Memorandum on the System of Cattle Advances in the Cape Colony.
47. CA NA 708/F2, CMT to SNA, 18.8.1908 and enclosures; *BBNA*, 1904 –9, reports by Pondoland magistrates.
48. CA PMO 145 A.
49. Cape of Good Hope, Henry Burton, *Memorandum on a Visit to the Native Territories Submitted to the Prime Minister John X. Merriman*, unnumbered confidential print (Cape Town, 1909).
50. CA NA 557/950, A. H. Stanford and W. T. Brownlee to SNA, 15.3.1906.
51. CA NA 708/F2, SNA circular, 10.12.1907.
52. CA NA 557/950, A. H. Stanford and W. T. Brownlee to SNA, 15.3.1906.
53. Information on contracts from sources cited and CA NA 554/950, RM Umzimkulu to SNA, 16.10.1906; CA NA 557/950, SNA Transvaal to SNA Cape, 27.2.1906 and enclosures; CA NA 708/F2, SNA to Sec., Law Department, 29.4.1908; CA NA 712/F2, RM Port St Johns to Asst CMT, 15.3. 1907; CA NA 740/F76, RM Ngqeleni, report 30.1.1911.
54. Interview, Vulizibhaya.
55. CA NA 708/F2, Petition from Pondoland West and Umtata Recruiters, 8.8.1908 in CMT to SNA, 18.8.1908.
56. Cape, Burton, *Memorandum*.
57. CA NA 710/F2, Acting Asst Director GNLB to SNA, 6.1.1910 and Acting RM Libode to SNA, 20.1.1910.
58. PTA TAB SNA 7/742 and 7/745, letters by M. S. Erskine in WNLA reports; C of M, Memo on the System of Cattle Advances; CA NA 557/950, SNA Transvaal to SNA Cape, 27.2.1906 and enclosures.
59. PTA TAB SNA 46/1794, Sec. WNLA to SNA Transvaal, 28.7.1904.
60. PTA TAB SNA 59/3280 and 63/664, *passim*; CA NA 555/950, SNA circular, 28.9.1906; CA NA 609/1701, SNA Transvaal to SNA Cape, 13.4.1903; CA NA 718/F73, RM Mount Frere to CMT, 7.1.1910.
61. CA NA 554/950, RM Umzimkulu to SNA, 16.10.1906; CA NA 708/F2, SNA to Director GNLB, 27.3.1908; CA NA 709/F2, *passim*; CA NA 711/F2, A. M. Mostert to Minister of Native Affairs, 17.6.1910; Cape Archives, Lewis papers, Acc. 2044, vol. I.
62. CA NA 709/F2, SNA circular, 13.1.1910.
63. C of M, N.A. 1825/09, Memorandum on the Position of the Natives Labour Supply in the Proclaimed Labour Districts of the Transvaal as at 31st March, 1909.
64. CA NA 554/950, correspondence on Cape of Good Hope proclamations 101 of 1899 and 191 of 1902.

65. CA NA 527/516, SNA circular, 2.5.1899.
66. CA NA 554/950, cutting from *Cape Times*, 20.7.1899.
67. CA NA 557/950, A. H. Stanford and W. T. Brownlee to SNA, 15.3.1906.
68. CA NA 708/F2, CMT to SNA, 6.4.1908, SNA to Director GNLB, 27.3.1908 and SNA circular, 20.7.1908; CA NA 710/F2, SNA circular, 5.9.1908; CA NA 708/F2, CMT to SNA, 18.8.1908 and enclosures.
69. Cape Burton, *Memorandum*; P. Lewsen, 'Merriman as Last Cape Prime Minister', *South African Historical Journal*, 7 (1975).
70. CA NA 709/F2, SNA Cape to SNA Transvaal, 3.12.1909 and SNA to RM Ngqeleni, 18.2.1910; CA NA 710/F2, SNA circular, 18.6.1910.
71. CA NA 685/2608, S. J. Mabengu to RM Lusikisiki, 23.7.1904.
72. PTA TAB SNA 59/3280 (1905), Statement by Mfitshane to C. Pietersen, Boksburg, 24.10.1905.
73. Cape, Burton, *Memorandum*.
74. CA NA 708/F2, SNA to Sec., Law Department, 29.4.1908.
75. Cape, Lewis papers, vol. I, P. C. Hawkins to Lewis, 7.10.1906.
76. CA NA 718/F473 (1), RM Mount Frere to SNA, 7.1.1910.
77. CA CMT 3/607/49 (8), Conference of Merchants, Traders, Labour Recruiters and Farmers' Associations to Minister of Native Affairs, 22.1.1914.
78. CA CMT 3/607/49 (8), Tshongwana to RM Lusikisiki, 6.3.1914.
79. See *Kokstad Advertiser*, 27.4.1914, letter from G. Lawrence, Flagstaff for evidence of this after East Coast fever.
80. See Hunter, *Reaction to Conquest*, 190ff.
81. CA NA 708/F2, CMT to SNA, 18.8.1908 and enclosures.
82. CA NA 554/950, Acting RM Bizana to SNA, 13.10.1906.
83. PTA TAB SNA 59/3280 (1905), Inspector Native Affairs Department to District Controller, Boksburg, 13.10.1905 and statements by Mpondo workers.
84. CA NA 708/F2, CMT to SNA, 18.8.1908 and enclosures.
85. CA CMT 3/882/670, RM Ngqeleni to CMT, 25.1.1911. in CMT to SNA 12.9.1911.
86. For a fuller discussion of chiefs and headmen, see ch. 4.
87. Rural differentiation is discussed in more detail in ch. 5.

3. Rural production and the South African state, 1911–1930

1. Union, *Blue Book*, U. 17 – 1911, 185; Union, *Census of 1911*, 1357.
2. Union, *Blue Book*, U. 17 – 1911, 62–3.
3. This section is based largely on PTA SA NA 100; CA CMT 3/902 and 3/903; J. R. L. Kingon, 'The Economics of East Coast Fever as Illustrated by the Transkeian Territories', *Report of the South African Association for the Advancement of Science, 1915* (Cape Town, 1916).
4. CA NA 691/2683, enclosing W. Robertson, 'African Coast Fever', *Agricultural Journal*, 1904.
5. CA CMT 3/573/40. See ch. 4, sect. 1 for a more detailed analysis of dipping.

6. *Kokstad Advertiser*, 19.3.1910, 2.4.1910, 28.5.1910 and 1911 and 1912, *passim*; CA CMT 3/884–9/692–4.
7. CA 1/LSK 2/2/2/3, Report by H. Tucker, Stock Inspector, February and March 1914 in Tucker to RM Lusikisiki, 29.3.1914.
8. CA O'D 23, 24. Calculated from figures in diaries.
9. PTA SA NA 98/6011/F179.
10. Paragraph based on CA CMT 3/902/725 (1), RM Bizana to CMT, 18.11.1912; *Kokstad Advertiser*, 22.11.1912; PTA SA NA 100, *passim.*
11. PTA SA NA 100, Minutes of a Meeting of a Deputation from Chief Mare-lane with the Chief Magistrate, 20.11.1912 in CMT to SNA, 23.11.1912.
12. CA CMT 3/902/725 (1), Qanqiso Ndamase to CMT, 8.11.1912.
13. E.g. PTA SA NA 100, RM Lusikisiki to SNA, 25.10.1912 and Callaway to SNA, 30.10.1912; cutting from *Transvaal Daily Mail*, 1.11.1912; CMT to SNA, 2.11.1912.
14. PTA SA NA 100, cutting from *Cape Argus*, no date, report dated 25.10.1912.
15. E.g. CA NA 516/355, RM Kentani to CMT, 30.11.1900 and following cor-respondence.
16. CA CMT 3/902/725 (1), RM Bizana to CMT, 30.10.1912; PTA SA NA 100, C. E. S. King to Ashfield, 8.12.1912; CA O'D 22, 24; CA CMT 3/902/725 (1), RM Bizana to CMT, 18.11.1912; PTA SA NA 100, Director of Native Labour to SNA, 2.12.1912; CMT to SNA, 27.11.1912, 2.12.1912.
17. PTA SA NA 100, CMT to SNA, 4.12.1912, 9.12.1912.
18. PTA SA NA 100, Minute by Director of Native Labour in SNA to CMT, 17.10.1912; Pritchard to SNA, 2.12.1912.
19. CA 1/LSK 6/13/2/6, W. P. Nicol, District Surgeon of Lusikisiki, Reports, 5.3.1913, 20.1.1914, 24.1.1915; RM Lusikisiki, Health Report, 21.1.1914.
20. PTA SA NA 101/351/16/179; CA CMT 3/920/774.3; CA 1/LSK, 6/13/2 for influenza deaths.
21. CA CMT 3/607/49 (7), RM Bizana to CMT, 31.10.1913; CA CMT 3/607/49 (9)), Acting Director of Native Labour circular, 4.10.1916; CA CMT 3/605/49 (2), Director of Native Labour circular, 12.1.1920. For discussion on advances, Union of South Africa, *Report of the Native Grievances Inquiry, 1913–1914*, U.G. 37 – 1914; CA CMT 3/607/49 (7), RM Bizana to CMT, 31.10.1913; RM Port St Johns to CMT, 9.2.1914.
22. CA CMT 3/918/774 (1).
23. E.g. CA CMT 3/902/728.1, Extracts from Debates of Pondoland General Council and TTGC in CMT to SNA, 2.5.1916; CA CMT 3/918/774 (1), Extracts from TTGC Debate, 1917.
24. CA CMT 3/552/36, Sec., Mount Frere Traders' Association to CMT, 20.3.1917 and correspondence following; PTA SA NA 80, SNA to CMT, 9.8.1917.
25. See ch. 4, sect. 1.
26. CA 1/LSK 3/4/2/2 (27.1); CA CMT 3/941/183 and 3/884–92/692–6.
27. CA 1/LSK 3/4/2/2 (27.1), Senior Veterinary Surgeon (Transkei) to RM Lusikisiki, 23.5.1913 and following correspondence concerning permits. For permits to remove hides, see also CA CMT 3/892/696.

187

28. CA 1/LSK 4/27/1, RM Lusikisiki to Senior Veterinary Surgeon, 2.5.1918.
29. Library of Parliament, Unprinted Annexures to House of Assembly Debates, An. 242 – 1915, Report by W. Stanford on the Disturbances in East Griqualand, 1914; CA CMT 3/918/774 (1), RM Mount Fletcher to CMT, 14.9.1914; CA CMT 3/903/728.2, RM Engcobo to CMT, 31.12.1918.
30. Hunter, *Reaction to Conquest*, 141.
31. Interview, Lawrence.
32. House of Assembly, An. 242 – 1915, Stanford's Report; CA 1/LSK 3/4/2/2 (27.1), CMT circular, 10.8.1915.
33. CA CMT 3/903/728.2, CMT to SNA, 4.2.1919; Senior Vet (Transkei) to CMT, 15.2.1919.
34. CA CMT 3/921/774.3 (2), RM Engcobo to CMT, 22.1.1920.
35. F. Wilson and D. Perrot, *Outlook on a Century: South Africa 1870–1970* (Lovedale/Johannesburg, 1973), 320.
36. Hunter, *Reaction to Conquest*, 388.
37. *PGC, 1916*, 12; see *PGC, 1917*, 22; *PGC, 1918*, 17. For discussion of bridewealth, see ch. 3, sect. 3.
38. *PGC, 1914*, 38; *PGC, 1917*, 13; *PGC, 1918*, 8; *PGC, 1919*, 9, 15.
39. F. Wilson, *Labour in the South African Gold Mines 1911–1969* (Cambridge, 1972), 146.
40. See ch. 3, sect. 4.
41. Hunter, *Reaction to Conquest*, 68–9.
42. CA 1/LBE 4/2/3/22/9, Asst RM Libode to Mangala, 22.9.1914; CA CMT 3/918/774 (1), RM Mount Ayliff to CMT, 1.9.1914 and CMT to Sec. for Finance, 15.9.1914; CA CMT 3/903/782 (2), CMT to SNA 4.2.1919; *PGC, 1920*, 14; *PGC, 1922*, 9; *Umcebisi Womlimi Nomfuyi*, 3, 4 (Dec. 1927), 27ff.
43. *Umcebisi*, 4, 6 (Dec. 1928), 4.
44. CA CMT 3/918/774 (1), Malcolmess and Co. to CMT, 1.9.1915, RM Tabankulu to CMT, 27.2.1918 and F. Meth to RM Tabankulu, 26.3.1918; *Umcebisi*, 3, 1 (March 1927), 4; interview, Moncur.
45. Interview, Xinwa.
46. *PGC, 1929*, 31.
47. F. W. Fox and D. Back, 'A Preliminary Survey of the Agricultural and Nutritional Problems of the Ciskei and Transkeian Territories, with Special Reference to Their Bearing upon the Recruiting of Labourers for the Gold Mining Industry', unpublished typescript, Johannesburg, 1938?, 9.
48. CA 1/LBE 9/2/9/2, Annual Report, 1931; Union of South Africa, *Report of the Native Economic Commission, 1930–1932*, U.G. 22 – 1932, 10.
49. J. P. H. Acocks, *Veld Types of South Africa* (Pretoria, 1975), 19–21; interviews, J. Norton, Mathanda and Thandekhaya, Mgeyana, Hall-Green, Mathandabuzo.
50. CA PMO, Asst CMT to Sec., Prime Minister's Office, 22.7.1898.
51. Union, *Native Economic Commission*, U.G. 22 – 1932, 11ff; Hunter, *Reaction to Conquest*, 65–71, 550; *Umcebisi*, 3, 1 (March 1927).
52. *Umcebisi*, 3, 4 (Dec. 1927), 27.
53. Fox and Back, 'Preliminary Survey', 44.

54. CA 1/LSK 38/2/9/2, Annual Reports, 1932–6.
55. CA 1/LSK, 38/2/9/2, RM Lusikisiki, Annual Report, 1934.
56. The following paragraphs are based on extensive records of the agricultural demonstration scheme in CA CMT 3/847–50/593. See also *Umcebisi*, 1925–33, *passim*; interviews with agricultural demonstrators Nkonya, Sigwili, Mpateni and Magazi and agricultural official Hall-Green; Fox and Back, 'Preliminary Survey', 70–80.
57. *Umcebisi*, 2, 4 (Dec. 1926), 2.
58. *Umcebisi*, 4, 4 (Aug. 1928), 13.
59. CA CMT 3/848/593.1 (1) and (2), Hughes to CMT, 8.6.1920, 18.7.1922; *Umcebisi*, 2, 4 (Dec. 1926), 3.
60. Interviews, Mathandabuzo, Nkonya; see ch. 5, sect. 1.
61. CA CMK 1/114, G. C. Brisley to RM Umzimkulu, 24.12.1886 in Annual Report, 1886.
62. CA CMT 3/772/353, Savage and Sons to SNA, 27.3.1906 and *passim*; *Izwi Labantu*, 28.8.1906, 27.11.1906, 18.2.1907.
63. A. van Reyneveld, 'The Pondoland Cotton Experiment', *Practical Agriculture*, 1, 2 (March 1914), 72–5; interview, Birkett; Dominions Royal Commission, *Royal Commission on the Natural Resources, Trade, and Legislation of Certain Portions of His Majesty's Dominions, Part I*, Cd. 7706 (1914), 274–84; *Kokstad Advertiser*, 14.11.1911, 30.8.1912, 4.10.1912.
64. See ch. 4, sect. 3.
65. CA CMT 3/714/281.5, RM Port St Johns to CMT, 6.2.1915.
66. CA CMT 3/849–50/593 (5)–(8); CA CMT 3/818/774 (1), CMT to SNA, 29.6.1915 and following correspondence.
67. CA CMT 3/848/593.1 (1), Reports by Hughes to CMT, 1919 and 1920; *Territorial News*, 10.1.1924, 31.1.1924; Union of South Africa, Department of Agriculture, *Report*, U.G. 13 – 1921, 53; Department of Native Affairs, *Report*, U.G. 34 – 1922, 15.
68. Following based on *Royal Commission on Natural Resources, Part I*, Cd. 7706, 191ff, 199ff, 235ff, 278ff; newspaper advertisements; CA O'D 47, 50; interviews, Ned Xinwa, H. W. Clarke.
69. CA CMT 3/930/778.3, Director of Supplies, Defence Department to CMT, ?.2.1917 and correspondence following.
70. CA CMT 3/919/774 (3), Census of Agriculture Returns, 1920–1; cf. Cape, *Census, 1904*.
71. CA CMT 3/875/648, Sec., Ngqeleni Traders' Association to Senator W. Stanford, 29.7.1921 and *passim*.
72. CA CMT 3/875/648.
73. CA CMT 3/875/648, Sec., Ngqeleni Traders' Association to W. Stanford, 29.7.1921; CA CMT 3/851/596, Meetings, 12.9.1921, 12.5.1922; *East London Daily Dispatch*, 21.10.1921, 1.11.1921; *Territorial News*, 1924, *passim*; *PGC, 1922*, 9; *Umcebisi*, 9, 5 (Oct. 1933).
74. Union, *Agricultural Censuses*, 1924–37.
75. See ch. 4, sect. 3.
76. CA CMT 3/919/774 (2); CA CMT 3/942/817.

77. CA CMT 3/827/561 (1)–(3), SNA to CMT, 18.12.1914 and correspondence following.
78. CA CMT 3/827/561 (2), RM Libode to CMT, 5.1.1916; RM Lusikisiki to CMT, 12.1.1916.
79. 3/827/561 (2), W. Stuart to CMT, 26.1.1916; *PGC, 1916*, 10, 18.
80. *Territorial News*, 24.4.1919.
81. T. Bell, *Industrial Decentralisation in South Africa* (Cape Town, 1973), 26–30.
82. Calculations based on age breakdowns in Union Censuses.
83. See ch. 5, sects. 1, 2.
84. See ch. 4, sect. 3.
85. CA CMT 3/604/49, RM Flagstaff to Director of Native Labour, 22.11.1919 and enclosures; CA CMT 3/605/49 (2), SNA to CMT, 6.9.1916; CA 1/LSK Criminal Cases, 1912–24, *R. v. George Wardle, Neil Mackenzie and J. B. Mackenzie*; interview, Bartwell Nkonya.
86. CA CMT 3/604–8/49, 49 (2), 49 (8).
87. Hunter, *Reaction to Conquest*, 60, 546ff.
88. CA 1/LSK 38/2/9/2, Annual Report for 1932.
89. Interview, Ned Xinwa.
90. Hunter, 'Status of Pondo Women' and 'The Pondo and Xhosa Family'; Hunter, *Reaction to Conquest*, 189–203; CA 1/LSK Civil Cases; CA 1/LBE 9/2/9/2, Annual Report 1930; interviews, esp. Mgeyana.
91. P. Harries, 'Kinship, Ideology and the Origins of Migrant Labour', unpublished, 1980; C. Murray, 'High Bridewealth, Migrant Labour and the Position of Women in Lesotho', *Journal of African Law*, 21, 1 (1977).
92. See ch. 4, sect. 3.
93. Hunter, *Reaction to Conquest*, 1, 61–4; interviews, esp. Kohlabantu, Vulizibhaya. Cf. D. H. Reader, *Zulu Tribe in Transition* (Manchester, 1966), 76ff.
94. G. M. B. Whitfield, *South African Native Law*, 2nd edn (Cape Town, 1949), 257–64; CA CMT 3/868/635 (3), Tshongwana to RM Lusikisiki and following correspondence; *PGC, 1918*, 19; *PGC, 1919*, 13; *PGC, 1921*, 10; cf. CA CMT 3/880/663, RM Mount Ayliff to CMT, 5.10.1915.
95. Interview, Kohlabantu.
96. Following two paragraphs based on interviews, esp. Bartwell Nkonya, Mpateni, Kohlabantu, Mathandabuzo, Mathanda, Fono, Xinwa, Mgeyana, Sihlobo, Daisy Ball. CA CMT 3/919/774/3, G. J. Bosman, Report on the Status of the Maize Industry in the Transkeian Territories, 1922?.
97. See ch. 4, sect. 1.
98. Interviews, Kohlabantu, Mpateni, Nkonya.
99. Interviews, Hedding, Heathcote; National Institute for Personnel Research (South Africa), 'A Study of the Factors Influencing the Seasonal Flow of Migratory Labour from Three Districts of the Transkeian Territories', unpublished interim report, Sept. 1958.
100. Ch. 4, sect. 3.
101. See correspondence about census returns and crops in CA CMT 3/919–20/774 and 3/903/728.

102. CA CMT 3/846/585 (10), Extract from Officials' Conference.
103. CA CMT 3/919/774 (3), E. Muller, Census Supervisor, to Acting Director of Census, 1.12.1919. See also CA CMT 3/918/774 (1).
104. See ch. 5, sects. 1, 2.
105. For imports, see CA CMT 3/920/774.3 (3). Interviews, Deutschmann, Lawrence, Heathcote, Gregory. There are figures in the TTGC reports on quantities bought in the 1920s, but they appear to be too unreliable to use in the analysis.
106. S. B. Ngcobo, 'Taxation of Africans in South Africa, 1849–1939', unpublished Ph.D. thesis, University of London, 1964; McLoughlin papers, 'The Transkeian System of Native Administration'; H. Rogers, *Native Administration in the Union of South Africa* (Johannesburg, 1933); McLoughlin papers, Meeting between CMT and Mswakeli, 30.11.1925.

4. Chiefs and headmen in Pondoland, 1905–1930

1. See ch. 1, sect. 3.
2. CA NA 686/2610; CA NA 751/F142.
3. See ch. 5, sect. 3; interview, G. Dana.
4. CA NA 751/F142, J. Henderson to SNA, 31.8.1908 and correspondence following.
5. CA NA 526/509 and 691/2683 for correspondence on Councils and tanks.
6. CA CMT 3/824/558, Report of Meeting between Chief Magistrate and the Pondos, 17.12.1909; CA CMT 3/829/567, RM Lusikisiki to CMT, 11.11. 1909 and correspondence following.
7. CA CMT 3/824/558, Meeting, 17.12.1909.
8. CA CMT 3/829/567, CMT to SNA, 13.11.1909; RM Lusikisiki to CMT, 20.11.1909 and Meeting, Lusikisiki, 12.11.1909, esp. statement by Bodweni.
9. CA CMT 3/829/567, Meeting, 12.11.1909.
10. CA CMT 3/824/558, Meeting, 17.12.1909.
11. Poto, *Ama-Mpondo*, 51; Hunter, *Reaction to Conquest*, 400; A Groser, *South African Experiences in Cape Colony, Natal, and Pondoland* (London, 1891), 38; CA CMT 3/824/582, RM Bizana to CMT, 9.5.1922; CA 1/LBE 4/2/3/22/9, Acting CMT to RM Libode, 28.12.1915.
12. CA CMT 3/824/558, Meeting, 17.12.1909.
13. CA CMT 3/829/567, SNA to CMT, 25.11.1909.
14. CA NA 751/F142, CMT to SNA, 23.2.1910 and following correspondence; CA CMT 3/842/582, Meeting, 18.2.1910.
15. CA CMT 3/842/582, Marelane to CMT, 25.8.1911.
16. For this episode, see CA CMT 3/868/635, 635 (3) and 635 (4). File 635 (2), covering the height of the crisis in 1914, is missing. See also Rhodes University, Cory Library, PR 1140–2, Obituaries in *E.G.* (*Education Gazette*), 9.9.1921, *Christian Express*, 1.9.1921, *Territorial News*.
17. House of Assembly, An. 242 – 1915, Stanford's Report; PTA SA NA 83, 84; CA CMT 3/790–1/425; CA 1/QBU 1/1, RM Qumbu to CMT, 20.11.1914.

18. E.g. CA CMT 3/714/281.5, Meeting at Port St Johns, 25.6.1915; CA CMT 3/824/558, Meeting, Lusikisiki, 12.12.1919; CA CMT 3/835/572.21.

19. *Christian Express*, 1.6.1921; W. D. Cingo in *Territorial News*, 11.8.1921.

20. On education, see CA 1/LSK 8/29/14; *PGC, 1912–30*, including Accounts of the Eastern Pondoland Trust Fund; Province of the Cape of Good Hope, Department of Public Education, *Reports of the Superintendent-General of Education, 1915–1921*. For Cingo's views, see *Kokstad Advertiser*, 11.9.1914; *Territorial News*, 11.8.1921; *Forward*, Dec. 1928.

21. Cape Province, *Report of the Superintendent-General of Education for the Year ended 31st. December 1919*, C.P. 4 – 1920, including *Report of the Commission on Native Education*, 60–106.

22. CA CMT 3/842/582 (3), CMT to RM Lusikisiki, 14.7.1919 and CMT to SNA, 22.7.1919; CA 1/LSK 2/2/2/3, RM Lusikisiki to CMT, 7.2.1921 and following correspondence.

23. Interview, G. Dana; CA 1/LSK 2/2/2/3, Dana to RM Lusikisiki, 18.3.1921.

24. For an outline of segregationist thinking, see M. Legassick, 'The Making of South African "Native Policy", 1903–1923'.

25. CA 1/LSK 2/2/2/3, Acting CMT circular, 2.1.1914.

26. See this ch. sect. 2 for analysis of disputes.

27. S. Marks, 'Natal, the Zulu Royal Family'; CA CMT 3/842/582 (3), RM Lusikisiki to CMT, 4.9.1917.

28. Following paragraph based on CA CMT 3/851/596 (1); Poto, *Ama-Mpondo*, introduction. For South African Native Labour Contingent, see CA CMT 3/925–9/778.

29. CA CMT 3/846/585 (10), Draft for Minute by CMT, 30.8.1920.

30. For further information on immigrants, see ch. 5, sect. 1; CA CMT 3/594/45 (4), RM Tabankulu to CMT and correspondence following; CA CMT 3/851/596 (1), RM Ngqeleni to CMT, 8.9.1915 and CMT to RM Ngqeleni, 22.11.1915.

31. CA CMT 3/593/45, *passim*; Bundy, *South African Peasantry*, 136–7; Lewsen, 'Merriman as Last Cape Prime Minister'.

32. CA CMT 3/595/45 (7), Statement of Mazangazanga, Tabankulu, 4.1.1913 and CA CMT 3/593–6/45 to 45 (9), *passim*.

33. CA NA 499 deals with Mhlangaso during his exile. For details of this dispute, see CA CMT 3/793/422, esp. CMT to SNA, 21.9.1911 and enclosures; CA CMT 3/842/582, SNA to CMT, 16.3.1910 and *passim*; PTA SA NA 89, Notes of a Meeting of Chief Marelane and Pondos with the Chief Magistrate, 7.9.1911 and Interview of a Deputation from Chief Marelane, 8.3.1912.

34. CA CMT 3/824/558, Meeting, 17.12.1909; CA NA 751/F142, CMT to SNA, 19.2.1910.

35. See ch. 1, sect. 3.

36. Hammond-Tooke papers, files 11-605 and 11-650, CMT to RMs Pondoland, 29.11.1924; RM Bizana to CMT, 11.11.1924; Statement by I. Godlwana to Hammond-Tooke, 10.2.1956; CA 1/LSK 38/2/9/2, Report on Tribal Matters.

37. Hunter, *Reaction to Conquest*, 428.
38. Interviews, Mgeyana, Dana, Xinwa, Laqwela.
39. For extensive correspondence on Toli, see McLoughlin papers (Toli's new location was called Bomvini); CA CMT 3/713/271; CA CMT 3/959/3/213; CA CMT 3/824/558, Meeting, 7.9.1911; CA CMT 3/842/582, Meeting, 18.2.1910; CA 1/LSK 2/2/2/3, Acting CMT to RM Lusikisiki, 8.8.1914 and correspondence following. The quotation is from CA CMT 3/842/582, Marelane to CMT, 26.3.1911 in CMT to Under SNA, 17.12.1909.
40. PTA SA NA 79, RM Lusikisiki to RM Flagstaff, 13.5.1908 and following correspondence; CA CMT 3/713/271, Asst CMT to SNA, 22.12.1911 and following correspondence.
41. For other disputes over headmanship, see CA CMT 3/713/271, 3/851/596 (2), 3/959/3/213, 3/954/2/62, 3/954/2/29, 3/714/281.5; McLoughlin papers; District Record Books; 1/LSK 2/2/2/3.
42. See esp. dispute over location no. 9, Bizana, in McLoughlin papers.
43. CA 1/LSK 2/2/2/3, Acting CMT to RM Lusikisiki, 17.6.1914, Tshongwana to RM Lusikisiki, 11.5.1912 and Meeting, 7.2.1911; CA 1/LSK 184/2/28/2/24; interview, Laqwela; McLoughlin papers; CMT 3/959/2/29, RM Lusikisiki to CMT, 23.7.1925.
44. CA CMT 3/959/3/212.
45. CA CMT 3/954/2/29, Meeting between Mswakeli and CMT, 7.4.1925.
46. CA CMT 3/959/3/213, Meeting between Mswakeli and CMT, 30.11.1925.
47. CA CMT 3/954/2/62, CMT to RM Libode, 1.9.1922 and enclosure, Meeting, 22.8.1922.
48. CA CMT 3/609/50.
49. CA CMT 3/609/50, CMT to SNA, 9.5.1911 and previous correspondence.
50. Paragraph based on *PGC, 1912–19, passim*; PTA SA NA 134/5195/12/F253, Minutes of Libode District Council, 25.1.1912; *PGC, 1917*, 10; *PGC, 1918*, 9; *TTGC, Minutes of Convention Held ... to Consider the Amalgamation of the Transkeian Territories General Council and the Pondoland General Council* (Umtata, 1929?), 2; CA CMT 3/846/585 (10), Draft for CMT Minute, 30.8.1920; CA CMT 3/851/596 (2), Meeting, 4.1.1922.
51. CA CMT 3/822/545, Carmichael to CMT, 5.1.1917 and notes.
52. CA CMT 3/951/4/212, CMT to SNA, 11.3.1926 and following correspondence.
53. Interview, Dana.
54. TTGC, *Minutes of Convention; PGC, 1928–30.*
55. CA 1/LSK 8/29/14.
56. Poto. *Ama-Mpondo*; cf. W. Cingo, *Ibali lama-Mpondo* (Palmerton, 1925).
57. J. T. Kenyon, *An Address on the General Council Administrative System of the Transkeian Territories, October 1932* (Umtata, 193?), 12–15; Hunter, *Reaction to Conquest*, 421–6; J. Lewin, *Studies in African Native Law* (Cape Town, 1947), 13–31.
58. *PGC, 1917*, 11; CA NA 686/2609, Meeting, 17.2.1903 in CMT to SNA, 3.3.1903 and Mabengu to Asst CMT, 24.3.1904; cf. CA CMT 3/827/561 (2), CMT circular, 29.10.1915.

59. E.g. Henkel, *Native Territories*, 124; *BBNA*, G. 24 – 1908, 24; *Daily Dispatch*, 5.2.1920.
60. CA CMT 3/714/281.5, Minutes of Meeting between Mangala and CMT, 17.5.1916.
61. P. Walshe, *The Rise of African Nationalism in South Africa* (London, 1970).
62. *Kokstad Advertiser*, 16.1.1914. For Msimang's reply and subsequent debate, see *ibid.* 23.1.1914, 6.2.1914, 13.3.1914, 3.4.1914.
63. PTA SA NA 61, CMT to SNA, 25.5.1905; CA CMT 3/824/558, Meeting, 7.9.1911 in CMT to SNA, 18.9.1911. See Beinart, 'Political Economy of Pondoland', ch. 2.
64. CA CMT 3/714/281.5, Meeting, 17.5.1916.
65. CA CMT 3/880/663, *passim*, esp. CMT to RM Qumbu, 22.8.1918; Hunter, *Reaction to Conquest*, 112–7, 119.
66. McLoughlin papers, 'Transkeian System of Native Administration', 131 and *passim*; *PGC 1926*, 9, 10.
67. *PGC, 1920*, 11; CA CMT 3/959/15/415 and 416; CA CMT 3/851/596 (2), Notes of Meeting between CMT and Poto, 4.1.1922; CA CMT 3/824/558, Skeleton Report of Meeting Held in Lusikisiki, 11.4.1922; Hammond-Tooke files, CMT to RM Libode, 20.12.1923.
68. CA CMT 3/714/281.5, Meeting, 17.5.1916.
69. See ch. 5, sect. 1.
70. *Territorial News*, 6.3.1919.
71. Ch. 1, sect. 1; Hunter, *Reaction to Conquest*, 71–5, 112–17 and *passim*. The question of land tenure and allocation was touched on in many interviews.
72. E.g. CA CMT 3/918/774 (1), RM Tabankulu to CMT, 4.1.1918.
73. *PGC, 1928*, 44–6, 51; *PGC, 1929*, 37; interviews, Xinwa, Mpateni; Fox and Back, 'Preliminary Survey', 32, 33; CA CMT 3/880/667, esp. RM Mount Ayliff to CMT, 7.10.1920 and following correspondence.
74. CA CMT 3/712/270.4 (1), RM Libode to CMT, 16.1.1911 and previous correspondence; CA NA 676/B2555.
75. *PGC, 1928*, 44–6; *PGC, 1929*, 37; Fox and Back, 'Preliminary Survey'.
76. CA 1/LBE 4/2/3/22/9, RM Libode to CMT, 19.3.1914; CA CMT, 3/842/582 (3), Meeting, 25.6.1914.
77. CA CMT 3/880/667.
78. *PGC, 1927*, 25.
79. CA CMT 3/851/596 (2), Report of Meeting, 1920 in SNA to CMT, 12.8.1920; *PGC, 1929*, 36ff; *PGC, 1930*, 61.

5. Rural differentiation, alliance and conflict, 1910–1930

1. Bundy, *South African Peasantry*.
2. Information has been taken from a limited number of interviews, but tends to accord with the leading themes emerging in the interviews as a whole and with available documentary evidence.
3. Interviews, Dana, MacGowan; *PGC, 1929*, 45; *BBNA*, G. 5 – 1896, 116; CA CMT 3/842/582 (3), Meeting between Mpondo Deputation and CMT, 25.6.1914.

4. Interview, Vulizibhaya.
5. Following based on interviews, Mpateni, Nkonya, Mathanda, Heathcote; *PGC, 1914*, 30ff; *PGC, 1929*, 37; PTA SA NA 100, CMT to SNA, 7.11.1912 and enclosures; Hunter, *Reaction to Conquest*, 386–8.
6. Interview, Mpateni.
7. Interviews, Nkonya, Mpateni, Mathanda, Stanford Sigcau, Fono, Nonkonyana, Lanyazima.
8. Interview, Mathanda. The number of cattle probably refers only to those in the kraal, not those out on loan; cf. Hunter, *Reaction to Conquest*, 143.
9. Interview, Xatsha Cingo.
10. Hunter, *Reaction to Conquest*, 61ff.
11. *PGC, 1916*, 18.
12. For discussions on employment, see *PGC, passim*.
13. Hunter, *Reaction to Conquest*, 110; *PGC, passim*. For a comparison of teachers' pay to that received by others in urban and rural employment, see Cape Province, *Report of the Superintendent-General of Education, 1919*, C.P. 4 – 1920, 106.
14. See N. A. Etherington, *Preachers, Peasants and Politics in Southeast Africa, 1835–1880: African Christian Communities in Natal, Pondoland and Zululand* (London, 1978), 71–4 for a brief assessment of mission work in Pondoland.
15. G. Callaway, *Pioneers in Pondoland*, (Lovedale, 1939), chs. 12, 13; E. Green and E. Eldridge, *A Pondoland Hilltop* (London, 1938?); Hunter, *Reaction to Conquest*.
16. CA CMT 3/593–7/45 to 45 (14); interviews, J. Mhatu, E. Mhatu, Nkonya, Mpateni.
17. Interviews, Xinwa, Mathandabuzo, Godlwana, Ben Siposo Ndabeni.
18. For early contact between the Cingo family and the missionaries, see WMMS, SA Box 21, W. Milward to Secs., 20.4.1874.
19. Interviews, Dana, Nkonya, Magazi, Mvunelo; R. Hunt-Davis, 'School vs. Blanket and Settler: Elijah Makiwane and the Leadership of the Cape School Community', *African Affairs*, 78, 310 (1979); W. Beinart, 'Conflict in Qumbu: Rural Consciousness, Ethnicity and Violence in the Colonial Transkei (1880–1913)', paper for Conference on History and Anthropology in Southern Africa, Manchester, 1980.
20. Interview, Mpateni.
21. Figures from Union, *Census, 1936*; MLO, Umtata, back files. Sporadic figures for migrancy to Natal in e.g. CA CMT 3/604/49, CMT circular, 19.12.1920 and replies; MLO, Johannesburg office, Kokstad files 1947–8; see Union, *Native Economic Commission*, U.G. 22 – 1932, 129.
22. Interview, E. Mhatu.
23. Interview, Elliot Jamjam.
24. Interview, Vulizibhaya. For general information on mine labour, see e.g. Union, *Native Economic Commission*; Fox and Back, 'Preliminary Survey'; F. Wilson, *Labour in the Gold Mines*; MLO, Umtata Office, back files; interviews, W. Hedding, Xatsha Cingo, Kohlabantu, Nkwakwa and Mbokoma, Vulizibhaya.

25. C. van Onselen, *Chibaro* (London, 1976).
26. Fox and Back, 'Preliminary Survey', 247; MLO, back files; Hunter, *Reaction to Conquest*, 108–10.
27. Interviews, Kohlabantu, Xatsha Cingo.
28. Union, *Native Economic Commission*, 128–34, 301; Herbst papers, Minutes of Evidence to the Native Economic Commission, 1971, 2102, 2132; Hunter, *Reaction to Conquest*, 109; R. G. T. Watson, *Tongaati: An African Experiment* (London, 1960); CA CMT 3/607-8/49 (9)-(10), *passim*; interviews, Heathcote, Mgeyana, J. Norton.
29. *PGC, 1921*, 11; *PGC, 1930*, 26–30; CA 1/LSK 15/2/18/22, Meeting between Mswakeli and RM, Lusikisiki, 4.7.1924; CA 1/LSK 38/2/9/2, Annual Reports, 1934 and 1936.
30. Interview, Mgeyana.
31. These averages, drawn from stock figures, estimates of production and estimates of family size, cannot be calculated with any accuracy. Cf. Union, *Native Economic Commission*, 41; Fox and Back, 'Preliminary Survey', 39, 108. See ch. 3, sect. 4.
32. Hunter, *Reaction to Conquest*, 142.
33. Union of South Africa, Department of Native Affairs, Report of the Departmental Committee Regarding the Culling of Livestock in the Native Areas, unpublished, (1951?), 98, 99.
34. Hunter, *Reaction to Conquest*, 434 – 502.
35. Esp. P. Mayer, *Townsmen or Tribesmen* (Cape Town, 1971); Wilson, 'Growth of Peasant Communities'; See Bundy, *South African Peasantry*, 95–100, for a sensitive discussion of areas of conflict.
36. Beinart, 'Conflict in Qumbu'.
37. CA CMT 3/594/45 (4), Tshongwana to RM Lusikisiki, 15.9.1910.
38. *PGC, 1914*, 18.
39. C. C. Saunders, 'Tile and the Thembu Church', *Journal of African History*, 11, 4 (1970); Cory Library, MS. 15,799, H. Rock, 'Reminiscences'; CA NA 497, 498; CA CMT 3/196A, RM Lusikisiki to CMT, 6.6.1900; CA CMT 3/938/787; CA CMT 3/594/45 (4), RM Bizana to CMT, 23.10.1912.
40. CA CMT 3/714/281.5, Meeting, 17.5.1916; ch. 4, sect. 3; interview, Majambe; CA CMT 3/851/596 (2), Meeting of a Deputation of the Western Pondos with the Chief Magistrate, 4.1.1922; Hunter, *Reaction to Conquest*, 432; See regular reports from Qaukeni in *Imvo Zabantsundu*, 1921, 1922 for the milieu at the eastern Mpondo Great Place.
41. *Imvo Zabantsundu*, 2.5.1922; 1/LSK 38/2/9/2, Annual Report 1929 and Report on Farmers' Associations by R. Bennie, 1934; CA CMT 43/919/774 (2); CA CMT 3/968/35/50, CMT to SNA, 15.12.1931; interview, R. Bennie; *Umcebisi*, 1926–30, *passim*; Hunter, *Reaction to Conquest*, 143.
42. Walshe, *Rise of African Nationalism; Territorial News*, 6.3.1919; CA CMT 3/851/596 (2), SNA to CMT, 13.9.1920 and following correspondence; Hammond-Tooke papers, CMT minute, 30.8.1920 and enclosures; interview, Dana.
43. Ch. 4, sect. 1.

44. Interview, Nkonya.
45. Hunter, *Reaction to Conquest*, 428; *PGC, passim*: e.g. *1913*, 14ff; *1915*, 10; *1918*, 18; *1920*, 9; *1921*, 12ff; CA CMT 3/592/45, Evidence to the Departmental Commission on Native Passes.
46. W. Beinart and C. Bundy, 'State Intervention and Rural Resistance: The Transkei, 1900–1965', in Klein, *Peasants in Africa*.
47. BPP, C. 5022, 177; T. R. Beattie, *A Ride through the Transkei* (Kingwilliamstown, 1891), 66; MacQuarrie, *Stanford*, vol. II, 61; CA CMT 3/918/774.1, CMT circular 23.12.1916 and correspondence; CA NA 707/2966.
48. R. Edgar, 'Garveyism in Africa: Dr Wellington and the "American" Movement in the Transkei', *ICS, SA Seminar*, 6 (1976); Beinart and Bundy, 'State Intervention'; Hunter, *Reaction to Conquest*, 570–2; interviews, Soji, Nkonya, Gqambuleni *et al.*, Mvunelo; S. Trapido (ed.), C. Kadalie, *My Life and the ICU* (London, 1970); P. Wickins, *The Industrial and Commercial Workers' Union of Africa* (Cape Town, 1978); 1/LSK 38/2/9/2, Annual Report for 1929; Natal Archives, Chief Native Commissioner 348/ 1/29/7 (reference from R. Edgar).
49. *PGC, 1928*, 49; cf. CA 1/LBE, 9/2/9/2, Annual Report for 1930.
50. PTA TAB SNA 59/3280 (1905); Union of South Africa, *Judicial Commission of Inquiry into the Witwatersrand Disturbances, June–July 1913*, U.G. 56 – 1913, 235; P. Bonner, 'The 1920 Black Mine-Workers' Strike: A Preliminary Account', unpublished, 1978; microfilms from Department of Justice files, School of Oriental and African Studies, University of London.
51. C. van Onselen, 'The Regiment of the Hills: South Africa's Lumpenproletariat Army, 1890–1920', *Past and Present*, 80 (1978); van Onselen, 'The Witches of Suburbia: Domestic Servants in Johannesburg', unpublished, 1977.
52. *Daily Dispatch*, 21.1.1930, 30.1.1930; CA 1/LSK 38/2/9/2, Annual Report, 1934; *PGC, 1928*, 41; *United Transkeian Territories General Council: Proceedings and Reports*, 1928, 1933, 92; CA 1/LBE 5, RM Libode to Poto, 9.10.1928; information from F. Deyi.
53. Interviews, Nelson Sigcau, Heathcote, Dana, Deyi; Hammond-Tooke files, J. S. de Villiers and Son to Lt-Col. R. Fyfe King, 7.7.1942 and following correspondence and memoranda on *Sigcau* v. *Sigcau*; District Record Book, Flagstaff, esp. speech by Chief Magistrate on Botha's installation; Beinart and Bundy, 'State Intervention'.

Postscript

1. For comparative material see Bundy, *South African Peasantry*, ch.8; Palmer and Parsons, *Roots of Rural Poverty*; Union, *Native Economic Commission*; Wilson, 'Growth of Peasant Communities', in Wilson and Thompson, *Oxford History of South Africa*, vol. II.
2. See ch. 4, sect. 3.
3. See ch. 3, sect. 2.

Select bibliography

GOVERNMENT ARCHIVES AND PRIVATE PAPERS

Official papers
(Grouped by archival location and series.)

Public Record Office, London
Great Britain, Colonial Office (PRO CO), series 48 and 179.

Cape Town Archives Depot
(The South African Archives were open till 1925, when the bulk of research was done. Since 1979 they have been open till 1950, and a few documents have been obtained from boxes previously closed to research.)
Cape of Good Hope, Prime Minister's Office (CA PMO).
Cape of Good Hope, Native Affairs Department (CA NA), especially vols. 505–760; correspondence files on all aspects of administration from 1896 to 1912, when the series ends.
Cape of Good Hope and Union of South Africa, Chief Magistrate of the Transkeian Territories (CA CMT). Union brought no sharp break in the administration of the Transkeian Territories. The papers of the Chief Magistrate continued to be received by the Cape Archives depot and were classified in series 3 of the archive, begun in 1891. Volumes 3/47–52 and 3/55 (papers received from Assistant Chief Magistrate and Resident Magistrates, Eastern Pondoland) and 3/592–3/959 (correspondence files on all aspects of administration, *c.* 1906–30) were especially important.
Union of South Africa, Resident Magistrates. There are separate series, in the Cape Archives, for each of the Resident Magistrates (RMs) in the Transkeian Territories. Few had been sorted or inventoried when archival research was done. References to the RM Lusikisiki (CA 1/LSK) series were taken from the initial transfer boxes. Since then the series has been sorted, and copies of documents have been obtained from the newly numbered boxes. It has not been possible to relocate the old references. References beginning 1/ to 6/ are to the old boxes; the rest are to the new. Reference has been made to the archives of the RM Libode (1/LBE), RM Flagstaff (1/FSF) and RM Qumbu (1/QBU).

198

Union Buildings, Pretoria

Transvaal Colony, Native Affairs Department (PTA TAB SNA), correspondence files of the Secretary of Native Affairs, 1902–10.
Union of South Africa, Secretary of Native Affairs (PTA SA NA), correspondence files on all aspects of administration, 1910–25.

Magisterial Headquarters, Transkei

District Record books, Bizana, Flagstaff, Libode, Lusikisiki, Port St Johns, Tabankulu. (The district record books are kept at the various magisterial offices. Most were started in the 1930s and contain information, often dating back to the nineteenth century, on the genealogies of local chiefs, the demarcation of district and location boundaries, names of state employees, rainfall figures etc.)

Non-official papers

British and Foreign Anti-Slavery and Aborigines Protection Society (APS) (Rhodes House, Oxford). Series G, no. 10; Series C, 126, 141, 149. Correspondence received from and concerning Pondoland.
Chamber of Mines (C of M), Johannesburg. Back files on Native Labour and Native Unrest, N9–N20. Various memoranda. References provided by R. Mendelsohn and D. Yudelman.
W.D. Hammond-Tooke (papers in his possession in Johannesburg). Files marked 11–605 amaPondo and 11–650 amaPondo Eastern containing various unpublished official correspondence, anthropological notes and interviews covering the period from annexation to the 1950s.
Herbst papers (University of Cape Town Library, BC 79). Official in the Native Affairs Department and Secretary of Native Affairs. Includes part of minutes of evidence to the Native Economic Commission, 1930–2.
R. T. A. James (Witwatersrand University, Church of the Province Library, A55). Trader in Pondoland, 1860s. Reminiscences, 'The Diary of Trader James'.
Thomas Jenkins (Rhodes University, Cory Library). Methodist missionary in Eastern Pondoland 1838–68. Fragments of his diary, 1845–52 (MS. 15,014). Letters to the General Secretaries of the Missionary Society, 1862–7 (MS. 15,391).
V. Leibbrandt (papers in his possession, Durban). Former official in Native Affairs Department, and Chief Magistrate of Transkeian Territories, 1960–2. Papers include unpublished report of Departmental Committee on Stock Reduction in the Native Areas, 1951.
W. S. Lewis (Cape Archives Accession 2044). Correspondence of a Bizana trader.
A. G. McLoughlin (Rhodes University, Cory Library MSS. 14,304, 14,305). Official in Transkeian Territories. Papers include official documents on disputes in Eastern Pondoland, genealogies, oral traditions, notes on law and customs and unpublished thesis entitled 'The Transkeian System of Native Administration', presented to University of South Africa, 1936.

199

Select bibliography

Mine Labour Organisation (MLO) (Johannesburg office). Back files, Kokstad recruiting office, series 12, monthly reports and statistics. Records in this file go back only to 1939.

Mine Labour Organisation (MLO) (Umtata office). Back files and especially statistical book recording Cape Province branch outputs, deferred pay and remittances, 1923–50.

M. H. O'Donnell (CA O'D) (Cape Town Archives Depot, Accession no. 1403). Trader in Eastern Pondoland, 1882–1915. Vols. 1–25 are diaries covering 1886–1915. Vols. 26–57 are letter books, account books and invoice books, 1881–3 and 1887–1912. There are, in addition, a number of unsorted and unnumbered volumes, including Daily Balance Books. Further papers relating to the firm's activities are in the possession of Mr B. Gallagher, Durban.

H. Rock (Rhodes University, Cory Library, MS. 15,799). Missionary and trader in Eastern Pondoland in the late nineteenth century. Typescript entitled 'Reminiscences'.

H. C. Shepstone (Natal Archives Depot, Pietermaritzburg). Resident Magistrate at Alfred, southern Natal. Diaries, 1870–4.

W. E. Stanford (University of Cape Town Library). Chief Magistrate of East Griqualand, Secretary of Native Affairs and Chief Magistrate of the Transkeian Territories. Published and unpublished official papers. Includes letters from Peter Hargreaves, 1885–98 (Schedule Ca.).

Wesleyan Methodist Missionary Society (WMSS) archives (London). Correspondence from South Africa (some was published in the *Missionary Notices* of the Society); Jenkins papers, typescript collection of 171 letters to and from Jenkins, 1838–80.

PUBLISHED AND SECONDARY MATERIAL

Published government papers

Great Britain
British Parliamentary Papers (BPP)

Correspondence Respecting the Affairs of Pondoland, C. 4590 (1885).
Correspondence Respecting the Affairs of Pondoland, C. 5022 (1887).
Further Correspondence Respecting the Affairs of Pondoland, C. 5410 (1888).
Report of the Transvaal Labour Commission, Minutes of Proceedings and Evidence, Cd. 1896, 1897 (1904).
Dominions Royal Commission, *Royal Commission on the Natural Resources, Trade, and Legislation of Certain Portions of His Majesty's Dominions*, Cd. 7706, 7707 (1914).

Cape of Good Hope
Series

Department of Native Affairs, *Blue Books on Native Affairs*, 1874–1909.
Department of Agriculture, *Reports of the Chief Inspector of Sheep*, 1896–1909.

200

Statistical Registers of the Colony of the Cape of Good Hope, 1895–1909.
Government Gazette, 1899–1910.
Miscellaneous Parliamentary Papers
Report of the Commission of Enquiry on the East Griqualand Rebellion, G. 58 – 1879.
Return of Papers on Pondo Affairs, A. 105 – 1880.
Report and Proceedings of the Commission on Native Laws and Customs, G. 4 – 1883.
Report of the Commission of Enquiry into the Disease among Cattle, Known as Redwater, G. 85 – 1883.
Memorandum on the Pondo Settlement of 1886, G. 10 – 1887.
Correspondence Respecting the Affairs of Pondoland, G. 59 – 1894.
Reports on the Affairs of Eastern Pondoland, G. 67 – 1895.
Census of the Colony of the Cape of Good Hope, 1904, G. 19 – 1905.
Department of the Treasury, *Report on Trade with the Native Territories,* G. 22 – 1905.
Henry Burton, *Memorandum on a Visit to the Native Territories Submitted to the Prime Minister John X. Merriman,* unnumbered confidential print, 1909.

Natal
Report of the Trade Commission, 1885–1886 (Pietermaritzburg, 1886).

South Africa
South African Native Affairs Commission, Report and Minutes of Evidence, vols. I–V (Cape Town, 1905).

Series
Department of Native Affairs, later Department of Bantu Administration and Development
Blue Book on Native Affairs, 1910, U. 17 – 1911.
Reports, U.G. 10 – 1913, U.G. 33 – 1913, U.G. 7 – 1919, U.G. 34 – 1922, U.G. 14 – 1927.
van Warmelo, N. J., *A Preliminary Survey of the Bantu Tribes of South Africa,* Ethnological Publications, vol. 5 (1935).
Jackson, A. O., *The Ethnic Composition of the Ciskei and Transkei,* Ethnological Publications, vol. 53 (1975).
Revised Proclamations and Other Legislation in Force in the Transkeian Territories . . . in Force on the 31 December, 1935 (1937).
Department of Census and Statistics (later Office of . . . *and* Bureau of . . .)
Censuses of the Population of the Union, 1911, 1921, 1936, 1946. (Census counts between these dates did not include the African population.)
Agricultural Censuses, 1918–39. (Figures for Transkeian districts appear from 1923; no census was taken between 1931 and 1933.)
Miscellaneous
Judicial Commission of Inquiry into the Witwatersrand Disturbances, June–July 1913, U.G. 56 – 1913.

Select bibliography

Report of the Native Grievances Inquiry, 1913–1914, U.G. 37 –1914.

Native Land Commission, Report and Evidence, 1916, U.G. 19 – 1916.

Department of Agriculture, Report, U.G. 13 – 1921.

Report of the Inter-Departmental Committee on the Native Pass Laws, U.G. 41 – 1922.

Report of the Native Economic Commission, 1930–1932, U.G. 22 – 1932.

Report of the Witwatersrand Mine Native Wages Commission, 1943, U.G. 21 – 1944.

Social and Economic Planning Council, Report No. 9, The Native Reserves and their Place in the Economy of the Union of South Africa, U.G. 32 – 1946.

Report of the Native Laws Commission, 1946–1948, U.G. 28 –1948.

Summary of the Report of the Commission for the Socio-Economic Development of the Bantu Areas within the Union of South Africa, U.G. 61 – 1955.

Transkeian Territories

Transkeian Territories General Council, Proceedings and Reports, 1908–30. (Used for specific debates and statistics.)

United Transkeian Territories General Council, Proceedings and Reports, 1931–9. (Used for specific debates and statistics.)

Pondoland General Council, Proceedings and Reports, 1911–1930. (The only full run of the PGC that could be found is in the Library of Parliament, Cape Town.)

Umcebisi Womlimi Nomfuyi, 1925–33. Journal of the Department of Agriculture of the General Council. First published in 1924. Appeared four times a year 1925–8, then six times a year. Articles in Xhosa only till 1926, then Xhosa and English. (Title means, literally, 'advisor to the cultivator and stock-keeper'.)

Minutes of the Convention Held at Umtata on 10 and 11 September, 1929, To Consider the Amalgamation of the Transkeian Territories General Council and the Pondoland General Council (Umtata, 1929?).

Cape Province

Reports of the Superintendent-General of Education, 1915–1921. The report for 1920 (C.P. 4 – 1920) includes the Report of the Commission on Native Education.

Newspapers and periodicals

Christian Express (from 1923, South African Outlook)
East London Daily Dispatch
Imvo Zabantsundu
Izwi Labantu
Kaffrarian Watchman
Kokstad Advertiser
Natal Mercury
Territorial News (formerly Umtata Herald)

202

Contemporary material

Algar, F., *Handbook to the Colony of Natal: 1865* (London, 1865).

Bachmann, F., *Sudafrika: Reisen, Erlebnisse und Beobachtunge während eines Sechsjährigen Auftenhaltes in der Kapkolonie, Natal und Pondoland* (Berlin, 1901).

Beattie, T. R., *A Ride through the Transkei* (Kingwilliamstown, 1891).

Brownlee, C. P., *Reminiscences of Kafir Life and History* (Lovedale, 1916).

Brownlee, F., *The Transkeian Native Territories: Historical Records* (Lovedale, 1923).

Bryant, A. T., *Olden Times in Zululand and Natal* (London, 1929).

Callaway, G., *Pioneers in Pondoland* (Lovedale, 1939).

Cingo, W. D., *Ibali lama-Mpondo* (Palmerton, 1925).

'The Pondos: Their History, Psychology and Development', pt 5, *Forward*, Dec. 1926.

Dower, W., *Early Annals of Kokstad and Griqualand East* (Port Elizabeth, 1902).

Edmonds, C. R., *Diseases of Animals in South Africa* (London, 1922).

Fortes, M. and E. Evans-Pritchard (eds.), *African Political Systems* (London, 1940).

Gardiner, A. F., *Narrative of a Journey to the Zoolu Country in South Africa* (London, 1836; facs. repr. Cape Town, 1966).

Green, E. and E. Eldridge, *A Pondoland Hilltop* (London, 1938?).

Groser, A., *South African Experiences in Cape Colony, Natal, and Pondoland* (London, 1891).

Guthrie, F. H., *Frontier Magistrate* (Cape Town, 194?).

Haines, E. S., 'The Transkeian Trader', *South African Journal of Economics*, 1, 2 (June 1933).

Hammond-Tooke, W. D. (ed.), *The Journal of William Shaw* (Cape Town, 1972).

Henkel, C. C., *The Native or Transkeian Territories: The Country between the Cape Colony and Natal* (Hamburg, 1903).

Hunter, Monica, 'Results of Culture Contact on the Pondo and Xhosa Family', *South African Journal of Science*, 29 (1932).

'The Effects of Contact with Europeans on the Status of Pondo Women', *Africa*, 6 (1933).

'Methods of Study of Culture Contact', *Africa*, 7 (1934).

Reaction to Conquest (London, 1936, 1964).

Jabavu, D. D. T., *The Black Problem* (Lovedale, 1921?).

Kenyon, J. T., *An Address on the General Council Administrative System of the Transkeian Territories, October 1932* (Umtata, 193?).

Kingon, J. R. L., 'The Economics of East Coast Fever as Illustrated by Transkeian Territories', *Report of the South African Association for the Advancement of Science, 1915* (Cape Town, 1916).

Kirby, P. R., *Jacob van Reenen and the Grosvenor Expedition of 1790–1791* (Johannesburg, 1958).

Kropf, A., *A Kafir–English Dictionary*, 2nd edn, ed. R. Godfrey (Lovedale, 1915).

Lister, M. H., *Journals of Andrew Geddes Bain* (Cape Town, 1949).

Select bibliography

Maclean, C. B., *A Compendium of Kafir Laws and Customs* (Grahamstown, 1906).

MacQuarrie, J. W., *The Reminiscences of Sir Walter Stanford*, vols. I, II (Cape Town, 1958, 1962).

Muller, E. H. W., *Address on the Administration of the Transkeian Territories* (Umtata, 1924?).

Pim, Howard, *A Transkei Enquiry* (Lovedale, 1934).

Poto Ndamase, Victor, *Ama-Mpondo: Ibali ne-Ntlalo* (Lovedale, 1927).

Rogers, Howard, *Native Administration in the Union of South Africa* (Johannesburg, 1933).

Sampson, V., 'A Trip through Pondoland to the Mouth of the St Johns River', *Cape Quarterly Review*, 2, 5 (1882).

Seymour, W. M., *Native Law and Custom* (Cape Town, 1911).

Shaw, E. M. and N. J. van Warmelo, 'The Material Culture of the Cape Nguni', pt 1, 'Settlement', pt 2, 'Technology', *Annals of the South African Museum*, 58, 1 and 2 (1972, 1974).

Shaw, W., *The Story of My Mission in South Eastern Africa* (London, 1860).

Sim, T. R., *The Forests and Forest Flora of the Colony of the Cape of Good Hope* (Aberdeen, 1907).

Skota, T. D. Mweli, *African Yearly Register* (Johannesburg, 1932).

Sneesby, G. W., 'Eastern Pondoland – a Geographical Study', *South African Geographical Journal*, 16 (1933).

Soga, J. H., *The South Eastern Bantu* (Johannesburg, 1930).

Steedman, A., *Wanderings and Adventures in the Interior of Southern Africa*, 2 vols. (London, 1835; repr. Cape Town, 1966).

Stewart, J., *Lovedale, Past and Present* (Lovedale, 1887).

Stuart, J. and D. McK. Malcolm, *The Diary of Henry Francis Fynn* (Pietermaritzburg, 1969).

Taylor, W., *Christian Adventures in South Africa* (London, 1867).

Trapido, S. (ed.), Clements Kadalie, *My Life and the ICU* (London, 1970).

Tredgold, C. H. and W. P. Buchanan, *Decisions of the Supreme Court, Cape of Good Hope*, 12 (1895).

van Reyneveld, A., 'The Pondoland Cotton Experiment', *Practical Agriculture*, 1, 2 (March 1914).

Vindex, *Cecil Rhodes: His Political Life and Speeches, 1881–1900* (London, 1900).

Whitfield, G. M. B., *South African Native Law*, 2nd edn (Cape Town, 1949).

Wright, J. and C. de B. Webb (eds. and trans.), *The James Stuart Archive of Recorded Oral Evidence Relating to the History of the Zulu and Neighbouring Peoples*, vols. I, and II (Pietermaritzburg, 1976, 1979).

Other books and articles

Acocks, J. P. H., *Veld Types of South Africa*, Memoirs of the Botanical Survey of South Africa, no. 40 (Pretoria, 1975).

Allen, W., *The African Husbandman* (Edinburgh, 1965).

Amin, S. 'Underdevelopment and Dependence in Black Africa', *Journal of Modern African Studies*, 10, 4 (1972).
Neo-Colonialism in West Africa (Harmondsworth, 1973).
Arrighi, G., 'Labour Supplies in Historical Perspective: A Study of the Proletarianisation of the African Peasantry in Rhodesia', *Journal of Development Studies*, 6, 3 (April 1970).
Arrighi, G. and J. S. Saul (eds.), *Essays on the Political Economy of Africa* (New York, 1973).
Atmore, A. and S. Marks, 'The Imperial Factor in South Africa in the Nineteenth Century: Towards a Reassessment', *Journal of Imperial and Commonwealth History*, 3, 1 (1974).
Atmore, A. and P. Sanders, 'Sotho Arms and Ammunition in the Nineteenth Century', *Journal of African History*, 12, 4 (1971).
Banaji, J., 'Modes of Production in a Materialist Conception of History', *Capital and Class*, 3 (1977).
Baran, P. A., *The Political Economy of Growth* (New York, 1957).
Beinart, W., 'European Traders and the Mpondo Paramountcy, 1878–1886', *Journal of African History*, 20 (1979).
'Economic Change in Pondoland in the Nineteenth Century', *ICS, SA Seminar*, 7 (1977).
Bell, T., *Industrial Decentralisation in South Africa* (Cape Town, 1973).
Bernstein, H., 'Notes on Capital and Peasantry', *Review of African Political Economy*, 10 (1977).
Brenner, R., 'The Origins of Capitalist Development: A Critique of Neo-Smithian Marxism', *New Left Review*, 104 (1976).
Brett, E. A., *Colonialism and Underdevelopment in East Africa: The Politics of Economic Change, 1919–1939* (London, 1973).
Bundy, C., 'The Response of African Peasants in the Cape to Economic Changes 1870–1910', *ICS, SA Seminar*, 3 (1971–2).
'The Emergence and Decline of a South African Peasantry', *African Affairs*, 71, 285 (Oct. 1972).
The Rise and Fall of the South African Peasantry (London, 1979).
Campbell, W. B., 'The South African Frontier, 1865–1885: A Study in Expansion', *Archives Year Book for South African History*, 1959, pt 1.
Carter, C. M., T. Karis and N. Stulz, *South Africa's Transkei: The Politics of Domestic Colonialism* (London, 1967).
Chayanov, A. V., *The Theory of Peasant Economy* (Homewood, Ill., 1966).
Clarence-Smith, W. G. and R. Moorsom, 'Underdevelopment and Class Formation in Ovamboland, 1845–1915', *Journal of African History*, 16, 3 (1975).
Cook, P. A. W., *Social Organisation and Ceremonial Institutions of the Bomvana* (Cape Town, 1934).
Dalton, G. (ed.), *Tribal and Peasant Economies* (New York, 1967).
Daniel, J. B. McI., 'A Geographical Study of Pre-Shakan Zululand', *South African Geographical Journal*, 55, 1 (1973).
Davenport, T. R. H., *The Afrikaner Bond: The History of a South African Party, 1880–1911* (Cape Town, 1976).

Select bibliography

de Kiewiet, C. W., *The Imperial Factor in South Africa: A Study in Politics and Economics* (Cambridge, 1937).

A History of South Africa, Social and Economic (London, 1941).

Edgar, R., 'Garveyism in Africa: Dr Wellington and the "American" Movement in the Transkei', *ICS, SA Seminar,* 6 (1976).

Ennew, J., D. Hirst and K. Tribe, '"Peasantry" as an Economic Category', *Journal of Peasant Studies,* 4, 4 (1977).

Etherington, N. A., *Preachers, Peasants and Politics in Southeast Africa, 1835–1880: African Christian Communities in Natal, Pondoland and Zululand* (London, 1978).

'Labour Supply and the Genesis of South African Confederation in the 1870s', *Journal of African History,* 20, 2 (1979).

Frank, A. Gunder, *Capitalism and Underdevelopment in Latin America* (Harmondsworth, 1971).

Franklin, N., 'Co-operative Credit Societies in the Transkeian Territories', *South African Journal of Economics,* 10, 2 (1942).

Friedmann, H., 'Household Production and the National Economy: Concepts for the Analysis of Agrarian Formations', *Journal of Peasant Studies,* 7, 2 (1980).

Gluckman, M., 'Analysis of a Social Situation in Modern Zululand', *Bantu Studies,* 14 (1940).

Order and Rebellion in Tribal Africa (London, 1963).

Goodfellow, D. M., *Principles of Economic Sociology: The Economics of Primitive Life as Illustrated from the Bantu Peoples of South and East Africa* (London, 1939).

Goody, J., *Technology, Tradition and the State* (Oxford, 1971).

Production and Reproduction: A Comparative Study of the Domestic Domain (Cambridge, 1976).

Goody, J. (ed.), *The Developmental Cycle in Domestic Groups* (Cambridge, 1958).

Gray, R. and D. Birmingham, *Pre-Colonial African Trade* (London, 1970).

Gulliver, P. (ed.), *Tradition and Transition in East Africa* (London, 1969).

Guy, J. J., 'A Note on Firearms in the Zulu Kingdom with Special Reference to the Anglo-Zulu War, 1879', *Journal of African History,* 12, 4 (1971).

The Destruction of the Zulu Kingdom (London, 1979).

Hammond-Tooke, W. D., *Bhaca Society: A People of the Transkeian Uplands, South Africa* (Cape Town, 1962).

'Chieftainship in Transkeian Political Development', *Journal of Modern African Studies,* 2, 4 (1964).

'Segmentation and Fission in Cape Nguni Political Units', *Africa,* 35, 2 (April 1965).

'The Transkeian Council System, 1895–1955: An Appraisal', *Journal of African History,* 9, 3 (1968).

The Bantu Speaking Peoples of Southern Africa (London, 1974).

Command or Consensus (Cape Town, 1975).

Harries, P., 'Labour Migration from the Delagoa Bay Hinterland to South Africa: 1852–1895', *ICS, SA Seminar,* 7 (1977).

206

Hill, Polly, *Studies in Rural Capitalism in West Africa* (Cambridge, 1970).

Hobsbawm, E., *Primitive Rebels* (Manchester, 1959, 1974).

Hopkins, A. G., *An Economic History of West Africa* (London, 1973).

Hunt-Davis, R., 'School vs. Blanket and Settler: Elijah Makiwane and the Leadership of the Cape School Community', *African Affairs*, 78, 310 (1979).

Jeeves, A., 'The Control of Migratory Labour on the South African Gold Mines in the Era of Kruger and Milner', *Journal of Southern African Studies*, 2, 1 (1975).

Kay, G., *Development and Underdevelopment: A Marxist Analysis* (London, 1975).

Keegan, T., 'The Restructuring of Agrarian Class Relations in a Colonial Economy: The Orange River Colony, 1902–1910', *Journal of Southern African Studies*, 5, 2 (1979).

Klein, M. (ed.), *Peasants in Africa* (Beverly Hills, Calif. 1980).

Krige, E. J., 'Economics of Exchange in a Primitive Society', *South African Journal of Economics*, 9 (1951).

Laclau, E., 'Feudalism and Capitalism in Latin America', *New Left Review*, 67 (1971).

le Cordeur, B. A., 'The Relations between the Cape and Natal, 1846–1879', *Archives Yearbook for South African History*, 1965, pt 1.

Legassick, M., 'South Africa: Capital Accumulation and Violence', *Economy and Society*, 3, 3 (Aug. 1974).

'South Africa:Forced Labour, Industrialisation and Racial Differentiation', in R. Harris (ed.), *The Political Economy of Africa* (Cambridge, Mass., 1975).

'Race, Industrialisation and Social Change in South Africa: The Case of R. F. A. Hoernle', *African Affairs*, 75, 299 (1976).

Lenin, V. I., *The Development of Capitalism in Russia* (Moscow, 1974).

Lewin, J., *Studies in African Native Law* (Cape Town, 1947).

Lewis, C. and G. E. Edwards, *Historical Records of the Church of the Province of South Africa* (London, 1934).

Lewsen, P., 'Merriman as Last Cape Prime Minister', *South African Historical Journal*, 7 (1975).

Lonsdale, J. and B. Berman, 'Coping with the Contradictions: The Development of the Colonial State in Kenya, 1895–1914', *Journal of African History*, 20 (1979).

Marks, S., *Reluctant Rebellion: The 1906–1908 Disturbance in Natal* (Oxford, 1970).

'Firearms in Southern Africa: A Survey', *Journal of African History*, 12 (1971).

'Natal, the Zulu Royal Family and the Ideology of Segregation', *Journal of Southern African Studies*, 4, 2 (1978).

Marks, S. and A. Atmore (eds.), *Economy and Society in Pre-Industrial South Africa* (London, 1980).

Marks, S. and S. Trapido, 'Lord Milner and the South African State', *History Workshop Journal*, 8 (1979).

Mayer, P., *Townsmen or Tribesmen* (Cape Town, 1971).

Mbeki, G., *The Peasants' Revolt* (Harmondsworth, 1964).

Meillassoux, C., 'From Reproduction to Production: A Marxist Approach to Economic Anthropology', *Economy and Society*, 1 (1972).

Miracle, M. P., *Maize in Tropical Africa* (Madison, Wisc., 1966).

Moore, Barrington, *Social Origins of Dictatorship and Democracy: Lord and Peasant in the Making of the Modern World* (London, 1967).

Morris, M., 'The Development of Capitalism in South African Agriculture: Class Struggle in the Countryside', *Economy and Society*, 5 (1976).

Murray, C., 'High Bridewealth, Migrant Labour and the Position of Women in Lesotho', *Journal of African Law*, 21, 1 (1977).

Omer-Cooper, J., *Zulu Aftermath* (London, 1966).

Palmer, R. and N. Parsons (eds.), *The Roots of Rural Poverty in Central and Southern Africa* (London, 1977).

Parkin, D. J., *Palms, Wine and Witnesses: Public Spirit and Private Gain in an African Farming Community* (London, 1972).

Peires, J. B., 'The Rise of the "Right Hand House" in the History and Historiography of the Xhosa', *History in Africa*, 2 (1975).

Ranger, T., 'Growing from the Roots: Reflections on Peasant Research in Central and Southern Africa', *Journal of Southern African Studies*, 5, 1 (1978).

Reader, D. H., *Zulu Tribe in Transition* (Manchester, 1966).

Redfield, R., *Peasant Society and Culture* (Chicago, 1956).

Rhodes, R. I. (ed.), *Imperialism and Underdevelopment: A Reader* (New York, 1970).

Robertson, H. M., '150 Years of Economic Contact between White and Black', *South African Journal of Economics*, 2 (1934).

Ross, R., *Adam Kok's Griquas: A Study in the Development of Stratification in South Africa* (Cambridge, 1976).

Roux, E., 'Land and Agriculture in the Native Reserves', in *Handbook of Race Relations in South Africa* (Johannesburg, 1949).

Saunders, C. C., 'Tile and the Thembu Church', *Journal of African History*, 11, 4 (1970).

Saunders, C. C., and R. Derricourt (eds.), *Beyond the Cape Frontier* (London, 1974).

Schapera, I., *Tribal Legislation among the Tswana of Bechuanaland Protectorate* (London, 1943).

Migrant Labour and Tribal Life (London, 1947).

Tribal Innovators: Tswana Chiefs and Social Change 1795–1940 (London, 1970).

The Tswana (London, 1976).

Schapera, I. (ed.), *The Bantu-Speaking Tribes of South Africa* (London, 1937).

Schneider, H. K., 'Economics in East African Aboriginal Societies', in M. Herskowits and M. Harwitz (eds.), *Economic Transition in Africa* (London, 1964).

Seddon, D. (ed.), *Relations of Production: Marxist Approaches to Economic Anthropology* (London, 1978).

Shanin, T., *The Awkward Class* (Oxford, 1972).

Shanin, T. (ed.), *Peasants and Peasant Society* (Harmondsworth, 1971).

Tatz, C. M., *Shadow and Substance: A Study in Land and Franchise Policies Affecting Africans, 1910–1960* (Pietermaritzbug, 1962).

Terray, E., *Marxism and 'Primitive' Societies* (New York, 1972).

'Long-Distance Exchange and the Formation of the State: The Case of the Abron Kingdom of Gyama', *Economy and Society*, 3, 3 (1974).

Thompson, L., *Survival in Two Worlds: Moshoeshoe of Lesotho 1786–1870* (Oxford, 1975).

Thompson, L. (ed.), *African Societies in Southern Africa* (London, 1969).

Trapido, S., 'African Divisional Politics in the Cape Colony, 1884 to 1910', *Journal of African History*, 9, 1 (1968).

'Landlord and Tenant in a Colonial Economy: The Transvaal 1880–1910', *Journal of Southern African Studies*, 5, 1 (1978).

van der Horst, S. T., *Native Labour in South Africa* (London, 1942).

van Onselen, C., 'Reactions to Rinderpest in Southern Africa, 1896–1897', *Journal of African History*, 13, 3 (1972).

'Worker Consciousness in Black Miners: Southern Rhodesia, 1900–1930', *Journal of African History*, 14, 2 (1973).

Chibaro (London, 1976).

'The Regiment of the Hills: South Africa's Lumpenproletariat Army, 1890–1910', *Past and Present*, 80 (1978).

van Tromp, J., *Xhosa Law of Persons* (Cape Town, 1947).

van Velsen, J., 'Labour Migration as a Positive Factor in the Continuity of Tonga Tribal Society', *Economic Development and Cultural Change*, 8 (April 1960).

Walshe, P., *The Rise of African Nationalism in South Africa* (London, 1970).

Walton, J., 'South African Peasant Architecture: Nguni Folk Building', *African Studies*, 8, 2 (1949).

Watson, R. G. T., *Tongaati: An African Experiment* (London, 1960).

Welsh, D., *The Roots of Segregation: Native Policy in Colonial Natal, 1845–1910* (Cape Town, 1971).

Wickins, P., *The Industrial and Commercial Workers' Union of Africa* (Cape Town, 1978).

Wilson, F., *Labour in the South African Gold Mines 1911–1969* (Cambridge, 1972).

Wilson, F. and D. Perrot, *Outlook on a Century: South Africa 1870–1970* (Lovedale/Johannesburg, 1973).

Wilson, M. and L. Thompson (eds.), *Oxford History of South Africa*, 2 vols. (Oxford, 1969, 1971).

Wolf, E., *Peasants* (Englewood Cliffs, N.J., 1966).

Wolpe, H., 'Capitalism and Cheap Labour-Power in South Africa: From Segregation to Apartheid', *Economy and Society*, 1 (1972).

Wolpe, H. (ed.), *The Articulation of Modes of Production* (London, 1980).

Wright, J. B., *Bushmen Raiders of the Drakensberg 1840–1870* (Pietermaritzburg, 1971).

Wrigley, C. C., *Crops and Wealth in Uganda* (Kampala, 1959).

Select bibliography

Unpublished theses and papers

Beinart, W., 'Production, Labour Migrancy and the Chieftaincy: Aspects of the Political Economy of Pondoland, ca. 1860–1930', Ph.D., University of London, 1979.

'Conflict in Qumbu: Rural Consciousness, Ethnicity and Violence in the Colonial Transkei (1880–1913)', paper for Conference on History and Anthropology in Southern Africa, Manchester, 1980.

Bonner, P., 'The Rise, Consolidation and Disintegration of Dhlamini Power in Swaziland between 1820 and 1899', Ph.D., University of London, 1977.

'The 1920 Black Mine-Workers' Strike: A Preliminary Account', 1978.

Cobbing, J. R. D., 'The Ndebele under the Khumalos, 1820–1896', Ph.D., University of Lancaster, 1976.

Cragg, D. G. L., 'The Relations of the Amampondo and the Colonial Authorities (1830–1886) with Special Reference to the Role of the Wesleyan Missionaries', D.Phil., University of Oxford, 1959.

Delius, P., 'The Pedi Polity under Sekwati and Sekhukhune, 1828–1880', Ph.D., University of London, 1980.

Guy, J., 'Cattle-Keeping in Zululand', paper presented to the Language and History in Africa Seminar, School of Oriental and African Studies, University of London, 1970.

Harries, P., 'Kinship, Ideology and the Origins of Migrant Labour', 1980.

Hedges, D., 'Trade and Politics in Southern Mocambique and Zululand in the Eighteenth and Early Nineteenth Centuries', Ph.D., University of London, 1978.

Hutton, A. M., 'Pondoland: Her Cape and Natal Neighbours, 1878–1894', M.A., University of the Witwatersrand, 1935.

Legassick, M., 'Development and Underdevelopment in South Africa', 1971.

'The Making of South African "Native Policy", 1903–1923: The Origins of Segregation', paper presented at the Institute of Commonwealth Studies, London, 1973.

Leverton, B. J. T., 'Government Finance and Political Development in Natal, 1843 to 1893', Ph.D., University of South Africa, 1968.

Ngcobo, S. B., 'Taxation of Africans in South Africa, 1849–1939', Ph.D., University of London, 1964.

Peires, J. B., 'A History of the Xhosa c. 1700–1835', M.A., Rhodes University, 1976.

Purkis, A. J., 'The Politics, Capital and Labour of Railway Building in the Cape Colony, 1870–1885', D.Phil., University of Oxford, 1978.

Saunders, C. C., 'The Annexation of the Transkeian Territories (1872–1895) with Special Reference to British and Cape Policy', D.Phil., University of Oxford, 1972.

Sieborger, R. F., 'The Recruitment and Organisation of African Labour for the Kimberley Diamond Mines, 1871–1888', M.A., Rhodes University, 1972.

Trapido, S., 'White Conflict and Non-White Participation in the Politics of the Cape of Good Hope, 1853–1910', Ph.D., University of London, 1970.

van Onselen, C., 'The Witches of Suburbia: Domestic Servants in Johannesburg', paper presented to the Institute of Commonwealth Studies, London, 1977.

Unpublished reports

Fox, F. W. and D. Back, 'A Preliminary Survey of the Agricultural and Nutritional Problems of the Ciskei and Transkeian Territories, with Special Reference to Their Bearing upon the Recruiting of Labourers for the Gold Mining Industry', Johannesburg, 1938? (in Chamber of Mines Library).

Jokl, E., 'A Labour and Man-Power Survey of the Transkeian Territories', Johannesburg, 1943 (in South African Institute of Race Relations Library, Johannesburg).

National Institute for Personnel Research (South Africa), 'A Study of the Factors Influencing the Seasonal Flow of Migratory Labour from Three Districts of the Transkeian Territories', interim report, Sept. 1958.

Union of South Africa, Department of Native Affairs, Report of the Departmental Committee Regarding the Culling of Livestock in the Native Areas, 1951? (in Leibbrandt papers).

ORAL MATERIAL

This list covers only material mentioned in the text. Translation of Xhosa in the interviews is based on simultaneous interpretation by Mr F. Deyi and has been modified in certain cases. Quotations from the tapes have in some cases involved the reordering of material.

Interviews and discussions on tape

Allison, Frank and Stanley, Ludonga Trading Store, Lusikisiki, 16.2.1977. English.

Ball, Daisy, Lusikisiki, 12.2.1977. English.

Cingo, Xatsha, Ngobozana Administrative Authority (AA), Lusikisiki, 8.2.1977. Xhosa.

Dana, G., Tsweleni AA, Lusikisiki, 22.6.1976, 7.1.1977, 4.2.1977, 17.3.1977. English and Xhosa.

Fono, Calvin, Caguba AA, Port St Johns, 26.2.1977. Xhosa.

Godlwana, I., Flagstaff, 21.1.1977. English.

Gqambuleni, Gqude and others, Ngcoya AA, Lusikisiki, 25.3.1977. Xhosa.

Gregory, Sydney, Mount Bleak Trading Station, Lusikisiki, 9.2.1977. English.

Hall-Green, C. E., Kenton on Sea, 10.12.1976. English.

Heathcote, I. M., Port St Johns, 3.1.1977, 15.1.1977. English. Further interviews not on tape.

Hedding, W., Gonubie, 16.12.1976. English.

Jamjam, Elliot, Zalu AA, Lusikisiki, 6.1.1977, 17.1.1977. Xhosa.

Kohlabantu ka Mduduma, Zalu Heights AA, Lusikisiki, 9.2.1977. Xhosa.

Lanyazima, Lutengele AA, Port St Johns, 26.2.1977. Xhosa.

Select bibliography

Laqwela, Merriman, Lusikisiki, 21.2.1977, 7.3.1977. Xhosa.

MacGowan, James, Mzintlava AA, Lusikisiki, 20.1.1977. English.

Magazi, Dubana AA, Lusikisiki, 18.1.1977. English.

Majambe, Gomolo AA, Port St Johns, 13.3.1977, Xhosa.

Mathanda of Mateko AA and Thandekhaya of Xura AA (headmen), Lusikisiki, 22.2.1977. Xhosa.

Mathandabuzo, Lionel, Mfinizo AA, Lusikisiki, 17.2.1977, 23.2.1977, 18.3.1977. Xhosa.

Mbola, Oliver, Zalu AA, Lusikisiki, 11.1.1977. Xhosa.

Mgeyana, Msikaba AA, Lusikisiki, 14.1.1977. Xhosa.

Mgibe, Nkwakwa ka and Mbokoma ka Nompentshu, Mtambalala AA, Lusikisiki, 11.3.1977. Xhosa.

Mhatu, E., Xurana AA, Lusikisiki, 21.1.1977. Xhosa.

Mhatu, J., Malengeni AA, Lusikisiki, 13.1.1977. English.

Moncur, D., Tabankulu, 8.3.1977. English.

Mpateni, E., Flagstaff and Mhlumba AA, Lusikisiki, 12.1.1977 and 17.1.1977. English.

Mvunelo, James, Mtambalala AA, Lusikisiki, 13.3.1977. English.

Ndabeni, Ben Siposo, Mkanzini AA, Port St Johns, 25.2.1977. Xhosa.

Nkonya, Bartwell, Zalu AA, Lusikisiki, 10.1.1977. English.

Nonkonyana, Chief David, Bala AA, Flagstaff, 6.3.1977. Xhosa.

Norton, J., Gonubie, 1.2.1977. English.

Ntobe, Moses, Ntsimbini AA, Port St Johns, 12.3.1977. English.

Sigcau, Chief Nelson, Mxopo AA, Flagstaff, 4.3.1977. Xhosa.

Sigcau, Chief Stanford, Ngobozana AA, Lusikisiki, 8.2.1977. Xhosa.

Sigwili, Malengeni AA, Lusikisiki, 13.1.1977. Xhosa.

Sihlobo, Zalu Heights AA, Lusikisiki, 3.2.1977. Xhosa.

Soji, Alexander, Hombe AA, Lusikisiki, 21.3.1977. English.

Thompson, R., Lusikisiki, 14.1.1977. English. Further interview in Kokstad not on tape.

Vulizibhaya, Bomvini AA, Lusikisiki, 18.1.1977, 10.2.1977. Xhosa. Another interview not on tape.

Xinwa, Ned, Gomolo AA, Port St Johns, 27.2.1977 and 13.3.1977. Xhosa.

Interviews and discussions not on tape

Bennie, R., Howick, 8.7.1976.

Birkett, Mrs M., Port St Johns, 16.1.1976.

Clarke, H. W., Port St Johns, 12.5.1976.

Deutschmann, G., Port St Johns, 12.5.1976.

Lawrence, Mr and Mrs, Mzintlavana Store, Lusikisiki, 25.1.1977.

Mgoduka, J., Ngobozana AA, Lusikisiki, Feb. and March 1977.

Norton, A. J., Gonubie, 3.5.1976.

212

Index

213

BOOKS IN THIS SERIES

Books in this series